THE END OF DETROIT

THE END

— OF —

DETROIT

HOW THE BIG THREE LOST THEIR GRIP ON THE AMERICAN CAR MARKET

MICHELINE MAYNARD

CURRENCY

DOUBLEDAY

NEW YORK   LONDON   TORONTO   SYDNEY   AUCKLAND

A CURRENCY BOOK
Published by Doubleday
A division of Random House, Inc.

CURRENCY is a trademark of Random House, Inc., and
DOUBLEDAY is a registered trademark of Random House, Inc.

The End of Detroit was originally published in hardcover by Currency in October 2003.

Book design by Erin L. Matherne and Tina Thompson

The Library of Congress has cataloged the hardcover edition of this book as follows:
Maynard, Micheline.
    The end of Detroit : how the Big Three lost their grip on the American car market /
    Micheline Maynard — 1st ed.
    327 p. ; 25 cm.
    Includes bibliographical references p. [339] and index.
    1. Automobile industry and trade—United States. 2. Automobile industry and trade—
United States—Forecasting. 3. Competition, International. I. Title: How the Big Three lost
their grip on the American car market. II. Title.

HD9710.U52M39.2003
338.476292220973—dc22   2003055493

ISBN 0-385-50770-4

FIRST EDITION: October 2003
FIRST CURRENCY PAPERBACK EDITION: November 2004

All trademarks are the property of their respective companies

SPECIAL SALES
Currency Books are available at special discounts for bulk purchases for sales
promotions or premiums. Special editions, including personalized covers, excerpts
of existing books, and corporate imprints, can be created in large quantities for
special needs. For more information, write to Special Markets, Currency Books,
specialmarkets@randomhouse.com.

10 9 8 7 6 5 4 3 2 1

For Benjamin Maynard and Parker Maynard

Go confidently in the direction of your dreams.
Live the life you've imagined.

—HENRY DAVID THOREAU

CONTENTS

A LIGHT FOG ENVELOPED the Detroit area on September 3, 2003, as thousands of automobile-industry employees made their way into auto plants, company offices and industrial parks. Thanks to an early Labor Day holiday, that Wednesday morning, for many, was only the second day back after summer vacation. A relaxed feeling hung in the air. Few people had any sense that by the end of that late summer day, the American automobile industry would be changed forever. By mid-afternoon, e-mail traffic was flying thick and fast across the country and around the world, as the August automobile sales results were made public. An e-mail from Ron Pinelli, an industry analyst with Autodata Corp. in Woodcliff Lake, New Jersey, whose firm tracked monthly sales results, said it all: "The big news is that Toyota beat Chrysler."

No earthquake could have rattled Detroit more. For the first time since Toyota began selling cars in the United States more than four decades before, it had taken the No. 3 position in American car and truck sales. After the most aggressive August sales campaign the industry had ever seen, Toyota's sales for the month topped 200,000. That was 10,000 more cars than Chrysler, whose sales had been sliding all year, due to a stale lineup and a reluctance to match the hefty rebates and interest-free loans that other Detroit companies were offering.

Chrysler's chief executive, Dieter Zetsche, had dubbed such deals "automotive heroin." But without them, Chrysler could not keep pace. And as a result, that month Detroit's automakers no longer comprised the country's Big Three carmakers. The lineup was General Motors, Ford and Toyota.

That was not the only bad news for Detroit companies. That August, their combined share of the American car and truck market had fallen to just 57 percent, a level they had not seen since 1981. That depressing figure was what the *Detroit News* chose to make the lead of its story, splashed the next day across its front page. But editors at the *Detroit Free Press* and countless newspapers around the country saw it otherwise. The next morning's *New York Times* story, datelined September 3, began like this: "The day that the American automobile industry has been dreading for years arrived today. Toyota outsold Chrysler, the first time one of Detroit's Big Three has fallen to fourth place."

The news, though monumental, was not completely unexpected. A few months earlier, Toyota had come within about 5,000 sales of Chrysler for the month, and it had ended 2002 as close to Chrysler as it had ever been in any year. At an industry conference in August 2003, David Cole, the veteran automobile industry expert whose father, Ed, had been president of General Motors, proclaimed that the industry in essence consisted of a Big Two—meaning GM and Toyota. Yet Toyota executives, famed for an outward modesty that camouflaged an unflinching ambition, insisted that the company's goal was not to pass Chrysler, only to please customers. Whether it wound up beating Chrysler was irrelevant, as long as buyers were content, they maintained.

Other executives in the industry, and indeed, even some within Toyota, argued that any Toyota victory would be only a partial one. That was because Toyota's monthly sales figures included those of Lexus, its luxury brand, while those at Chrysler included only its traditional brands—the Chrysler division, Dodge and Jeep. If Chrysler were to include Mercedes-Benz, the luxury carmaker owned by its German parent, DaimlerChrysler, then Chrysler easily kept its lead. But at the outset of the merger between Chrysler and Daimler-Benz in 1998, meant to create the world's first truly global automaker, DaimlerChrysler officials emphasized that there were no plans to combine the American carmaker and the German luxury company. They were to remain separate, with separate marketing approaches and separate sales reports, even though GM and Ford had always folded the sales of Cadillac and Lincoln respectively into their monthly reports, along with those of their other luxury marks.

When it came time to explain what happened with August sales, Chrysler officials seemed sanguine. They certainly gave no sense of the historic event that had just transpired and if they felt rattled, they did not show it. "Nobody's going to question the fact that Toyota's having a great run in the U.S. car and truck business right now," said Chrysler vice president Gary Dilts, in what was clearly the understatement of the day. The emphasis at Chrysler, which lost $900 million in 2003's second quarter, would be on "selling cars and trucks profitably," he said. Speaking about the event six months later, CEO Zetsche was equally blasé. "It was much more of a media event than it was an event for us," he maintained.

But on that September day, Toyota, for once, was not modest. James Press, chief executive of the company's American sales operations, said the sales report was inevitable. "This was a day that had to happen. I'm glad it happened," said Press, who had joined the company in 1970. But he did not predict more monthly victories in the near future—in part because the flurry of sales had exhausted Toyota dealers' supply of vehicles. "Next month, they may beat us," Press said.

In fact, Chrysler did beat Toyota in October 2003 and maintained its lead, though often a slim one, over Toyota in the following months. Yet that September afternoon would not quickly be forgotten, in Detroit or elsewhere in the industry. Toyota's victory over Chrysler was the most visible sign yet that Detroit's long grip on the American car market had been loosened, if not lost. But it was far from the only such evidence.

As anniversary celebrations go, Honda's ceremony back in November 2002, marking the twentieth anniversary of its first American car plant in Marysville, Ohio, was decidedly low key. There were no marching bands and no balloons, and not even sunny skies to brighten the day, just the cold, gray, dreary weather that blankets the Midwest pretty much continuously after the autumn leaves fall. Only about a hundred or so local dignitaries, a few state representatives and some county officials showed up for the reception, chatting jovially around round tables, kicking the tires of Honda's newest cars, sipping coffee (no champagne was in sight) and munching on sugar cookies in the shape of the state with the number 20 written in pink icing on top. The event's only headliner, lanky Governor Robert Taft, thoughtful scion of the longtime Ohio political family, arrived in his typically quiet fashion, trailed by a small knot of television cameras and reporters from the state capitol in Columbus, 30 miles away.

The journalists and some Honda officials dodged raindrops in front of the factory, watching as Taft climbed inside a Honda Element, a boxy, unconventional SUV that Honda itself referred to as a "dorm room on wheels." The Element had just gone into production at Honda's East Liberty plant, a few miles away, marking the first time a sport utility had been built at Honda's Ohio manufacturing complex. The Element was targeted at a far younger and hipper buyer than the middle-aged governor, who had a politely bemused look on his face as he sat inside and examined the vehicle's vast cargo space. The governor then obligingly met the owner of a Honda Accord with more than a million miles on its odometer, which had been built at the Marysville plant eight years earlier. With the grip-and-grin complete, Taft and his entourage ducked inside out of the cold.

A few minutes later, standing at a podium in the plant's small auditorium, the governor launched into remarks that illustrated just how important the plant had become to his state, and indeed, the critical role that Honda had come to play in the American automobile industry. In the 20 years that Honda had been building cars in Marysville, the Japanese auto company had become the single biggest manufacturer of cars in Ohio, producing more than 700,000 Accords, small Civics, luxury Acura sedans, and now the quirky Element, every year. Honda's production was significantly above the number of vehicles built in the state by either GM, Ford or Chrysler, despite the fact that those American companies had been building cars in Ohio for decades, at factories in towns like Youngstown, Dayton and Toledo. Moreover, Honda had progressed from a modest start to become the state's biggest manufacturer in terms of employees.

When it had struck the $5 million deal that clinched the Marysville factory nearly a quarter-century before, Honda had promised the state that it would eventually hire 1,000 people. By 2002, counting all of its operations in the state, including the Marysville plant and the one nearby in East Liberty, an engine plant 60 miles away in Anna, and its gleaming research and development center in Marysville, Honda had 14,000 employees on its Ohio payroll, far greater than the population of many of the small towns in the surrounding farmland near the plant. Turning to Honda's North American manufacturing director, a cordial executive named Koki Hirashima, the governor bowed his head in thanks, saying, "Arigato, Koki. Arigato." Though he slightly mangled the Japanese, the governor's gratitude for everything Honda had brought to his state was clear.

Koki Hirashima had come to this manufacturing complex 10 years earlier, when Honda's lineup was only cars—no minivans or SUVs or pickups. Although the Accords and Civics that were built here sold well and their owners seemed very satisfied with them, many experts doubted that Honda would ever become a major player in the industry without a full lineup of vehicles. But Hirashima had learned not to doubt Honda's capabilities. In the mid-1980s, Hirashima was a young engineer in Japan assigned to develop the Acura Integra hatchback, one of the original cars in the luxury Acura lineup that was introduced in the United States in 1986. One day, unexpectedly, Soichiro Honda, the founder of the company, showed up at the plant in Suzuka, Japan, where the Integra's development was taking place, and asked to drive a prototype. Hirashima accompanied the company's founder to the plant's short test track, where Honda jumped behind the wheel of the Integra, gunned the engine and went barreling down the straightaway. Suddenly, he slammed on the brakes.

Hirashima instinctively closed his eyes and gripped the armrest, bracing himself in case the test model didn't stop. It did, however, and Hirashima opened his eyes to find Honda glaring at him. "What's the matter with you?" the company founder thundered. "Don't you believe in your own brakes?" Recalling the episode later, Hirashima said he had never again doubted what Honda could accomplish.

Like the ceremony, like the company's entire approach to the car market, Honda's philosophy was simple. Unlike its American competition, which made sweeping declarations every year about the vast numbers of vehicles they expected to sell, Honda approached the American market one customer at a time. Its vehicles might have originally been bought by young, ecology-minded buyers eager to find an alternative to gas guzzlers from Detroit, but by the time it celebrated its twentieth anniversary as an American manufacturer, Honda's appeal cut across all strata of backgrounds and income levels, reaching beyond the import-focused West Coast to every corner of the United States. Honda's name had become synonymous with quality and durability, and its customers' loyalty was second to none.

Whenever it decided to introduce a new vehicle, whether the Odyssey minivan, the Pilot sport utility or the boxy, unusual Element, Honda already had thousands of customers on waiting lists at dealerships across the country willing to purchase one based solely on their confidence in Honda's past performance. Honda saw no need to continuously offer rebates or low-interest financing plans to convince buyers to take a chance on something new. Honda had proved, time and again, that it would not let its buyers down. By 2002, Honda's annual American sales, including its Acura luxury division, had climbed well above 1 million vehicles; the company earned more money in 2002 than the Detroit companies combined.

At the beginning of that year, only 200 miles to the north in Dearborn, Michigan, the home of Ford Motor Company, journalists and Ford Motor officials had gathered to hear news of a very different sort. Amid the whir of motor drives and the flash of camera bulbs, William Clay Ford, Jr., sat at a conference table to somberly announce that, after posting its first annual loss in nine years for 2001, his family's auto company would cut 23,000 jobs, close five factories and eliminate five vehicles from its lineup. It had been a terrible few months for the 44-year-old Ford, a member of the fourth generation of the Ford family, and the strain showed on his still-boyish face. Clad in a dark gray suit and white shirt, his sandy hair closely cropped, at one point during the two-hour presentation, and a lunch that followed, he folded his fingertips in an unconscious prayer, leaning his forehead against his hands as the magnitude of his task bore down on him.

The auto company was mired in a crisis that had begun about a year and a half earlier, in the summer of 2000, when the world discovered that the Ford Explorer SUV, the industry's most popular SUV, was plagued by defective Firestone tires that could explode, sending the vehicles hurtling into rollover accidents; already the problem had resulted in dozens of deaths. Ford, then the company's chairman, had dispatched his handpicked chief executive, a feisty, ambitious Australian named Jacques Nasser, to deal with the situation. Nasser and Ford had joined forces only a year before in a plan that ultimately would elevate Ford, then only 41 years old, to the chairman's job, and Nasser, not yet 50, to the job of chief executive. At the time that they took control, Ford's annual profits topped $7.2 billion. The pair seemed to be a golden duo, hailed in newspaper articles and on magazine covers as the perfect combination of family dominance and management expertise.

As Chrysler foundered in the early days of the DaimlerChrysler merger and General Motors struggled to stop its market share plunge, Ford seemed to have a master touch. It gobbled up luxury nameplates, paid $6.45 billion to buy Volvo Cars and added Land Rover to a stable that included Aston Martin and Jaguar. Sales of its popular sport utilities continued to grow, fueling speculation that Ford was on its way to passing GM as the world's largest auto company. Nasser, known for his boundless energy and his ceaseless store of new ideas, spent millions of dollars on e-commerce ventures and bought a collection of junkyards, an electric car company and an auto-repair business in Europe; he vowed to build Ford into a consumer company as beloved by its customers as Disney or Nordstrom.

But when the Firestone tires began to disintegrate, so, too, did Nasser's dreams for Ford. Making a critical mistake at a high point in the crisis, he refused to testify before a congressional inquiry into the Explorer rollovers. He quickly reversed himself, but he was forced to spend an entire day sitting silently in a hearing room, visible to anyone who tuned in on C-SPAN, forced to wait until early evening for his chance to speak. While Ford's sales of the Explorer held firm throughout the crisis, the relationship between Ford and Firestone, forged by heritage and family connection—Ford's own mother was a Firestone, and

Firestone had been supplying Ford with tires for 94 years—soured. By the fall of 2001, Ford was drowning in red ink (it would lose $2 billion that year), its auto sales had stumbled in the strongest market that the industry had ever known and Ford's reputation for quality, so carefully honed throughout the 1980s and 1990s, when it insisted "Quality Is Job One," was in shambles.

So, Nasser had to go. Ford himself would have to take Nasser's place as chief executive. He now needed to come up with a plan to save the company his great-grandfather had founded 98 years before. At the January 2002 news conference, Ford explained how the auto company had failed. "Our success may have caused us to underestimate our competition," he said. "We strayed from what got us to the top of the mountain. We perceived some strategies that were poorly conceived and poorly timed." His words, though reflective that morning merely of Ford's position, echoed what auto industry analysts said of America's two other major car companies. For in 2002, the mistakes Detroit's auto companies had made with their customers were clear. Once among the biggest, most profitable and most glamorous of industries, the American automobile companies were no longer the industry's leaders and its guiding light. Detroit's 100-year grip on the American industry had ended.

CHAPTER ONE

HOW DETROIT
LOST ITS GRIP

DETROIT'S LONG REIGN as the dominant force in the American car industry is over.

More than 100 years after Henry Ford sold his first automobile in 1903, imports have taken an unshakable hold on the American consumer and are leading to the demise of inarguably the most important industrial force that America has ever produced. Like the steel industry before it, like the airline industry to an increasing extent, as with retailers, the balance of power in the car industry has shifted away from Detroit's giant companies—General Motors, Ford Motor Co. and Chrysler Corp.—toward smaller, more nimble players that can react faster to the competitive landscape.

It's an unthinkable but undeniable reality, one with tremendous ramifications for American life and the business world in general. During the twentieth century, the automobile changed everything in the United States, from the way people commuted to work, to where they lived, to the way they conducted romance. The automobile triggered the development of the interstate highway system, allowing Americans to see every corner of their country at ease. It created suburbs and exurbs, beginning with bedroom communities within a few minutes' drive of downtown areas, to sprawling developments that extend for 50 miles or more outside major cities. At their peak a scant 40 years ago, Detroit-built vehicles accounted for more than 9 of 10 automobile sales in the United States. Nearly a million people worked in automobile plants, and every manufacturing job created by Detroit generated five more, at auto parts suppliers scattered across the country, at steel mills in Pittsburgh, Cleveland, Detroit and Chicago, and at coal mines in West Virginia and in the Deep South. The neon lights of car dealerships from Maine to California lit the night sky, and the arrival of the year's new vehicles every autumn generated long lines of automobile enthusiasts eager to see the latest models.

But Detroit's single-handed control of the American automobile industry has been lost forever. From small cars to luxury cars, from family sedans to minivans, vehicles made by foreign-based companies are escalating in popularity, attracting an unending stream of converts every year from among owners of vehicles built by Detroit's Big Three. Four of every 10 vehicles sold in the United States in 2003 were be built by companies with foreign nameplates. That is a vivid contrast to 1960, when General Motors alone controlled 60 percent of the automobile market and the U.S. government constantly threatened to use the Sherman Anti-Trust Act to break up its operations. Few could have imagined imports' popularity in 1964, when the Ford Mustang and its creator, Lee Iacocca, accomplished the almost-impossible feat of landing simultaneously on the covers of both *Time* and

Newsweek. At the time, the only imported car that most people knew about was the Volkswagen Beetle. Toyota was selling only a few thousand cars a year in the United States, and Honda had yet to produce its first car in Japan.

Yet today, GM, Ford and Chrysler together control barely the market share that GM itself held four decades ago. Buyers of all ages, incomes, ethnic backgrounds and social strata are choosing foreign companies' cars and trucks over those produced by Detroit. Consumers may sigh nostalgically over the cars their parents drove, and they still crowd curiously around the vehicles that Detroit puts on display at auto shows and in shopping malls. But when it comes to spending their hard-earned dollars, their decisions tell a much different story.

Thanks to their record of quality and reliability, Toyotas and Hondas have become today's Chevrolets and Fords. In the luxury market, Lexus and BMW cars have supplanted Cadillacs and Lincolns. Where once foreign cars were considered to be the domain of the wealthy, the eccentric or the unpatriotic, now everybody knows somebody who drives a foreign car—in part because foreign cars aren't really foreign anymore. Millions of them are built in the United States every year, to an enthusiastic reception from their owners: grandmothers in Michigan, computer programmers in Texas and high school students in Nevada. If the current sales trends continue, cars and trucks from foreign-based companies could easily, some say inevitably, account for 50 percent of all American sales by the year 2010.

How could this have happened? The automobile industry, after all, has been the biggest economic engine this country has ever known, save for the war effort during World War II (as plenty of people will remind you, this was led by Detroit, which transformed itself overnight into the Arsenal of Democracy). Thanks in part to Henry Ford's philosophy that factories should be built near where consumers bought products, automobile plants were established in all corners of the country, from Framingham, outside Boston, to Los Angeles, from Minneapolis to Atlanta. The center of production, and of the automotive universe, of course, was Detroit, where afternoon skies were clouded by a gray haze from the automobile, steel, glass and parts plants that churned out a seemingly endless supply. Well into the 1990s, GM produced 70 percent of all the parts that it used on its cars. In 1979, when Chrysler teetered perilously close to bankruptcy, the nation gasped at the idea that one of America's industrial giants might shut its doors. While there were cynics who argued that Chrysler should be allowed to go out of business, the victim of its own mismanagement, its supporters rallied to convince Congress to pass $1.5 billion in loan guarantees, giving the company time to find its way back.

Today, thanks to the failures of firms such as Enron, WorldCom and United Airlines, a call for help from the automobile industry might well go unheeded or, at the very least, face a much more difficult time being addressed. Indeed, there is a strong chance that by the end of this decade, at least one of Detroit's Big Three will not continue in the same form that it is in now. Already a German company owns Chrysler, and the difficult economy that has come about in the aftermath of the 1990s bubble is making it all the harder for Detroit to cling to market share. The dissolution of a Detroit automaker would be a tragedy for its employees and vendors. But, given the vast array of vehicles that they can choose from now, consumers might not even miss one of the Big Three companies should it disappear. The shift did not happen overnight. It has taken place slowly but steadily over the past 20 years. Either Detroit wasn't paying attention, or if it did notice, the center of the automotive universe plodded on blindly in a state of denial.

The ultimate irony of Detroit's demise is that it has been defeated by companies that do the job that Detroit once did with unquestioned expertise: turn out vehicles that consumers want to buy and vehicles that capture their imaginations. Toyota, Honda, Mercedes and BMW have never made industrial size their ultimate priority. They made vehicles their ultimate priority. They poured all their resources—human, financial, engineering, manufacturing, marketing and sales—into achieving their goal. They have not tried to be all things to all people, as GM strived to be with "a car for every purse and purpose," a philosophy from which it has not strayed since the phrase was crafted by Alfred P. Sloan in the 1920s. They have not focused on one category in their lineup to the detriment of all others, as Ford did during the 1990s with its slavish devotion to sport utility vehicles. With their efficient development methods, their focus on manufacturing, and most important, experienced engineers in critical management jobs, the foreign companies never forgot that they were in business to develop top-quality cars and trucks that appealed to customers, as opposed to rental-car models and government fleets.

The overriding goal of General Motors and Ford has never been to simply be good, but to be big and to grow as strategically as possible. Selling one vehicle at a time to one customer at a time, the way the best foreign companies approach growth, simply was too slow. Throughout the 1990s, GM and Ford poured billions of dollars into a variety of foreign companies, from Fiat at GM, to Jaguar and Volvo at Ford, with disappointing results. Daimler-Benz's purchase of Chrysler was supposed to provide the German company with a cash machine and easy access to the American mass market. Instead, Daimler-Chrysler wound up being bogged down in cultural clashes and product delays, suffering huge losses that set back its competitive drive for years.

Deals, not product development, have driven GM, Ford and Chrysler in the past decade—and no wonder. With only occasional exceptions, Detroit executives have traditionally been finance men who look at vehicles themselves as an end result of a great enterprise, rather than critical products to which the utmost attention should be paid. There has long been a saying in Detroit that General Motors, with its huge credit, financing and mortgage operations, is less of a car company than a bank that builds cars. Indeed, three of the last four GM chief executives, including its current CEO, G. Richard Wagoner, came up through its New York finance staff. Although William Clay Ford, Jr., is the fourth generation of his family to run the auto company that bears his name, he is yet another finance executive, schooled at Princeton and M.I.T. Only Dieter Zetsche, the Turkish-born German executive in charge at Chrysler, can claim an engineering background, and it is Zetsche, in fact, who is trying hardest to shift his company away from being seen as a Detroit carmaker. He is fully aware of what imports have done to Detroit's hold on the American industry and the unebbing erosion that lies ahead. Among all the executives in Detroit, it is Zetsche who is acting the most urgently to help Chrysler avoid that fate, at the same time fully aware that Chrysler's legacy of substandard quality is its biggest obstacle to success.

The companies that threaten Detroit are led by men who understand vehicles inside and out, who have dedicated their careers to meeting their customers' needs. There is Fujio Cho, the ebullient chief executive of Toyota, who spent years in charge of Toyota's giant manufacturing complex in Georgetown, Kentucky, where he walked the long assembly lines daily and spent endless hours getting to know his employees. When other executives at the company doubted that American Toyota workers could match the quality of Toyota's vehicles in Japan, Cho insisted that they could, and oversaw an expansion of the plant that brought workers the chance to build large sedans and minivans. A modest man—a rarity among CEOs—Cho is taking that same determination now to Toyota on a global scale. By the year 2010, he wants Toyota to sell 15 percent of automobiles worldwide, which would make it the world's biggest player, exceeding General Motors, which has been the world's leading car manufacturer since the 1920s.

Helmut Panke, the chief executive at BMW, is another such determined executive. He has made sure that his company has the clearest brand image among the world's automakers. Tall, lanky, with silver hair and bright eyes, Panke was trained as a nuclear engineer and began as a corporate consultant with McKinsey & Company. He was hired by BMW as it was looking to shift its image from specialty car-maker, with a narrow appeal, to a company all kinds of people could admire. Panke is holding a delicate balance between preserving the German company's tradition for performance automobiles and seiz-ing upon ideas to enhance BMW's position. While running BMW's American operations during the 1990s, Panke heeded his dealers' cry to develop a luxury sport utility vehicle that would be among the fastest on the road. Panke also saw the promise that the Mini Cooper offered in attracting younger buyers, and he turned the 1960s icon into a smash hit for the new millennium. That open-mindedness helped BMW spar with Lexus in 2003 as the best-selling luxury brand in the United States, and Panke is now aiming to increase sales in the years ahead as he broadens BMW's lineup. Even as he does so, he is pledging that a BMW will always be a BMW.

Carlos Ghosn, the charismatic chief executive at Nissan, is perhaps the most instantly recognizable automotive figure, aside from GM's Robert Lutz, in the industry today. With his hawklike face and quick, clipped speech, the Brazilian-born executive of Lebanese descent has become so popular since arriving in Japan in 1999 that he has starred in a series of comic books. Under Ghosn's leadership, Nissan has undergone a transformation. When he joined Nissan upon its alliance with the French automaker Renault, the Japanese company was saddled with more than $20 billion in automotive debt. Its product lineup was dotted with also-ran vehicles that required thousands of dollars of incentives to sell. And Nissan was bogged down by a corporate culture rooted in the past, with too many interlocking ties to suppliers. Today, Nissan has eliminated its debt. It has become one of the leanest, fastest-moving companies in the world, mirroring Ghosn's own impatience to push Nissan forward. In 2003, Nissan opened a new factory in Canton,

Mississippi, where it began building a crucial new series of vehicles, including the Quest minivan, the Titan pickup truck and two big SUVs. In addition, Nissan has even more vehicles coming, all developed swiftly and sharing components with Renault. By the middle of the decade, Ghosn is expected to take control at both Renault and Nissan, coordinating the attack of what he hopes will become one of the world's leading automotive giants.

Whether based in Tokyo or Munich or California, executives of these foreign companies share the same enthusiasm and drive and belief that their companies, though not the world's largest (at least not yet, in Toyota's case), can have a tremendous influence in individual markets such as the United States. In doing so, they shield themselves from the economic forces that have been Detroit's own undoing. With its emphasis on size and economies of scale, Detroit has always been vulnerable to the boom-and-bust cycles that have been a part of the car industry since its inception. As long as Detroit could rake in enough profits during good times to make up for the losses it encountered during lean years, that never mattered. Before imports' push began, Detroit's solution to any softening of sales was simply to shut down its plants to keep its vehicle inventories in line with sales, laying off workers for months on end. No more: Current United Auto Workers labor contracts at GM, Ford and Chrysler require the companies to pay their workers nearly all of their income, whether they are on the job or not. Moreover, the companies are limited from permanently closing factories without the union's agreement, and must finalize any such moves during contract negotiations, a process that ensures generous benefits for workers who are losing their jobs.

These contracts, as well as the pensions and health care that GM, Ford and Chrysler provide for their workers, active and retired, have led to a penalty of $1,200 per vehicle that must be overcome before they can book the first penny of profit. That is not the case at Toyota and Honda and the other foreign firms, whose non-union employees are for the most part at least a decade younger than their counterparts in Detroit, and whose health care and retirement costs are structured in a far different way.

Detroit has spent countless hours and millions of dollars trying to figure out the imports' secrets, studying their marketing methods, dissecting the way their vehicles are assembled, replicating the way they are manufactured, all without being able to truly understand their approach. Each Detroit company entered into joint ventures with Japanese companies—GM with Toyota, Ford with Mazda and Chrysler with Mitsubishi—in a fruitless effort to find a silver bullet. Unable to find answers, Detroit has come up with countless excuses to explain the foreign companies' success. It has hurled unfair-competition accusations at its rivals, insinuating that they are dumping vehicles on the market at low prices, maintaining that foreign governments are propping up the companies by keeping currency rates abnormally weak. Detroit has even criticized buyers of foreign companies' cars for having bad taste, as Bob Lutz, GM's vice chairman, asserted in 2002. Deconstructing the success of the Toyota Camry, Lutz called it one of the ugliest cars ever to travel the nation's roadways, thereby slamming the choice of nearly 6 million consumers who might be potential customers for GM. (Even Lutz, however, had to concede the Camry's sterling quality.)

To understand why Detroit is faltering, however, you need to get out of Detroit and visit places like California, where legions of young "tuners" have transformed their vanilla-flavored Honda Civic compacts into automotive dream machines. Or New England, where more than half of all vehicles sold are now imports, a distinction that once only California could claim. Or visit the headquarters of the imports, in Japan and Korea, where the desks of some of the young engineers are situated right in the lobby of the development centers, where they work oblivious to the flocks of curious visitors who arrive for appointments each day. In these places, Detroit's illustrious past is merely a memory, and for some of the youngest buyers and employees, not even that.

However, if you attend the annual Dream Cruise, held one week each August on Woodward Avenue in Detroit's northern suburbs, it would be easy to assume that Detroit's glory days have continued. Throughout the week, travel slows to a crawl as classic cars from the twentieth century such as Cadillacs, Studebakers and Corvettes trundle up and down the boulevard in a rolling museum, gleaming in the summer sunshine. Here, on the long summer nights, women stroll in poodle skirts and men preen in Hawaiian finery, reliving Detroit's dominance and wallowing in the nostalgia that American companies still manipulate when they feel the need. A visit to the Dream Cruise would make any onlooker think that since 1965 time has stood still.

But the fact is that there is no longer a single segment of the car market where Detroit is clearly the leading player, either in profits, quality or buzz. Detroit lost its grip on the small-car market first, seeing Japanese companies take command in the 1970s and 1980s. Later, in the 1990s, the Korean manufacturers assumed the dominant position among the industry's entry-level vehicles. Mid-sized sedans, traditionally a Detroit strength, and still the heart of the automobile market, were ceded in the late 1980s and early 1990s to Toyota, with its bulletproof Camry and to Honda, with its Accord. More recently, they've been joined by Volkswagen, with the sturdy Passat, and Hyundai and its inexpensive Sonata. The highly profitable American luxury vehicle market, the source of numerous fantasy cars like the Lincoln Continentals of the 1930s and the Cadillacs of the 1950s, hasn't been led by those two brands since 1986. During the past 15 years, the leadership among the most expensive cars has been snared by Lexus, BMW and Mercedes-Benz, and trailed by such challengers as Audi, Acura and Infiniti, despite numerous attempts by the Detroit auto companies to revive their most heralded brands.

In the early 1990s, Detroit found itself on the verge of another near-collapse, beset by a weak economy and the impact of the Gulf War. It sought an answer that would convince customers to buy its vehicles in volume again. It found one in a category called sport utility vehicles. Single-handledly, the SUV became Detroit's ticket back to prosperity, with profits soaring as high as $15,000 a vehicle on luxury models like the Cadillac Escalade and Lincoln Navigator. Waits for the Jeep Grand Cherokee and Ford's Explorer stretched for months. By mid-decade, it seemed that Detroit had found one place where it was immune to a charge from the foreign companies. GM, Ford and Chrysler dominated the market, holding more than 90 percent of SUV sales. But imports recognized the new opportunity for sales growth and quickly jumped in.

By 2003, Toyota and Lexus together sold eight different SUVs, from the entry-level RAV-4 to Lexus's hulking LX 470. Honda, though late to this market, brought out the well-regarded Acura MDX and the Pilot sport utility. Mercedes and BMW entered the luxury SUV market with the M-Class and the X5, respectively. Even Porsche got into the fray with its controversial but breathtakingly fast Cayenne. And the Korean companies began to gobble sales, thanks to vehicles like the Hyundai Santa Fe.

Meanwhile, that most essential family market, minivans, which Chrysler virtually owned throughout the 1990s, was completely turned upside down by a new version of the Honda Odyssey minivan in 1998. With its three rows of seats and its solid handling, the Odyssey destroyed Chrysler's lock on a market to which it devoted the production of three of its factories. The downfall of its minivans triggered a financial crisis that sent the company into a tailspin and cost Chrysler's chief executive his job. As other foreign companies came forward with their minivans, such as the Toyota Sienna and the Nissan Quest, Detroit companies' share of the minivan market fell from 94 percent in 1992 to 70 percent in 2003.

With the intense loyalty that pickup owners feel for their trucks, the truck market was Detroit's last bastion. Detroit had a long history in the category, stretching back to the industry's earliest days. (One of the first variations that Henry Ford made on the Model A was a pickup truck.) Together, GM, Ford and Chrysler sell 2 million pickups each year, and the Ford F-series has been the best-selling vehicle in the United States since 1978. But in 1998, when Toyota, which had failed on its initial attempt at a full-sized pickup, created the Tundra, it instantly swept honors from *Consumer Reports* magazine as the nation's leading-quality truck, instantly making Toyota a force with which to be reckoned in a market that Detroit thought it would always own. More competition is on its way from the imports, with the Nissan Titan; a new, bigger version of Toyota Tundra; and a sporty pickup that Honda plans to build later this decade.

If the minivans, sedans and luxury cars that the foreign companies have introduced are any indication, those pickups will have customers waiting for them when they arrive at showrooms. Unfortunately for American automobile companies, in many cases the most desirable consumers, with high incomes, good educations and comfortable homes, have switched allegiances and have defected to imports. That has left Detroit to compete for increasingly older, less-educated, lower-income buyers whose sole priority is a good deal. Many of the vehicles that the foreign companies sell are now built in the United States, at plants that American car manufacturers insisted foreign companies build in order to compete on a level playing field. In the past 20 years, foreign companies have built 17 new factories in the United States, many of the newest in the South, and also in states like Ohio, Indiana and Kentucky, where Detroit companies have had plants for years.

Even as Ford, struggling to regain its former glory, proceeds to close factories as part of its bid to restructure and get its manufacturing capability in line with its dwindling sales, imports have continued to open new ones. Together, they now employ 85,000 factory workers, more than Chrysler and almost as many as Ford, and their factories produce nearly 5 million vehicles a year. Not a single one of these new factories has been organized by the UAW, whose only presence among these "transplants" is where the plants began in joint ventures with Detroit carmakers.

This is not the way things were supposed to turn out. Indeed, to many Americans, it is a big surprise that Detroit is in such dire straits. As recently as the middle of the 1990s, it looked as if GM, Ford and Chrysler had vanquished or at least outdistanced the foreign invaders. Customers waited months to buy the sexy Dodge Viper, the elegant Cadillac Seville STS sedan and Ford's seemingly endless variety of SUVs, each bigger and more luxurious than the one that had come before it. Profits were enormous, topping a collective $16 billion for the automakers in 1998. The companies were venturing into all sorts of new businesses, including Internet companies, junkyards and electric vehicle companies, flush with cash that they used to fund their acquisitions. It was fun, again, to be in the automobile business in Detroit. The industry abounded with celebrity CEOs, such as Robert Eaton at Chrysler and Jacques Nasser at Ford, gazing upon their kingdoms with confident smiles. A *Time* magazine cover portrayed the chief executives of all three companies in profile, aligned to mimic Mount Rushmore.

But the American companies declared victory over the imports long before the game was won. As has happened so frequently throughout the industry's history, the "good enough" mentality that has plagued the American automobile makers took hold once more by the year 2000. Sadly, the ground that Detroit conquered in the early 1990s had been lost again by the end of the decade, and the loss kept accelerating into the new millennium. In the wake of the 2001 recession and the terrorism that followed, the Big Three relentlessly enveloped consumers in a wave of incentives such as zero percent financing, no money down and no payments for months, and continued the offers for months afterward. Yet GM barely registered an increase in market share, while both Ford and Chrysler lost ground. The most desirable buyers simply shrugged and bought the higher-quality imports, even though the deals were not as widespread.

And this came at a time when the country was awash in patriotism, stirred by the horror of the September 11 attacks and fueled, at the end of 2002, by the specter of war with Iraq. There would probably never be a better climate for GM, Ford and Chrysler in which to gain sales.

What had gone wrong? First, *import companies have a better handle on consumers' tastes. They can react faster and they do not let up.* Toyota and Honda were at a huge disadvantage relative to Detroit when they first put their cars on sale in the United States. They didn't have a clue what American consumers wanted. They tripped up by simply shipping over the same vehicles that they sold in Japan and elsewhere in the world, which were small, fuel-efficient automobiles that appealed to only a small number of consumers. Toyota did so poorly with its initial car, the Toyopet, that it had to abandon the American market, returning two years later. The original Honda Civic, a two-door with a hatchback, was likened by its critics to one of Honda's riding lawn mowers, albeit with a roof and windshield wipers. And the quality of Hyundai's Korean-made vehicles was so dismal when they first went on sale in the mid-1980s that the company was almost forced to close up shop in the United States several years later.

But Toyota, Honda and Hyundai recognized that they didn't know American customers the way they knew their buyers back home. So they set out to ask the people who bought their cars what they really wanted. The first answer the Japanese companies got, in the wake of the nation's energy crises of the 1970s, was fuel economy. Subsequent feedback told them that quality and reliability and roominess, along with affordability, were key. And finally, they found an edge in appealing new body styles, like small SUVs and car-based wagons, called crossover vehicles, that no one else had dreamed up. As they were learning these lessons, Honda and Toyota were unhampered by the vast dealer organizations that Detroit companies had set up. Today, only 1,287 dealers sell approximately 2 million Toyota and Lexus cars a year, while there are 4,500 Chevrolet dealers selling a similar number of vehicles. Such a streamlined organization made two things possible: First, dealers made more money on each Toyota or Lexus they sold. Second, they were able to communicate with management much more easily to share news from the showroom floor and provide a heads-up when problems arose.

For quite a long while after they entered the U.S. market, the Japanese companies consistently delivered on their basic task, the small-car market. Detroit seemed willing to cede that market, because GM, Ford and Chrysler hadn't found a way to build cars to compete with these "rice burners" at a profit, and they really didn't want to be bothered figuring out how to do so. Japan's dominance here wasn't troublesome to them. Detroit's executives argued that the success of foreign vehicles was limited. Subcompacts and compacts might be desired by ecology-minded individuals or small families, but once consumers needed more space or comfort, buyers, Detroit assumed, would automatically come home to American automobiles. They assumed that the Japanese companies were content to stay small and dominate their niche. But the Japanese companies gradually gained expertise. Once they understood consumers' needs, they made their move upscale. By the late 1980s, they began building vehicles specifically for the American consumer—and building them at American plants, under the direction of skilled American executives, many of whom had trained at the Detroit companies. As American consumers' tastes evolved, so did the companies' lineups. The cars got bigger, the interiors more luxurious, the construction even more solid. The Toyota Camry, for example, grew six inches in 1992, and gained a smooth rounded styling that looked nothing like its boxy Japanese predecessor and everything like an American car.

And as their customers grew more affluent, Japanese companies sensed an opportunity in the luxury car market. In 1982, Toyota chairman Eiji Toyoda declared that he wanted to build "the finest car in the world." Toyota designers and engineers spent the next seven years studying American consumers and crafting a sedan they thought would attract aging baby boomers, who they felt were ready to shift to cars that cost more money and were more luxurious than the Toyotas they had originally owned. The result was the Lexus LS 400, which went on sale in 1989 to rave reviews, a rush of sales and the consternation of German and American luxury car companies. By 2003, Lexus outsold every other luxury brand, including century-old brands like Mercedes. And Lexus has been joined in the luxury car market by Nissan and Honda, with their Infiniti and Acura brands. They, too, have become solid luxury competitors.

Korea's Hyundai suffered a horrible sales disaster during its first decade in the United States, due to the horrendous quality of its small cars. Its former American president, Finbarr O'Neill, now trying to revive Mitsubishi, jolted Korean engineers into improvements, then decided to tackle Hyundai's poor image by offering consumers a generous 10-year, 100,000-mile warranty in order to convince customers that Hyundai believed in its cars and consumers could trust the company. The approach worked. Hyundai's sales quadrupled from 1998 to nearly 400,000 a year. It is now aiming to sell 1 million automobiles in the United States by the year 2010, which would make Hyundai the same size as Honda is now.

Only 10 years ago, European luxury makers, too, were in trouble. Like Detroit, they had completely miscalculated the ability of their

Japanese rivals to create high-quality luxury cars at reasonable prices that consumers would want to buy. Moreover, the European cars didn't have the features American consumers wanted, such as cup holders to hold coffee and Big Gulp drinks. On top of that, exchange rates and high manufacturing costs early in the decade put European cars well out of many consumers' reach. The collective market share for European vehicles in the United States hit bottom in 1994 at a mere 3.9 percent of the market. But like the Japanese and Koreans, they started over. One by one, Mercedes, BMW and Volkswagen retuned their lineups and their approaches, searching for the right mix of company heritage, performance and brand image that would win customers back. And their strategy has been enormously successful. Their vehicles have become the next choice for consumers who want to upgrade from their Asian imports. Today BMW, VW and Mercedes are expanding their lineups in both directions—smaller, cheaper vehicles intended to appeal to younger consumers, and ultra-luxury vehicles for the most demanding consumers. Overall, European vehicles have more than doubled their market share in just a decade and expect to gain even more sales.

What unites these foreign-based companies is that they have developed a better sense of what their American customers want than Detroit has. They have shown a willingness to change and go beyond the status quo that has made them leaders in the increasingly fast-paced car marketplace. Detroit companies, too often lagging behind, have fallen back on complaining that the Japanese, especially, have an unfair advantage because they are able to introduce their vehicles at home first, iron out the bugs, and then bring them to the United States, while Detroit has no such opportunity to hide its mistakes.

One could argue, however, that the imports have a tougher challenge than does Detroit. Unlike the Big Three, which rely on North America for three-quarters of their sales, the imports have to satisfy vast numbers of consumers in at least two key markets—their home market and the United States. They have to get it right more times than Detroit does. All anyone has to do is visit Tokyo—where hundreds of thousands of young people pour into districts like Shibuya and Harajuku on the weekends, to shop for clothes and electronics and sample the latest DVDs—to know just how hard a task pleasing the consumer in Japan can be. Tastes change daily, weekly, monthly, in a way that Americans have yet to experience. The platform shoes that were all the rage with Japanese teens in April are déclassé by May, and interest in automobiles is just as fickle.

What the imports learned was to not assume that their experience in their home markets automatically translates to the United States. The U.S. market may be the world's easiest to enter, but it is one of the toughest in which to compete. The scale and the outlook are completely different. Today, Toyota, Honda, Mazda, Mitsubishi and Nissan all sell more vehicles in the United States than they do in Japan. The weak Japanese market, in a slump for much of the past 10 years, no longer subsidizes the sales organizations in the United States. When they stumble here, as some of them have over the years, they hurt the parent company. So success in the United States has become paramount.

Although they excel at anticipating consumers' desires, foreign companies have become even more skittish about deciphering their success. Rarely do they boast about their vehicles in the fashion of Detroit's automakers. They would prefer to announce low sales expectations, and exceed them, than fall short of goals that are too optimistic. Another tactic is to focus primarily on pleasing current owners first, without publicly declaring that they will entice owners of other brands to defect, even if that is what ends up happening. When it introduced the Odyssey minivan, for example, Honda estimated that it would sell a mere 60,000 in its first year on the market; but it saw demand soar to more than 180,000 a year thanks to word of mouth from delighted consumers. Toyota posted record net income for the industry in 2002, yet its executives agonized over every investment in every new product, every plant and every dollar spent on marketing campaigns. This combination of humility, determination, careful attention and, above all, devotion to quality has been a formula that has worked time and again for them.

General Motors, Ford and Chrysler, however, have been unable to find a similar formula. And this is the second reason underlying the disintegration of the American auto manufacturers' position in the industry: *Detroit left the door wide open for the imports to walk right through.* The great tragedy of Detroit's decade-long demise is that it is self-inflicted. Detroit has been mired in a boom-and-bust cycle from which it cannot break free. Its sense of timing has been numbed by its own tendency to look inward and believe only in its own conclusions. GM, Ford and Chrysler shifted en masse in the early- to mid-1990s to focus most of their attention on pickups, SUVs and minivans. As a result, they ignored the car market, claiming that trucks were where consumers' tastes had shifted. They assumed that it would take years for the Japanese, the Germans and the Koreans to catch up in truck sales. Even when the foreign car manufacturers began to introduce their new light trucks, Detroit doubted that Americans would buy them.

When the foreign car manufacturers realized that they had missed consumers' initial shift toward light trucks, they made a concerted effort to catch up and to surpass Detroit. Yet in doing so, they continued to pay careful attention to the car market, introducing even better versions of their standard-bearers, like the Camry and the Corolla, the Accord and the Civic. In one sense, this was a no-brainer for the foreign manufacturers, because these cars are far more popular outside the United States. The imports had to develop them for their home markets in Japan and Europe, so why not spend the money to develop improved versions for the United States at the same time? In doing this, the imports showed yet again one of the secrets to their core strength: find a portion of the market that everyone else has abandoned and do well in it, and never relinquish their hold over that category as they go on to tackle a new one.

Detroit paid a steep price for its shortsighted approach. Not only did the imports get into the light truck category, they began outmaneuvering Detroit with several innovations. Toyota and Honda were first to introduce small SUVs based on car underpinnings that were easy to handle, and more sporty and affordable for young families while still offering plenty of room. The Toyota RAV-4 and the Honda CR-V might not have been able to vault a stack of logs or slough through the mud, as Chrysler's Jeeps could do. And sometimes the Japanese SUVs were noisy on the highway. But the reality was that most SUV owners never drove off-road in their vehicles. They never left their suburban streets and paved highways. And the noise level was something they were willing to endure. When Mercedes discovered that 30 percent of its wealthy sedan owners were purchasing Detroit's sport utilities as well, but would buy a Mercedes SUV instead if one was available, the German company brought out its M-Class, built at its first U.S. plant in Alabama. The M-Class handled as well as one of its well-engineered cars and gave Mercedes buyers a feeling of power, prestige and privilege. Soon there were two Mercedes vehicles in their driveways, instead of a Mercedes sedan and a Jeep or a Ford Explorer.

The same pattern was pursued by other foreign manufacturers. In 2001, the BMW 5-series won the highest score for any car in history from *Consumer Reports*, while its 3-series compact became the car to aspire to among younger buyers. And the imports continue to pursue new niches. When gasoline prices hit $2 a gallon in 2000 and soared even higher in subsequent years, it was Toyota and Honda who were ready with hybrid gasoline-electric vehicles. Ford, run by an environmentalist, delayed plans to introduce its own hybrids and, in fact, sold off its electric car company. At the end of 2002, Honda even had sold the industry's first hydrogen fuel-cell car to the governor of California, well before Detroit companies expected to have such vehicles available, despite their vows to beat the Japanese with better hydrogen fuel technology.

Why have the imports been able to prevail even at a time when the country has never been more patriotically inclined? That is a third reason for foreign manufacturers' success in the United States: the impact of the new global economy. In the 1990s, products from all parts of the world flooded American stores. At the same time, American manufacturers stumbled over themselves to open new factories in Mexico, Brazil, China, Thailand and in Eastern Europe, seeking to lower costs in order to compete. Joint ventures, too, became the order of the day, involving German banks, British telecommunications companies and all manner of Asian firms. American companies had become more international and seemed to show no loyalty to American consumers or workers. Americans began to show little loyalty back, whether it was a TV set or a DVD player or an automobile. To most car buyers, Toyota and Honda's Japanese heritage mattered less and less. To some it was even an advantage, because Japanese cars had come to symbolize quality. The same was true for European companies. As this mind-set change took shape, the import manufacturers took steps to ingratiate themselves with the people where they did business. In 1985, foreign manufacturers had factories in just a handful of American states, including California, Ohio and South Carolina. By 2003, Alabama alone was home to investments by Toyota, Honda, Mercedes and Hyundai, earning it the nickname "Detroit South." (Or, as David G. Bronner, the colorful head of Alabama's pension system and the chairman of US Airways puts it, Detroit is now known in his region as "Alabama North.") Import companies have established operations in a handful of states.

Of course, American consumers do not inherently dislike Detroit. In fact, they have shown a willingness to try just about anything innovative that General Motors, Ford and Chrysler can unveil. After the September 2001 terrorist attacks, Americans responded in record numbers to the Big Three companies' offers of zero percent financing on cars and trucks. Chrysler's PT Cruiser became an instant hit when Chrysler introduced it in 2001. The Ford Thunderbird made heads turn when it finally arrived in showrooms in 2002, months behind schedule. The Chevrolet Corvette, 50 years on, has legions of enthusiastic fans. Detroit can still summon its clout and its magic on occasion.

But GM, Ford and Chrysler suffer from a handicap that the imports do not. They are inconsistent—inconsistent in terms of quality, reliability, durability and styling—and as a result, they repeatedly leave their customers heartbroken, because it shows that the Big Three do not understand them and do not genuinely respect them. Detroit, deep down, has bought into the iconography that it has nurtured over the years. Its executives seem to truly believe that only they know what American buyers want. Because Detroit dominated the industry for its first 100 years, American car company executives feel they are the best arbiters of the industry. They think they know far more than their customers about the vehicles that these customers drive. They are convinced that should they stumble, as all companies are wont to do, consumers will be forgiving and return to Detroit anyway. Even in the face of vast research to the contrary, Detroit for years has convinced itself of the notion, completely unsubstantiated, that its vehicles are every bit as good as those built by the import companies. In fact, this was the very claim made one morning in November 2002 by General Motors vice chairman Bob Lutz when he declared GM's vehicles the equal of those built by Honda and Toyota. Yet that afternoon, GM recalled 1.5 million minivans.

Poor quality, as well as an inability to trust what Detroit tells us, continues to undermine Americans' faith in Detroit. In one of his television ads, created to convince consumers to believe in his family's struggling auto company, Bill Ford bubbled with enthusiasm for the small Ford Focus. He failed to mention that the Focus, designed in Europe, has been the subject of government defect investigations 11 times since it went on sale in the United States in 1999. A few months earlier, another

Ford car, the new T-bird, which should have been a standard-bearer for the company in design and excitement, had to have production shut down for several days after engine fans caught fire on the assembly line.

Detroit brings to mind a kind of automotive Oz, in which its simple announcement of a victory over imports is supposed to substitute for the real thing—despite the fact that its market share continues to fall and its profits have evaporated. Yet few are fooled. One need only look at the resale values of Detroit automobiles, far lower than the resale amounts for the best used foreign cars. This sense of unshaken superiority has been Detroit's most fatal flaw. For its hubris has led to blindness in the halls of the Big Three, disappointment and even a vague sense of betrayal among many American consumers.

Too many American car buyers are simply fed up with the vehicles that Detroit has tried to peddle to them. Millions of customers, loyal to GM for generations, finally got tired of tinny doors, keys that didn't fit both the door and the trunk, and instrument panels that simply looked cheap. Despite the improvements that Detroit has made, despite all its vows and promises, the list of flaws in its cars continues to exceed that of its rivals.

On the other hand, Toyota, Honda and the others realize full well that they cannot claim victory—that they can *never* do so. For as Detroit has shown, it is all too easy to lose one's advantage. The Japanese carmakers are frightened by the emergence of the resurgent Korean auto companies, such as Hyundai and Kia. The Koreans are battling for the hearts of the children of the Japanese and German consumers that they captured. These young buyers don't want to buy the same vehicles that Mom and Dad owned unless they can be convinced that these cars are what best fit their needs. And so Toyota created a whole new operation, called Scion, aimed at what it refers to as Generation Y buyers, confronting what it sees as a potential image problem long before it actually is in danger of losing sales.

No one dares to write off Detroit, however. Anger—as well as lost profits—is driving GM, Ford and Chrysler into action. Already this decade, Ford and DaimlerChrysler have replaced their chief executives and their top management. A Ford is back at the helm of Ford for the first time in 22 years. GM, which dominated the industry for so many years, has been forced to bring in fresh talent from outside. GM, Ford and Chrysler are spending vast amounts of money to develop new vehicles that they vow, yet again, will be their best ever and will provide the resounding answer to the imports on American ground.

But changing faces and making promises cannot change an attitude of indifference that has long grown among consumers. For too many years, Detroit companies' primary tactic for fighting back has been to shift consumers' attention to the future, while leveraging their past as a sentimental weapon that they have used to obscure the deficiencies of the present. But though consumers might appreciate the vehicles of the past, and express curiosity about what's coming down the road, they are focused, more than ever, on the present. The advent of the Internet has given them more access than ever before to information about the cars they are interested in. Comparing cars is easier than ever. Such mysteries as leasing, invoice prices and used car values are explained at the stroke of a few keys.

Rather than listen solely to Detroit, consumers now listen to each other. In an age of data, one of the most important criteria in buying a car is word of mouth. And what customers seem to be telling each other—in person, in e-mail and on the Internet—is that there are better choices than vehicles from Detroit. Satisfied customers have become the best selling tool foreign manufacturers could ever have. And they realize it, which is why they are so completely focused on consumers. No matter what GM, Ford and Chrysler have used in their attempt to fend off foreign competition, consumers' own resolve has been the one weapon that GM, Ford and Chrysler seem powerless to defend themselves against, for all their years of unquestioned industrial might.

CHAPTER TWO

A FALLEN COMRADE

THE DETROIT AUTO SHOW at times brings to mind the May Day military parades that were a perennial feature of the old Soviet Union. The two weeks at the beginning of every January mark the American automobile industry's time to show off all its prestige and might. In the past, the show has attracted presidents and senators, celebrities, talk-show hosts and every manner of corporate leaders, all drawn by a glittering array of vehicles to the Cobo Convention Center on the banks of the ice-strewn Detroit River. The 2003 show was no exception. Strolling the cavernous hall, it was hard to know where to cast one's eyes first. "A Proud and Primal Roar," the *New York Times* headline announced. It seemed to sum it up best. General Motors, Ford and Chrysler had thrust deep into their very core to come up with vehicles that marked the essence of their being as American companies and that represented the message that they wanted their audience to understand: We still have it and don't you forget it.

At one end of the show floor was the sprawling GM display, whose highlight was the gleaming Cadillac Sixteen, an expression of the ultimate in late-middle-aged male testosterone. Its proud creator was GM's vice chairman, Bob Lutz, who at age 71 had outlasted virtually his entire generation of industry executives to end up triumphantly as Detroit's best-known automotive figure. The Sixteen was only the latest exercise in automotive fantasy that had come to life under Lutz's direction, and one that he had long wanted to produce.

Years earlier, Lutz had sketched something that looked very much like the Sixteen on the back of a menu during a dinner at Die Ente Vom Lehel, the elegant restaurant in the Hotel Nassauer Hof in Wiesbaden, Germany, near Frankfurt. At the time, Lutz was the president of Chrysler, which was known for risk taking, spunk and its ability to stretch development dollars farther than any other firm in the industry. The fact that this led to vehicles with subpar quality, and that Chrysler's success was really based on the popularity of its Jeeps and minivans, was rarely discussed. The sketch was meant to show where Lutz would go if he had the resources to develop his ultimate dream car. It would have been a step beyond the Dodge Viper, the low-slung, sexy two-seater that jump-started Chrysler's image after its second brush with bankruptcy in the late 1980s.

Chrysler, in third place among the American companies, did not have the money or the inclination to produce Lutz's dream car. So he gave away the sketch to a journalist as a souvenir. But GM, where he had been given virtually a free hand since arriving in the late summer of 2001, had the resources and, moreover, the need for such an image-builder. With Lutz in charge of product development, GM wasn't about to let luxury car makers, like Mercedes and Bentley and Rolls-

Royce, get away with dominating the market for ultraluxury cars costing $150,000 and more.

Lutz fairly burst with cockiness and machismo as he showed off the Sixteen to the flocks of visiting executives and journalists. They crowded around the car, with its 16-cylinder, 1,000-horsepower engine and long, low-slung body, as he lounged, beaming, against the car body amid the popping of flashbulbs. Lutz had particular reason to preen, for his face that week stared out from the pages of *Newsweek*. The magazine's Detroit bureau chief, Keith Naughton, had been allowed to follow the development of the Sixteen during the past year. GM insiders whispered that Lutz would have landed on the cover of the magazine if not for a pesky political crisis in North Korea that bumped him in favor of the dictator Kim Jung Il.

The mere fact that GM would try to compete in such a hallowed segment of the market sparked waves of enthusiasm for its bravado. But the Sixteen wasn't the only such eye-catching car from Detroit. Ford had rolled out its own wave of vehicles, attempting to camouflage the fact that it had just been through one of the worst years in its history. Only a few years earlier, Ford had been in the spotlight at this show with a new version of the venerable Thunderbird. Now it was trying to leverage nostalgia once again. Its Mustang concept car, painted in dark teal, was modeled after the gutsy high-powered Mustangs of the 1970s, with their loud engines and getaway power. In fact, this concept version looked so much like the classic cars that passersby had to look twice to discern that it was a new model.

Its long hood and racing body seemed to reach back to a more glorious time, when the *vroom-vroom-VROOM* of engines and the squeal of tires could be heard on wide boulevards across the country late into summer nights. This Mustang drew such scrutiny among journalists that the company had to occasionally cordon off the car so that maintenance men in jumpsuits could wipe the fingerprints off its glistening sheet metal. The buzz about the Mustang overshadowed a more important vehicle—in fact, a far more important vehicle—that Ford also was unveiling at this show. The year 2003 ushered in the latest version of Ford's F-series pickup, which has been the best-selling vehicle in the country, car or truck, for the past 25 years. Yet this latest generation had come to life under a cloud. Just a few months before, Chrysler had introduced a restyled Dodge Ram pickup to a stronger reception than Ford had expected. Meanwhile, GM was pouring on rebates in advance of a face-lift on the Chevrolet Silverado and GMC Sierra, hoping that the incredible deals would lure customers away from Ford's trucks.

Feeling the competition bear down on its most critical vehicle, and knowing that it could not risk a defeat, Ford spent billions to revamp the F-series, so much that its costs soared more than $1,000 a vehicle above the investment it had made on the previous version. In another, more free-spending era, Ford might have been able to impress both Wall Street and its buyers with the attention it was giving the new F-series. But the cost increases came at a time when most auto companies were boasting that they were able to cut their product spending on each succeeding generation, thanks to computer-aided design and manufacturing techniques that were speeding up the development process. Ford looked wasteful for having gone in the opposite direction, especially when it had lost $6 billion over the past two years. So Ford instead chose to put its spotlight on the Mustang, and in light of the attention that the Sixteen was getting, the decision gave it a chance to say, "Look, we have something exciting, too."

But neither the Sixteen nor the Mustang could compete in sound and sheer gutsiness with what Chrysler roared out for the show's approval: the Dodge Tomahawk. It was not really a car at all, but a motorcycle with 500 horsepower and a 10-cylinder engine. It was ridden onto the floor by Wolfgang Bernhard, Chrysler's chief operating officer, who had accompanied Chrysler CEO Dieter Zetsche to Detroit from Germany a little over two years before in a desperate attempt to stop the hemorrhaging that had nearly laid the auto company flat. Bernhard sported a black leather jacket and a huge grin as he rode what was essentially the Dodge Viper's engine on wheels. Crowds instantly materialized, and within hours the Chrysler entry had become the talk of the show.

Even Lutz eventually strolled by with an entourage to look at the knife-precise contours and get a feel for its hard rubber seat. Chrysler had not planned to put the Tomahawk in production at all—it was simply a concept vehicle. But given the reaction, the company announced that it might build a few for $250,000 apiece. "Grown men fall to their knees and weep. I've never seen anything like it," Bernhard told the trade publication *Automotive News*. It was one of those moments that the American automobile manufacturers would like to freeze in time. For, just a few steps away inside Cobo Center, there was ample proof of the reality that GM, Ford and Chrysler faced outside the convention hall, where they had to compete for buyers with foreign competition.

In the first days of the show, GM had been showing off its wares like a grand pasha waving his jeweled hand over the fruits of his kingdom. But its largesse could not dispel a question lingering in the minds of everyone attending the show: What will the Nissan pickup look like? The question was justified. Only four years before, Nissan had been flat on its back, in danger of going out of business, nearly sunk by more than $30 billion in debt. Its recovery, under the leadership of Carlos Ghosn, had been swift and seemingly miraculous. By shutting plants, slicing costs and overhauling Nissan's product-development operations, Ghosn had wiped out billions of dollars of automotive debt and brought Nissan back to profitability in only three years. Now he was embarked on another ambitious challenge: to expand Nissan's vehicle lineup, boost its U.S. sales by about 30 percent to 1 million a year, and vault Nissan into position alongside Toyota and Honda in the top tier of Japanese companies.

The big pickup was the centerpiece of the strategy. Toyota had beat Nissan to the full-sized pickup truck market a few years earlier with the Tundra. But it was still big news that a Japanese company was attempting to take on the Detroit companies in the last remaining market that they still dominated. Bigger than the Tundra and as big as the largest Detroit trucks, the Nissan pickup was going to be produced at Nissan's new $1.5 billion factory in Canton, Mississippi, its second in the United States. Nissan planned to build a big sport utility later on, called the Pathfinder Armada, from the same chassis that it used to build the pickup, as well as a sister SUV for its Infiniti luxury division. Thus, if the pickup failed to live up to expectations, an enormous amount could be lost, not only for Nissan but for the imports' own reputation.

Nissan's game plan at the Cobo Convention Center called for the pickup to come barreling down a steep ramp amid exploding fireworks and screech to a fast stop at the bottom. If the special effects failed, the engine stalled or the brakes didn't work, the truck could easily take out an army of reporters. But everything went gloriously better than even Nissan could have dreamed. Right on schedule, the pickup, which Nissan had named Titan, revved its engine and zoomed down the ramp, hitting its mark perfectly. Big, and burnt orange, it had the unmistakable aura of a hit. Ghosn jumped up from a seat in the audience to illustrate the truck's features, which sent the crowd buzzing. Its exterior design was gutsy, angled and massive. And Nissan had stuffed a powerful V-8 engine under its hood, which guaranteed that it was able to offer enough performance and towing ability to please almost any pickup user.

But there were two other features that surprised the audience and showed that Nissan was thinking beyond its competition. Over the past few years, trucks with extended cabs had become the standard among truck buyers. The extended cab gave them an extra row of seats, for passengers or gear. But most extended cabs were configured so that the driver and passenger doors had to be opened all the way out to allow the smaller door to the cab, called the escape door, to be opened. Nissan, however, had installed a special hinge on its escape door that allowed it to be completely opened and laid almost flat against the side of the truck. The escape door could be opened regardless of whether the front doors were open, allowing more convenient access for passengers or cargo. And it closed completely flush with the front doors, allowing for a seamless side to the truck.

Nissan also was planning to offer another customer-friendly feature: a specially coated truck bed. Generally, auto companies' trucks came with unfinished or scantly painted beds, on the assumption that owners would buy a plastic liner. These liners were one of the easiest ways for dealers and aftermarket shops to make extra money on truck owners, since just about every pickup owner would buy one. But Nissan had developed a technology in which a pebbly graphite coating was sprayed on, offering an easy-to-clean surface without the need for a truck bed. Though company officials expected that some owners would buy a bed anyway, the coating was durable enough that they didn't need to. The features showed the thought that Nissan had put into its truck on behalf of consumers, while its size and stance were equally impressive, especially given that the only pickups the company had ever manufacturered were small models primarily popular with California surfers. "We will compete with nothing less than our best," Ghosn declared.

The Nissan pickup became every bit as much of a must-see at the auto show as the Cadillac Sixteen or the Chrysler Tomahawk. The next morning, Ghosn and the truck stared out from the front pages of both the *Detroit News* and *Detroit Free Press*, a two-for-two accomplishment that was akin, in the Motor City, to landing on the covers of both *Time* and *Newsweek*. And while grown men didn't weep at the sight of it, it did put a look of anxiety on the face of J. Davis Illingworth, a veteran Toyota executive who had run its Lexus division and who had led the company's efforts to discern what younger buyers wanted on future vehicles. "It's impressive," Illingworth acknowledged, adding that Toyota would have to take Nissan's pickup into account as it redesigned the Tundra.

Perhaps the best compliment that the truck received was paid by engineers from one of the Detroit auto companies early the next morning. According to the story told by Nissan, they had headed right for the Nissan pickup, and were caught by security guards with wrenches in their hands and the headlights from the truck lying on the floor as they attempted to dismantle the front end of the truck to figure out how Nissan had put it together.

Clearly, the message that the Detroit companies were getting from outside the doors of Cobo Center could not be ignored as 2003 began. The American economy was in the doldrums and the stock market was losing more ground. Threat of a war with Iraq hung over the world. Tensions between North and South Korea had reached a dangerous level. Oil prices had climbed due to a lengthening strike in Venezuela. Most important, sales figures for the year just ended revealed that the Big Three companies had again lost market share to foreign manufacturers during 2002, leaving GM, Ford and Chrysler with only 61.7 percent of car and light truck sales, their smallest share in history and down 10 percentage points in just five years. Only GM, among the three, had managed to eke out a gain, picking up 0.2 percent of share, though it had come at a tremendous cost. Throughout 2002, and particularly in December, GM had flooded the market with rebates and zero-interest financing, at a cost of nearly $4,000 for every car and truck that it sold. There were special lease deals, too, as low as $149 a month on a Chevrolet Malibu for family members, and enticements for leaseholders to turn in their cars for new ones. On top of it all, GM offered breathtakingly generous terms to its rental car customers like Enterprise and Hertz, putting an estimated 70,000 more cars than usual into their lots, easily enough to guarantee that it would end the year with a market share gain—albeit, in the end, a minuscule one.

GM's actions made a perverse kind of sense. Given that so much was at stake, it might have seemed timid had it not taken advantage of every sales trick at its disposal. Unfazed by complaints from their competitors that the incentives were ruining vehicles' resale value, and warnings from analysts that the constant stream of incentives were conditioning buyers to wait for better and better deals, GM's chief executive, Rick Wagoner, declared, "It's time to stop whining and play the game. At GM, we're going to do what works for us." (Only two months later, at the Geneva Motor Show in Switzerland, Wagoner admitted that the incentives were losing their pull and that GM needed a "new hook" to get customers into showrooms.)

What was good for GM, at least temporarily in 2002, was terrible for Ford. Including its 2002 decline, Ford had lost five points of market share over the past four years. The heady days of the late 1990s, when it seemed a surging Ford might have a chance to surpass a slipping GM in American sales, now seemed but a distant memory. Even as Ford tried to keep attention focused on its revitalization plan, which was meant to propel the company forward into its second century, it continued to lose ground with customers, and its profitability, long the company's hallmark, had evaporated.

Chrysler, too, had lost market share in 2002. But chief executive Zetsche had vowed not to match the onslaught of incentives that GM was throwing at the market. Long term, Zetsche was trying to fashion an identity for Chrysler that was like those of the best imports. He no longer wanted his company to be lumped in as part of Detroit's Big Three. Instead, he wanted its vehicles, like those of Toyota and Honda, to sell largely without hefty rebates and low-interest loans, applying them only when a car or truck was getting long in the tooth or in the most critical cases of stiff competition from its rivals. Zetsche was determined to stand his ground and change the way people thought of the auto company.

As Zetsche discovered, however, it was far too soon for Chrysler to be classified with its import competition. Consumers continued to lump its vehicles in with those from GM and Ford. When his dealers could not match GM's incentives, the company faltered. Without those incentives, Chrysler, which had held 15 percent of the car market in the late 1990s and seemed destined someday to capture 20 percent of American sales, saw its market share plummet to just 11 percent in fall 2002. Dealers were outraged and the company quickly brought the rebates and low-interest loan plans back, stabilizing its market share but frustrating Zetsche's attempts for the company to gain ground.

In addition to the challenge that the Detroit companies faced from the imports—and the economy—by 2003, the industry was under political assault from critics of all kinds, from Hollywood celebrities to officials of the heretofore business-friendly Bush administration. While executives tried to explain the criticism away, it seemed pretty clear that when it came to goodwill among the public, Detroit's residual balance had run low.

The initial criticism emerged from a coalition of church groups and ministers who denounced SUVs as wasteful and abusive of the environment. They called their campaign What Would Jesus Drive?—a takeoff on the admonishment to Christian teens, What Would Jesus Do?, that took root in the 1990s. The What Would Jesus Drive? campaign seemed to have little real religious content, but was meant to target gas-guzzling SUVs. Next came a group from Hollywood calling themselves The Detroit Project. Led by the conservative political commentator and gadfly Arianna Huffington, it launched a wave of television ads that equated ownership of SUVs with support for terrorism. The campaign, which ran during Sunday-morning public affairs talk shows, was a takeoff on a series of ads the previous fall that had linked illegal drugs with terrorism.

Huffington herself had owned a Lincoln Navigator, a big, imposing sport utility that had been the rage in Hollywood during the late

1990s. Her conversion had come after the September 2001 attacks, when her friend Laurie David, the wife of television writer and producer Larry David, convinced her that by driving a vehicle with single-digit gas mileage, she was inadvertently aiding and abetting Middle Eastern countries that allowed terrorists to flourish. Abandoning her Navigator, she bought a black Toyota Prius hybrid-electric vehicle (the car of choice for other celebrities who had been converted to the wisdom of better fuel economy) and took off after the Detroit automakers with a vengeance.

A final volley was fired by the federal regulator in charge of automobile safety. Jeffrey Runge, chief of the National Highway Transportation Safety Administration, denounced SUVs to a shocked audience at an industry conference in Dearborn that coincided with the auto show. Drivers who felt safer in sport utilities than in cars were deceiving themselves, Runge declared: SUVs had a far greater tendency to roll over than did cars. "The thing I don't understand is people, when they choose to buy a vehicle, they might go sit in it and say, 'Gee, I feel safe,'" said Runge, who had been an emergency room physician for 20 years before taking the federal post. "Well, sorry, but you know gut instinct is great for a lot of stuff, but it's not very good for buying an automobile."

He added that he would not let his own daughters ride in an SUV with a poor crash test record, and he vowed that his agency would take more action in coming months to stiffen safety regulations governing sport utilities. Industry officials quickly insisted that their SUVs were among the safest vehicles on the road. They had to—in 2002, sport utility sales accounted for one-quarter of all the vehicles that were sold in the United States, easily making them the top category among the different types of automobiles. The attacks, which were debated on talk radio and on evening cable television all week, dampened the excitement of the auto show.

A few weeks later, Peter DeLorenzo, scion of an automotive family and the prickly industry critic whose Web site, Autoextremist.com, was a weekly must-read even by executives who disagreed with him most, declared, "The pendulum has swung back." Auto companies, he declared, were about to find out that consumers were fickle and that they were likely to turn away from SUVs with the same fervor with which they had once flocked to them.

The weight of the criticism seemed one more obstacle in the effort by GM, Ford and Chrysler to convince consumers to trust Detroit vehicles, and that they were the equivalent of the imports that were gobbling up more sales each day. The irony was that these big SUVs had directly contributed to the demise of the vehicles that had been Detroit's best weapon in its battle against the import brands.

Only 10 years before, Detroit had cars that could compete head-on with the challengers from Japan. It had figured out the secret to convincing buyers to try its vehicles. But instead of supporting these cars with their best talent and resources, so that their gains could be perpetuated, Detroit got distracted by the opportunity to make bigger profits on SUVs than those cars could yield. Instead of focusing its efforts on making each generation better than the last, the companies revealed their true interest: easy, quick profits over long-term credibility.

There was no better example of how Detroit had dropped the ball than the Ford Taurus and its twin, the Mercury Sable, two family cars that had proved Detroit could triumph, given the right determination and approach. In the 1980s, the Taurus was the single best example of how Detroit could take on the Japanese and win. In the 1990s, the Taurus hung on to the title of best-selling car in the United States, despite a hard charge from Toyota and Honda. But by 2002, a mere 10 years later, the Taurus was forgotten. Ford, bent on maximizing the profits that its big SUVs and pickups could provide, thought so little of the Taurus that it did not run a single ad for the car for two years. The demise of the Taurus proved that Detroit, in the end, didn't really care. In a contest between short-term profitability and long-term customer satisfaction, profits won out every time. The irony was that those profits, earned so easily, could slip away just as fast. The much more difficult job of pleasing buyers and maintaining a car's heritage was seemingly beyond Detroit's grasp.

———————

When the Ford Taurus reached the car market in late 1985, it was absolutely revolutionary—in looks and in the way that Ford had brought it to life. Ford gambled that it could compete, and it won. Taurus was a tremendous victory for Ford and marked an impressive comeback for the American automobile industry, which had been in dire straits during the early 1980s. Taurus could proudly take its place with the Toyota Camry and the Honda Accord as one of the leading family cars of its day. From 1992 to 1995, it reigned as the country's best-selling car. Its owners could take pride in the knowledge that they were driving a symbol of American ingenuity and excellence. Along with Chrysler's minivans, the Taurus is one of the most important vehicles that Detroit developed during the late twentieth century. Had Ford continued to refine and improve the Taurus in the way that the Japanese companies have their cars, it still might be considered in their class. Instead, two decades after the Taurus made its mark, both the Camry and the Accord are still solidly on top of the nation's best-selling car list each year, with roughly 400,000 apiece.

They have remained the symbols of their respective companies, whose engineers focus intently on making the next generation of each better than the one before it. At Toyota, the Camry has served as the basis for half a dozen other vehicles, resulting in sales of nearly 1 million vehicles a year in the United States that use the Camry platform.

Meanwhile, the Accord, now in its twentieth year of production in the United States, continues to break new ground with each revision. "The Accord is the franchise," said a Honda executive. In comparison, however, the Taurus has fallen sadly behind in both sales and prestige.

The year 2002 marked the lowest Taurus sales in 10 years. From being a vehicle that consumers could own with pride, it has become essentially a rental car, or a company car, sold in bulk and at a discount to fleet purchases, far less often purchased by individual consumers. "Not many car companies in history have literally abandoned a best-seller," DeLorenzo, the Autoextremist, said. By 2005, Ford planned to phase out the Taurus, replacing it in its lineup with three different models—the Ford 500 family car, the Ford Freestyle crossover vehicle, and the Ford Futura, a hybrid-electric model—none of which was likely to reach the height of popularity that Taurus once achieved.

Yet, when Taurus reached the market in 1985, Ford was already awash in advance orders from buyers eager for the next great American car. Taurus had been born of adversity. Auto companies in the 1970s had been forced by two oil crises and a wave of federal regulations to severely overhaul their lineups, downsizing their cars to improve fuel economy and sending buyers fleeing to import companies that offered small, economical cars. By the early 1980s, Chrysler had nearly gone bankrupt, and Ford was hemorrhaging as well, pleading with the United Auto Workers for contract concessions, and relying on profits from its successful European division to see it through miserable years at home. Fuel-efficient imports were continuing to steal sales away from Detroit companies, and now the Japanese companies were starting to expand their lineups. When Honda opened its first U.S. automobile factory in Ohio in 1982, it signaled that it was serious about transforming itself from primarily a maker of motorcycles into a real competitor beyond small cars. Toyota had started a joint venture with GM in Fremont, California, and it, too, was looking for a site on which to build its first American plant. With Honda selling more than 350,000 Accords a year, and Toyota selling 150,000 Camrys, it seemed of utmost importance to Phillip Caldwell, Ford's chief executive at the time, that Ford prove it could compete with the Japanese.

In the early 1980s, Ford had a development team working on a new family car under the code name Project Sigma. Caldwell had handed the team its new challenge: develop a family sedan that would be world class. And so Team Taurus was born. The project became notable for two reasons: It broke with industry tradition, in which designers handed off to engineers, who handed off to manufacturing experts, and then on to the marketing department—each group fighting for its own priorities and slowing down vehicle development, causing introduction dates to repeatedly be pushed back. Instead, the Taurus development team worked close to one another within Ford's Dearborn operations, giving birth to the phrase "co-location."

They vowed that the Taurus would be introduced on time in late 1985—remarkable for an industry where delays in product development were routine. The team also embraced a new practice called benchmarking, in which they studied the features of competing vehicles to discern which manufacturer had the best features and components in a given area, and chose the ones they wanted to emulate. They decided that the Taurus needed to look distinctive, and borrowed from Audi what ultimately became known as the "aero look," with rounded body styling instead of square-cut corners. The look had several advantages. With rounded instead of angular sheet metal, air would flow more smoothly over the surface of the car, reducing drag and increasing fuel economy. The appearance also made the car look as if it could go faster, a plus at a time when Americans were chafing at a 55-miles-per-hour national speed limit. Calling to mind the favorite snack of President Reagan, Taurus was dubbed the "jellybean car."

The Taurus was priced at just above $10,000 when it went on sale, the average price for a car at the time. For their money, buyers got a roomy vehicle that could seat six passengers, or up to eight in a station wagon version, and which could be purchased with either bucket or bench seats, in contrast to the Japanese cars, which came with only front bucket seats. "It was packaged perfectly for the American market," said Gregory L. Kagay, an automotive industry analyst with Auto Market Scope. Buyers responded with enthusiasm, snapping up so many Taurus and sister Mercury Sable cars that Ford expanded production to two plants, in Chicago and Atlanta. Soon, suburban driveways were dotted with Tauruses. "You didn't have to be ashamed that you owned an American car," said Karl Brauer, editor in chief of Edmunds.com. Ford reveled in profits of up to $2,500 per car, an almost unknown figure at a time when most companies lost money on every car they sold.

Rivals across town, whose cars still looked like boxes of Velveeta, didn't get it. George Borst, now a Toyota executive, recalled taking part in a session at Chevrolet when his fellow managers took apart a Taurus piece by piece to try to figure out how it had been constructed, a practice in the industry that's called a "tear-down." The Chevrolet managers were ripping the Taurus apart verbally, too, saying that there was nothing so special about the Taurus that GM couldn't do. For political reasons, Borst said, he couldn't disagree, for fear the others would think him a traitor. But Borst also said he could see the design advantages of the aero look, and the solid construction of the car, which was better than anything Chevy offered at the time. (A few months after that, Borst jumped to Toyota, where his mentor at Chevrolet, Jim C. Perkins, had already defected to help start the Lexus luxury division.)

Japanese companies, however, wasted no time in responding to the Taurus. The first volley came from Toyota, which brought out the latest version of its Camry in 1988, followed by Honda, which surprised the industry in 1989 with a new version of the Accord that had grown in size and power. Sold as a 1990 model, this new Accord, five inches longer and light years ahead of previous Accord models in sophistication, was such an immediate hit that it became the country's best-selling car. It was the first time that a Japanese model had held the crown, and Accord's popularity spurred Ford to fight back. It did so with alacrity.

The 1990s marked a new phase for the Taurus. Initially, Ford played it safe as it proceeded with new versions of the car. The 1992 restyling of the Taurus didn't really change its appearance, but the car grew in size, as did its engine: Tauruses from here on out would be available only with a V-6, an effort to placate consumers who were seeking performance again after so many years of driving underpowered cars. At the same time, facing a stiff battle with the Japanese for individual customers, Ford saw an opportunity for Taurus in the rental car market.

The early 1990s saw the emergence of a new category of automobiles: the nearly new car. In order to keep factories running, auto companies encouraged rental car companies to buy new vehicles every four months instead of every six months or more, which had long been the industry's practice. In order to encourage the purchases, the companies agreed to buy back the former rental vehicles once the contracts were up, and take responsibility for reselling them at auctions. The continuous sales to rental car companies under these buyback programs helped the Detroit companies solve a problem that arose with their new union contracts. Under an agreement with the UAW in 1990, the auto companies pledged to lay off workers for only 13 weeks at a time. After that, workers would receive most of their take-home pay, even if they were sitting at home and their factories were idle. Since workers were going to be paid anyway, it behooved the auto companies to keep factories running. That meant the cars had to go somewhere, and rental car lots proved the answer.

Once the rental car companies were through with their cars, they would turn them back to the auto companies, which would sell them to dealers at auctions. The dealers couldn't be happier. Since there were so many of these rental cars, the dealers could get them for a song. And because they had just a few thousand miles on the odometer, they still looked new, meaning they could be displayed right on the showroom floors, next to the actual new cars. If a customer balked at paying full price for a brand-new vehicle, the dealer could show them the nearly new car, which could be had at a discount, but still at a price that ensured the dealer a bigger profit than he earned on a brand-new model. Thanks in part to the flood of business with rental car companies, the 1992 Taurus helped Ford grab the "best-seller" crown back from Accord. It was a devil's bargain, as the rental car business would come back to haunt the company and ultimately destroy Taurus's brand image.

Even as the new Taurus hit the streets, Toyota introduced a restyled Camry. Almost in homage to the Taurus, the Camry was redesigned from its previous squared-off look into an elegant, elongated car. Its rounded corners and slightly angled body seemed a fresher look than the jelly-bean-shaped Taurus, whose exterior was virtually unchanged. Moreover, Toyota's engines were quiet and smooth, its four-cylinder easily a match for the power of the Taurus's V-6, and with better fuel economy. It was essentially the first Camry to be designed with the tastes of American consumers in mind, rather than a Japanese car that Toyota adapted to American requirements. Also, this Camry reached the market three years after Toyota had launched its Lexus division, whose ES 250 sedan had been built from the Camry chassis but had a slightly more upscale appearance. For many people, the 1992 Camry brought to mind the Lexus, for many thousands of dollars less, and the family similarity became a valuable selling point for Toyota dealers.

Two years later, Honda stepped up with its own freshened Accord, with a comfortable interior, a cleanly designed exterior and, like the Camry, enviable fuel economy. Taurus clung to the lead, but the bar had been raised and Taurus was feeling the heat. Unlike the Taurus, whose sales had to be boosted, the Camry and Accord were selling without incentives and virtually without discounts. Toyota and Honda stayed away from doing all but minimal rental car business, which allowed them to protect the image of their cars along with their profits.

To fight back, Ford executives chose to gamble with an all-new version of the Taurus, due in late 1995, 10 years after the original. A sign reading "Beat Camry" hung on the wall of the conference room where the leaders of Taurus's development team, which included 700 engineers and designers, met to work on the next-generation Taurus. The team, whose story is told vividly in the book *Car*, by Mary Walton, decided that the new Taurus had to be as as revolutionary as the original Taurus had been when it first reached the market in 1985. "They thought they had to re-create the magic of that first Taurus," said Brauer at Edmunds.com. Seeing how well Toyota had done with the Camry, and how the Accord had also been able to rise in size and price from earlier versions, Ford officials decided that the next-generation Taurus would also be positioned as a more upscale model, moving it away from the reputation it had gained as a bargain car.

The approach was meant to attract the upper-middle-class baby boomers who had been defecting back to the Japanese. And it would help restore the profits on Taurus, which had dwindled to virtually nothing due to the incentives and steep discounts. Ford was certain that the formula of a higher-priced, dramatically different-looking car was just what it needed to beat back the competition and keep Taurus on top.

The result was one of the biggest mistakes in Ford's history. From an aesthetically pleasing, if now mundane-looking, aerodynamic car, the new Taurus seemed to have gone overboard on ovals. The ovoid shapes were everywhere—oval taillights, oval dials, an oval grille, oval rear windows. It had gone from jelly bean to egg, from simply modern to completely Jetsons. "They tried to use progressive styling as a shortcut, instead of honing an otherwise proven formula," Kagay said. More than the styling, however, was a marketing miscalculation that stalled the Taurus before it even hit the market. As development of the new Taurus proceeded, company officials were determined that Taurus had to remain the country's best-selling car. So Ford's marketing arm laid on every trick they could think of to expand Taurus's sales. They poured more Tauruses into rental car fleets. They piled on incentives, such as rebates and discounted lease deals, hoping to attract as many customers as they could. In the months right before the new Taurus was introduced, the offers got even more generous, with payments of as little as $199 a month on a Taurus lease, and rebates of $500 or more per car.

The deals worked in one unfortunate sense: Having heard and read all the ads for Taurus bargains, customers came to understand that the Taurus could always be had for a song—exactly the opposite of the upscale image that Ford wanted to achieve. When the new version came out, car shoppers came into dealerships expecting to get the same deals as before. What they found was a double disappointment: First, the looks of the Taurus had changed dramatically from the familiar car that had become such a beloved family sedan. It was as if a teddy bear had put on Spandex and a wig. Because its appearance had changed so much, the Taurus also seemed smaller than the vehicle it replaced, and customers complained that the new version wasn't as roomy inside. And the new Taurus cost hundreds to thousands of dollars more than its predecessor. The cheapest version cost close to $20,000, and once options were loaded on the car, the price approached $23,000. That was a steep price for a family car in the mid-1990s—still more than some Camry and Accord models cost today.

Thus, instead of a comfortable car that could be purchased at a reasonable price, the Taurus had become smaller, more expensive and less eye-pleasing. Dealers, who had ordered thousands of the cars in advance, weren't happy. But Ford provided them with an alternative that would prove to be another blow to Taurus. By the time the restyled Taurus reached the market, another Ford vehicle was entering its second generation: the Explorer. Introduced in 1990, Explorer had broken new ground in the SUV market. Until then, sport utilities emphasized their practicality and usefulness. The focus was primarily on the ways they could be used to traverse difficult territory and to transport camping gear and other equipment. The few people who bought them for regular driving gravitated to Jeeps, and the best-heeled moved to Range Rovers.

Ford, however, had seen how popular those vehicles were and experimented in the 1980s with a smaller version of its big Bronco SUV, called the Bronco II. Built on a truck chassis, the Bronco II's quality was subpar and its ride was uncomfortable, yet it offered a window into a potential market—namely, an SUV that could substitute for a car. Ford tapped into that market with Explorer, which by the mid-1990s was outselling many of the cars in Ford's lineup.

This was made abundantly clear when the new Taurus reached showrooms. Should consumers shake their heads in dismay at its radical new design and higher price, dealers could walk them over to an Explorer and suggest they give it a try. Some versions of the Explorer were even more expensive than the Taurus, but that seemed okay, given just how much bigger a vehicle the buyers were getting. Dealers were delighted to convince customers to make the switch, since profits on the Explorer were in the thousands of dollars, versus a few hundred on the Taurus. And customers were happy, both because SUVs were becoming chic and because they could avoid the hassle of shopping elsewhere. "They didn't even have to leave the showroom," said Brauer.

The defections from Taurus were immediate. By 1997, Taurus had slipped from first place to third in the best-selling-car list, behind the

Camry and the Accord. Ford seemed to take forever to respond to dealers' complaints that the car cost too much, most likely because it simply didn't want to admit that its gamble to go upscale had been wrong. It eventually did make a cheaper version available, but despite the uproar over the car's dramatic styling, it left the Taurus's appearance alone. Changing it right away would have meant millions of dollars in unbudgeted engineering expense. And by then, Ford had other priorities on its hands—namely, trucks. Jacques Nasser, who had become head of the Ford Automotive Group and was angling to become CEO, was convinced that the auto company needed to push full-bore into the SUV market. He saw all kinds of opportunities: Full-sized SUVs, bigger than Explorer—a vision that eventually led to the Expedition and the gargantuan Excursion. Small SUVs, such as the vehicle that Ford would call the Escape. Luxury SUVs, like the Lincoln Navigator. He also came up with an Explorer clone for Mercury called the Mountaineer. The company was SUV crazy, and its engineering resources were deployed to focus primarily on trucks.

As a result the Taurus, badly in need of attention, got left behind. "They thought totally corporate. They said, 'We've got all these truck products coming out, and they're going to be high margin,'" said a former Ford executive who is familiar with the decisions that were made on the Taurus. "They said, 'We can just let the Taurus sit there.'" Because of the company's obsession with trucks and its unwillingness to save its best-selling car, it took Ford five years, until the year 2000, to do anything about the styling that had been such an immediate disaster. On its next go-round, Ford calmed down the Taurus's appearance, removing the ovals and simplifying the interior, so that the car had a cleaner, understated look. It had cut back somewhat its flood of sales to fleets and rental car agencies, which had sliced into the car's profitability and destroyed its carefully crafted image.

But the changes hardly mattered by this time, because Taurus had long since been eclipsed again by the imports. In 2002, the Camry once again reigned as the nation's best-selling car, a title it has held since capturing it from Taurus in 1997. Accord was slightly behind, while Taurus trailed the pair by thousands of sales. Its sales in 2002 were nearly 100,000 fewer than at its peak. Ford executives belatedly admitted that they had made a major mistake. Speaking to journalists at the Chicago Auto Show in 2003, Ford executive vice president Jim Padilla said Taurus didn't deserve what Ford had done to it, saluting the car as if it were a fallen comrade.

Already gone from many buyers' shopping lists, the Taurus is destined to never again hold the crown as the nation's best-selling car. Ford is converting one of the factories that built the Taurus to produce the Freestyle, its first entry into the market for crossover vehicles, a kind of SUV that is a combination car and truck that it plans to introduce in 2004 as one of three models it has slated to compete for family buyers. But once again, Ford will trail its competition. The Japanese are already setting the pace with crossover vehicles like the Toyota Highlander and the Lexus RX 330, which are in their second generation, the Honda Pilot and the Nissan Murano, while Chrysler brought out the Pacifica in 2003. Later this decade, Ford also will introduce a family sedan, the Ford 500, and plans a hybrid-electric vehicle (which it had planned to call the Futura, but will have to rename because of a legal dispute), counting on those two vehicles and the Freestyle to fill the place in the market that Taurus alone once occupied.

Soon to be extinct, the Taurus is already a museum piece. The first one sits on display at the Henry Ford Museum and Greenfield Village in Dearborn, just a couple of blocks away from the styling studio where the first Taurus came to light 20 years ago. A sign tells the story of how Detroit once beat the Japanese and how the Taurus saved Ford from disaster. But the display doesn't go on to say how Ford then lost the game because it did not have the determination or focus to keep playing. It chose easy profits over difficult success. To a Japanese company, the outcome would have been no question. For proof, simply look at the latest Accords and Camrys, which remain stellar vehicles even as Honda and Toyota have expanded their focus into truck sales. Said Kagay, "Ford went from building a hit to misguided hubris. What does all of this say? To be humble is virtuous. And Ford forgot that."

CHAPTER THREE

TWO PATHS TO THE SAME CONCLUSION

TO THE AMERICAN CONSUMER, Toyota and Honda have become such interchangeable symbols of automotive reliability and quality that it's sometimes hard to tell them apart. They're often mentioned in the same breath—Toyota-and-Honda, all run together—as if they were one big company instead of two. They certainly have a lot in common. Toyota, the fourth-biggest seller in the United States, and Honda, the fifth biggest, are both based in Japan, where they rank No. 1 and No. 2 in size. They are both fiercely independent companies with clear operating philosophies that have endured for decades, a sharp contrast to the tendency of Detroit companies to follow the whims of whichever executive is at the top. While executives can certainly accelerate or shift the direction at Toyota and Honda, as is true in the case of their current management, the basic underlying values remain in place at each company no matter who is in charge. Despite the merger-and-acquisition craze that swept the automobile industry and indeed the business world during the past decade, both Toyota and Honda have stood steadfastly alone, although they have both participated in joint ventures with other companies when it met their needs.

The similarities extend to the showroom, as well. Both Honda's and Toyota's lineups in the United States feature cars and trucks that are known less for flashy styling than for their understated appearance and solid craftsmanship, although both have been experimenting lately with trendsetting vehicles aimed at Generation X consumers. Over the past two decades, both have built a network of factories in the American Midwest and South, which now produce the majority of vehicles that they sell in the United States. Toyota and Honda each got into the car business long after most of their global competitors. Ford and General Motors were already assembling cars at plants in Japan before Toyota built its first vehicle in 1936. Honda began as a motorcycle company after World War II. It didn't produce its first cars in Japan until 1966, and did not export cars to the United States until the 1970s. When both Toyota and Honda originally brought their vehicles to America, neither one was taken seriously as real competition for Detroit's automobiles. In retrospect, Detroit's indifferent attitude toward them gave the Japanese companies valuable time to get on their feet and hone their approach with American consumers.

But the perception that Toyota and Honda are carbon copies of each other is wrong. They have very different approaches toward developing vehicles, different corporate personalities and different strategies for global growth. Toyota is most like a traditional auto company, aiming to meet the needs of all kinds of customers with a broad lineup of cars and trucks. Honda has pursued a path all its own, picking its spots in the marketplace, introducing vehicles only when it is sure that they will stand out from the competition. Today, Honda's founding family plays no role in the company, while the Toyoda family remains an active participant in the company that bears its name, and someday soon could see one of the family again named to the chairman's job. What these companies share is a drive and determination to stay true to their mission, as they see it, which in the end focuses squarely on the customer.

One way to get a feel for just how different these companies are from each other is to visit their corporate headquarters in Tokyo. Honda's main office is located in a tall white building on a busy corner in Aoyama, one of the city's trendiest business districts, kitty-corner from the residence of Japan's crown prince. It sits squarely above a subway station, amid department stores, hotels, coffee shops and restaurants that are crowded at lunchtime and after work. The Honda building is just as popular a place to visit for people who work nearby. You can order a cappuccino or a light snack at the bar in the Honda headquarters lobby, shop in a boutique stocked with trendy merchandise, such as windbreakers with logos of Honda's Formula One cars, and look over dozens of Honda vehicles. Shoppers browse in air-conditioned comfort inside the vast lobby; those outside can examine a dozen or so vehicles that are parked on the sidewalk, in a display that changes every day. Here, Japanese office workers from nearby businesses can sit behind the wheel (on the right in Japan), examine the trunk and kick the tires on vehicles like the small Fit, the best-selling subcompact in Japan, or the Mobilio, a tall minivan that is built on the Fit's chassis. Visitors can pick up brochures about the vehicles or look up information about them on computer screens next to the coffee counter. But there's no hard sell, and no one ever buys a car here. Instead, buyers are directed to their local dealers.

When Honda constructed this building 15 years ago, the company's founder, Soichiro Honda, insisted that the headquarters be earthquake proof, and that the windows be set back from the street, behind balconies, so that broken glass would fall on balcony floors and not shower passersby below, making it one of the safest buildings in Tokyo. That same care extends to the welcome that visitors receive when they arrive for appointments. Unlike the silent formality that marks most Japanese business occasions, where the usual beverage is green tea and sessions start precisely on time, no meeting at Honda begins without an offer of espresso or orange juice or ice water, and a pleasant exchange about Formula One racing or plans for the weekend. And if the schedule slips by a few minutes and a spirited conversation runs overtime, no one seems rattled. As if to illustrate the company's friendliness, Honda's robot, Asimo, looks down on the visitors from the reception area, atop a steep flight of stairs in the showroom. About four feet tall and fully functional, without any guide wires or remote controls, Asimo is one of the most familiar and popular figures with Japanese consumers, and he is becoming increasingly familiar to Americans as well from Honda's lighthearted television commercials. A few lucky guests are greeted personally by Asimo (who spoke only Japanese at first, but has since been programmed to speak English) and escorted by him to a bank of elevators for their appointments.

The cordial atmosphere in Honda's headquarters is a sharp contrast to the starkness of Toyota's Tokyo headquarters a 10-minute taxi ride away. Toyota's imposing, black glass building sits in the shadow of the Tokyo Dome indoor stadium, home to the perennial champion Yomiuri Giants baseball team, whose winning ways have made them Japan's most-respected but probably least-loved sports team. The closeness to the home of the Giants is apt, for Toyota, too, inspires similar feelings of respect without real affection. Toyota's executives arrive in chauffeur-driven Crown sedans and disappear down a steep driveway to vanish behind garage doors. There is little to encourage anyone to linger. The leafy manicured park next to the building, though inviting, is generally deserted past the lunch hour. The near-empty lobby holds no such enticements as a coffee bar (the closest Starbucks is a few doors down). Instead, a security guard stands at attention as receptionists greet guests and phone upstairs to double-check their appointment before allowing them to enter. If a visitor is headed for the executive floor, he or she has to change elevators partway up. The corridors are starkly decorated and employees work silently away. The camaraderie at Honda is absent here, replaced by focus and formality. But in a way that's not surprising, because Toyota has an intensely serious focus. And because of that, it may well be that Toyota, rather than one of its American or European rivals, will become the world's first truly global automobile company, even though it is based in a country that until about 150 years ago was all but closed to the outside world.

Toyota's emergence as a world automotive power is the result of a journey that began 70 years ago, outside Nagoya, Japan, three hours west of Tokyo. Toyota was founded there in 1933 as the automotive department of the Toyoda Automatic Loom works, a company that made machinery for weaving vast bolts of industrial fabric. Unlike the United States or Europe, where automobile manufacturing had been under way since the turn of the century, the automobile craze was late to reach Japan. While it boasted major cities, like Tokyo and Yokohama to the east, Osaka in the center of the country and Hiroshima far to the west, Japan was still a largely rural nation in the years before the Second World War. Its automotive needs were being met by American automobile companies, through exports from the United States and the factories that they built in Japan in the 1920s. Only the firm that would later become Nissan had begun building vehicles when Kiichiro Toyoda appealed to his father, Sakichi Toyoda, to let him investigate the automobile industry. The Toyoda family by then was already well-known and prosperous, thanks to its enormously successful loom business. "By the time I had started going to school, Toyoda looms were as famous as Mikimoto pearls and Suzuki violins," wrote Eiji Toyoda, Sakichi's nephew and Kiichiro's cousin, who joined the auto company at its infancy and would later become one of its most influential chairmen.

But success in the automobile industry did not come quickly or easily. Kiichiro Toyoda, an engineer, had been fascinated by cars during his travels, including the trips he took to New York in 1921 and 1929, the first with his sister, Akio, and her new husband, Risaburo (who, in a fashion then common in Japan, forsook his more-modest family name to become a Toyoda). The testiness between Kiichiro and Risaburo, which would continue throughout their lives, began early. A well-known photo of the three Toyodas, taken on their first trip abroad, shows Akio and Risaburo sitting cozily together on one armchair, with Kiichiro across the room in another, turned away from them in a stiff pose. Kiichiro, always excited by new ideas, was convinced that the family's vast expertise in manufacturing could be leveraged in the car business. Shortly before his death in 1930, Sakichi gave his son permission to explore the new venture. It was not a popular decision among other members of the family and managers at the loom company, so as a result Kiichiro decided to keep his work clandestine.

Working at night in the corner of a factory on the loom works' grounds, Kiichiro and a group of loom company engineers began developing an automobile engine, feeling that the car had to be developed from the inside out. Kiichiro had set up a small casting forge in order to melt steel and pour it into molds to form the cylinder heads and blocks for the car's engine. Time and again, the engine blocks would crack, foiling the engineers on the most critical component of their vehicle. It took months to find a solution, but by 1933 Kiichiro and his team had built 10 prototype engines. He wanted to move the company forward into automobiles themselves, but for this he needed permission from Risaburo, who had become chairman of Toyoda upon his father-in-law's death, and from other company board members.

At a heated meeting in December 1933, Kiichiro pleaded his case, finally winning the board's approval to set up an automotive group. Kiichiro's engineers first tore apart a Chevrolet that they had shipped to Japan from the United States. They noted how many parts the vehicle had and how each piece fit together, lessons they would apply to their own design. Eventually, the team set up their own version of an automotive assembly line, finding sources for each of the parts and practicing how they would produce a car. Finally, in 1936, Toyoda was ready—and his timing was fortuitous. As the company was getting ready to show its first car, Japan's parliament, the Diet, passed legislation to encourage domestic automobile production and in effect curb production by Ford and GM by requiring that the companies be owned by Japanese citizens. "Looking back on it now, it was a very low blow by the government against foreign automakers," said Eiji Toyoda. Nonetheless, the measure gave Toyoda a much-needed boost.

At a motor show in Tokyo, the company unveiled a concept car it called the AA. It was essentially a copy of a Chrysler sedan, with a long hood and the kind of sculpted body that was so prevalent on vehicles from before World War II. There was nothing original about it that signaled the design direction that the company might ultimately take. But it was a start for the fledgling Toyota Motor Company, which had chosen a name that was slightly different from that of the loom manufacturer. (There are several different explanations for this: One is that the syllable "ta" was considered easier to pronounce in Japanese than "da." Another is that the name Toyota takes only eight brush strokes in Japanese writing, versus 10 for the name Toyoda. A third is that the family, concerned about the risks of the automotive project, didn't want it to share the same name as the loom works for fear that if it failed, the parent company's reputation might be harmed.)

Even as production of the first Toyota vehicles was under way, the culture that would permeate the company was taking shape. A year before the first Toyota car was introduced, Kiichiro and Risaboro sat down to draw up the principles under which they wanted all of the Toyoda group companies to operate. These would apply not only to the loom business but to the emerging automobile company as well. Known formally as the Toyota Precepts, they would eventually evolve into a cultural outlook that would become known as the Toyota Way. The first of the precepts was teamwork, followed by the determination to be at the forefront of technological and market developments. Employees were to be practical and avoid frivolity, be kind and generous and strive to create a comfortable atmosphere. Finally, Toyoda employees would be reverent and show gratitude to those around them.

Decades later, the Toyota Way has been refined into two main principles: continuous improvement and respect for people. It is deceptively simple, and incredibly difficult for many people to grasp, but it is cited around the company as the secret to what makes Toyota so successful. Its emphasis on always making things better leads to an unavoidable transparency, while its emphasis on teamwork and inclusion means no single executive can create a kingdom in which he is the sole ruler. "I don't think there's truly any way to hide in Toyota," said Dave Illingworth, senior vice president of planning and administration for Toyota Motor Sales USA, the company's American sales arm. "If you have a problem, you'd better tell somebody, because eventually you will be found out." The primary tool that Toyota would need to truly inculcate the auto company into its way of thinking would be created later, but the philosophical building blocks were put in place from the very beginning.

However, it took more than a decade for the auto company to build up a head of steam. Given the complexity and slow growth of the Japanese car market, Toyota decided not to produce cars in its early years, choosing to build simpler small trucks instead. Then World War II intervened, and the government stepped in to regulate production, although, unlike in the United States, automobile manufacturing never stopped in Japan. However, the bulk of orders for new vehicles during the war years came from the government, providing little incentive for companies to continue their investments beyond a minimum level or come up with new designs. Even so, Toyota came within a hairsbreadth of being completely destroyed in its infancy. American military documents, discovered by Eiji Toyoda after the war, showed that Toyota City was scheduled to be bombed on August 21, six days after Japan's surrender. The day of Japan's defeat was miserable and memorable for the workers who remained at the Toyota complex. The announcement of Japan's surrender, broadcast on radio, was the first time many of the workers at the Toyota complex had ever heard Emperor Hirohito's voice. The news of defeat stunned them. A number simply packed up their things and went home for the day. On August 16, a company executive, Hisayoshi Akai, called everyone in the complex together. "We lost the war," he said, "but mark my words, in five years we'll be on our feet again."

Rebuilding the company, like rebuilding the country, wasn't quite so simple. Immediately after the war, Toyota had no market for its small trucks. Instead, it produced dinnerware and fish paste, based on Kiichiro Toyoda's theory that even if they couldn't afford vehicles, people still had to eat. Then, as its trucks began to sell, boosted by liberal financing terms, the company was hit by two crises: a cash crunch and a series of labor strikes. Kiichiro and Risaboro Toyoda sparred on how to get the company out of danger. Risaboro, a better businessman than his brother-in-law, argued that the company had to cut more deeply. Kiichiro resisted, arguing that Toyota needed to be loyal to the workers who had seen it through its darkest days. But Toyota's fortunes worsened dramatically and the situation came to a head in 1950, when Kiichiro Toyoda tearfully stood before his workers and told them that he had to cut 1,600 jobs. One of them would be his own. Kiichiro stepped down from the company he had founded, heartbroken. But it was the right move. Under new management,

Toyota quickly regained its footing, becoming solvent in less than a year. The board invited Kiichiro to return. Sadly, it was a short comeback. In 1952, he suffered a fatal heart attack, never to see the vast global growth and accomplishment that Toyota would achieve.

It was the United States that saved Toyota in the 1950s and provided the stepping-stone to its future. Eiji Toyoda, who had joined his uncle's business after graduating from school in the 1930s, set off for Dearborn, Michigan, to visit Ford's sprawling operations. The company, which was producing just 40 trucks a day, decided to establish ties with an American company. There had always been symbiotic, if unofficial, relationships between Toyota and Ford. Kiichiro Toyoda was a deep admirer of Henry Ford's business practices and a great fan of Ford's book *My Life and Work*, which he made required reading for his staff. The pair had talked about a joint venture before World War II, only to see the idea scrapped by the outbreak of fighting. With Toyota on its feet again, Toyoda sent a letter to Ford to gauge the company's interest in reviving discussions. Ford didn't commit to a business deal, but its executives invited Toyoda to visit anything he wanted to see.

He combed its factories, studying how the massive Rouge complex turned out 800 vehicles a day, examining how Ford produced engines, learning about its international operations, which had then revved into action in Argentina, Israel, France and Spain. He talked his way into Chrysler's factories, too, looking for a point of comparison. As he was preparing to head back to Japan, Toyoda said to himself, "Detroit isn't doing anything that we don't already know." The joint venture didn't prove necessary, because as Toyoda returned home, he found that Toyota's plants were slowly increasing production, thanks to a slew of orders from both the United Nations and the American military. The U.S. Army decided to buy trucks from Japanese manufacturers in order to transport troops in Korea, where conflict had broken out. Ordering trucks from American companies would cost too much, and it would take too long to ship them overseas. Even after the Korean War ended, the military's orders from Toyota continued for years. But they didn't last beyond 1962, when American officials belatedly realized they were subsidizing a Japanese industry to the detriment of their own companies.

Shortly after Eiji Toyoda returned to Japan, one of the greatest figures in Toyota's history, Taiichi Ohno, who would become as famous as its founder, came forward to implement ideas that he, too, had learned in Dearborn. His concepts proved to be far more of a breakthrough for Toyota, and far more influential to the company's future, than any joint venture with an American company might have been. Ohno was an engineer who had joined Toyota in 1946, attracted by the company's long emphasis on mistake-free engineering. In an attempt to produce the best-quality textiles, the Toyoda loom company had invented a safeguard called *jidoka*, in which machinery would stop working in the event of any kind of manufacturing error. It kept the company from shipping flawed material, ensuring the company's reputation for quality, and it alerted the company instantly when its tools were broken and needed maintenance. Ohno thought that similar processes might be applied to the automotive assembly line. He decided to travel to the United States, where automobile factories had roared back to life after World War II, to learn more about production. Like Toyoda, Ohno explored Ford's Rouge operations, but with a slightly different motivation, which was to study the production process from start to finish.

He saw how Ford took in vast carloads of copper, iron ore and coal on its own freighters, which arrived at its own docks from its own mines in northern Michigan, and transformed the raw materials into steel, glass and auto parts that were fed to its assembly plants. He studied the manufacturing lines that had been Henry Ford's contribution to automotive greatness. And then he went to a supermarket. Here he made the real discovery that would lead to the Toyota Production System (TPS), which is the company's functional foundation and the secret that sets Toyota apart.

Back home in Japan, consumers relied on tiny "mom-and-pop" stores that stocked only a few kinds of goods. One might specialize in something as simple as bean-jam buns, called *ampan*. Another might sell dried snacks, a third fresh fruit. Shopping trips were quick: One asked the merchant for the quantity required, and it was provided. In America, however, customers chose from a vast array of products, in precisely the quantities they wanted, and shopped according to the pace they desired. As supermarket shelves emptied, they were restocked, often from the front, allowing merchandise like cartons of milk or containers of eggs to be constantly pushed forward within consumers' reach. Ohno saw that markets didn't keep huge stocks of cornflakes or boxes of paper towels piled up in back. They received constant deliveries, so money wasn't tied up in unneeded merchandise.

From his observations, Ohno created three basic principles that required the involvement of everyone in the company. First, management had to make a strong commitment to the system, participate in implementing it and reinforce its philosophy constantly with middle management. Second, all employees, from the shop floor to the executive offices, had to participate. Third, everyone involved in making an automobile, from hourly workers, to suppliers, to dealers, had to accept that this was the way Toyota was run, and to be constantly trained and updated on the system.

Under TPS, every Toyota factory, whether in Tahara, Japan; Cambridge, Ontario; or Huntsville, Alabama, is run on the same key principles. A fundamental element is the concept of just-in-time delivery, which has been widely applied in all manner of factories around the world, including those of Detroit companies. As with the replenishment of goods in a supermarket, every component that Toyota uses, whether engines on the assembly line floor or SUVs shipped to dealers, arrives as it is needed. This is called a "pull system," meaning that the required goods are pulled out of inventory according to demand. It's vastly different from, and more difficult than, Detroit companies' traditional practice of stockpiling supplies of parts and automobiles and selling down the supply, which is called a "push system."

The pull system requires a daisy chain of communication. As Toyota engineers set out to develop new vehicles, they spend months talking to consumers and dealers to find out what kind of features they want. Likewise, once those vehicles reach the showroom, dealers must keep track of what consumers are requesting and stock their lots with vehicles that will move quickly. They relay these sales trends back to the company, which then orders parts and builds vehicles according to customer demand. As those vehicles are being produced, Toyota's workers follow a preestablished series of steps called standardized work, another important TPS concept that applies all through the company. Near every workstation in a Toyota plant hangs a laminated card that shows how a task is to be performed, and workers are expected to do so to the letter, in the amount of time and with the number of steps that are prescribed. That is not to say that such tasks are set in stone; in fact, Toyota employees at all levels of the company are drilled in another key TPS concept, called continuous improvement, or *kaizen*. If there is a better way to do the work, from handling customer service telephone calls to installing headlights, Toyota wants to hear its employees' suggestions, and it implements them on a regular basis.

Nobody buys a car just because of the Toyota Production System, and probably most of the people who own Toyota vehicles have never even heard of it. But it's what makes Toyota cars and the company itself so sound. TPS isn't just the way Toyota cars are built; it's the foundation that the company is built upon. TPS is the reason that Toyota can bring out cars and trucks that fit together and run perfectly. TPS refines the concept of continuous improvement, using every kind of resource as efficiently as possible, and giving employees a real say in their jobs. It is both a set of guidelines for the factory floor, and a philosophy that guides the company. Because Toyota has TPS, it doesn't have to reinvent the wheel every time it wants to try something new. It doesn't have to communicate new slogans or rely on the personality of a new chief executive to motivate the troops. TPS basically puts everyone at Toyota on the same page and gives them the same frame of reference, which is the customer. The customers' needs and desires are the starting and ending point of TPS. The most humbling and frustrating aspect of TPS is that it is impossible to become completely proficient. Even now, when Toyota is the biggest, most profitable and most powerful company that it has ever been, Toyota executives say they have mastered only 50 to 60 percent of what Ohno hoped Toyota could achieve through the production system. That kind of thinking all but guarantees that Toyota will not become complacent.

One of the executives who best understood TPS went right to the top of the company: Fujio Cho, Toyota's chief executive, whose own career mirrors Toyota's most important steps during the past 35 years. Cho, along with Toyota's chairman, Hiroshi Okuda, is the architect of the plan that Toyota hopes will result in its becoming the world's largest automobile company by the end of the decade. Unlike the founders of the company, Cho did not have an engineering degree or any background in manufacturing. He studied law at Tokyo University, joining Toyota in 1960 and serving in a variety of staff jobs across the company. Were it not for an unusual assignment, Cho might have simply ended up in the ranks of Toyota's salarymen, with a modicum of responsibilities and no substantial authority.

Cho had been at the auto company for 14 years when he was assigned in 1974 to work with Ohno on improving the efficiency of Toyota's administrative operations. Previously, TPS had been applied only within its factories. Cho had paid deep attention during all the lectures, workshops and plant visits that had been part of his education and training process at the company. And when it came time to attack his assignment, he did so with zeal. Like many world economies that had suffered setbacks during the early 1970s, Japan's economy was in a recession as Cho took on his assignment. Keeping in mind TPS's emphasis on streamlined supplies, he decided that the company needed to reduce its inventories of all types of goods and services, from office furniture to typing staff, to the minimum amounts that would allow it to function properly.

And so he squeezed the excess out of Toyota's operations all across Japan, saving millions of yen. He expected that the activity would earn Ohno's praise. Instead, he received his master's scorn. "Are you stupid?" Ohno thundered. Cho, in slimming down the inventory levels, had paid no attention to company forecasts that showed that Japan was about to emerge from its economic doldrums. "We are going to be in a boom. We will need more inventories, not less!" Ohno said. He told Cho that he had to learn to look forward, not backward. It was a lesson that Cho learned well and applied many times in the future. It paid off for him not long after, when he convinced Ohno to publish TPS in English. Though noticed by only a few academics at the outset, the decision to make TPS available in another language raised Toyota's profile in the global auto industry—and raised Cho's standing in Toyota as well.

But before Toyota could run, it had to learn to walk. And as with all toddlers, its first steps were stumbles. Its first attempt to sell a car in the United States, the Toyopet, was a disaster. The Toyopet was a linchpin of Toyota's lineup in Japan, a small, inexpensive car meant to coax cash-strapped customers back into the market. It arrived in the middle of the most ostentatious era in American automobile history, when cars were draped with chrome, interiors resembled living rooms, with plush, sofalike seats, and rear ends were shaped like fins. In short, the Toyopet was nothing like what American buyers were used to, and Toyota was forced to retreat from the market and rethink what it would take to compete. It was a slow process. Returning in 1959, it took Toyota 10 years to sell 100,000 cars a year in the United States, a mark that it achieved in 1970. During that time, the company began setting up its dealer organization, which would eventually prove to be one of its most valuable tools. Unlike Detroit companies, which seemed to have a showroom in every sizable town across the United States, Toyota decided to be selective and choose areas where population growth was taking place. For one thing, it did not have the money to seed the kind of vast dealer network that the Big Three had established. Even today, GM has more than 7,400 dealerships, and nearly 5,000 at Chevrolet alone. The total number of Toyota dealerships is 1,287.

But Detroit barely took notice as Toyota was putting together its dealer network, because Toyota's sales were dwarfed by a far bigger foreign competitor: Volkswagen. Through the 1960s and into the 1970s, VW was at the height of its postwar popularity, thanks to the perennial Beetle, the Volkswagen Bus and specialty cars like the Karmann Ghia, all of which appealed to young, hip customers (a good portion of them hippies). Even so, Detroit companies considered VW to be an irritation at best, and hardly a real threat. Toyota was barely on their radar screen. And if VW and Toyota sparked little concern, executives in Detroit were even less cognizant of another Japanese competitor that was about to arrive in the United States: Honda.

———————

His employees called him "the old man" with both affection and sarcasm. In fact, Soichiro Honda was close to retirement age when he finally got into the car business. Born on a Japanese farm in 1906, Honda was 60 years old as Honda's first car, the N360, went on sale in Japan in 1966, and it wasn't until 1972 that Honda cars debuted in the United States. By then, Honda had achieved acclaim as a motorcycle company and had won respect for its recent and audacious success in Formula One racing, but it was extraordinarily late among Japanese companies in getting into the automobile business. It nearly missed its chance altogether.

Honda had founded an auto parts company before World War II but sold it to Toyota as the war ended, choosing to start over from scratch. He began with a small bicycle engine, which became the power source for the small motorcycle, called the Dream, which Honda put on sale in 1947. Even as he was getting on his feet, Honda was brazen enough to issue a challenge to his troops: He wanted to win the famous Isle of Mann Tourist Trophy motorcycle race. (Known as the TT, its name would later be borrowed by Audi for a two-seater sports car.) Honda entered the TT in 1954 and won in its category in 1959. By then, the company had sold more than a million Dreams, had introduced its next best-seller, the Super Cub, and was well into its next research venture, automobiles. Honda had been in a rush to get into the motorcycle business, but with cars he deliberately took his time. He'd actually passed on an early opportunity to enter a minicar contest put on by the Japanese government in 1955, surprising his potential automotive competitors, who were sure that Honda's competitive nature would spur him into the field.

There is an automobile industry legend that the Japanese government barred Honda from entering the auto industry, only to have the company disobey its orders. That was not the case. But in 1961, the Japanese government proposed legislation regulating the auto industry, and said it would apply only to companies that could prove they were building cars before the law took effect. The legislation seemed squarely aimed at Honda, almost an effort to get it to make up its mind, since Honda had been toying with the idea of automobiles as far back as 1957, when it set up a separate research division to look into the possibility. The threat of the law lit a fire under Honda, and in early 1962 the company immediately began producing prototype versions of mini sports cars and trucks.

In June of that year, Honda himself sped around the unfinished racetrack at Suzuka, Japan, in a Honda prototype, a display meant to prove to the Japanese government—and potential customers—that Honda was serious about getting into the car business. That was enough to satisfy the government, but it took four more years for Honda to begin selling its first car. The sterling reputation of its motorcycles was enough to convince Japanese customers to try the new Honda, and within three months its small car was the most popular minicar sold in Japan. Though few realized it then, Soichiro Honda was thinking about international sales from the very beginning. For he had already made Honda motorcycles a household name around the world, thanks to Honda's presence in motorcycle racing and its peppy approach to making motorcycles fun to ride, as opposed to the big, intimidating vehicles ridden by leather-jacket-clad bikers in movies like *The Wild One*. Honda's ads, in Japan and elsewhere, featured laughing young people on the backs of its bikes. Even its slogan was meant to evoke a smile: "You meet the nicest people on a Honda," its commercials declared.

That pleasant public face wasn't always in sync with the way Soichiro Honda ran his business or interacted with other people. From the start, when he first got his engine company up and running in 1948, Honda could be a driven employer, so intent on his tasks that he could enter a zone of deep concentration in which all other concerns fell away. His wife, Sachi, once was forced to trek down to Honda's workshop to ask for money because her husband had forgotten to give her the weekly allowance she was supposed to receive to pay the household accounts. He demanded superior performance out of both his employees and his factories. On a tour of a foundry in Japan, Soichiro Honda was outraged to watch molten metal splashing onto the floor as it was poured into molds for engine blocks. According to one witness, he walked up to the worker in charge and slapped him across the face, berating him for the dangerous conditions. And yet Honda loved being with his employees, to an almost fatherly extent.

Though he had his own children, three boys and a girl, Honda had barred them from entering the automobile business, for fear that the company would be perceived as nepotistic. His engineers in a sense became their substitutes, and Honda made a habit of going out drinking with them at the end of each week. Corporate imbibing is a common practice in Japan, where office relations between employees and supervisors are rigid and formality reigns. The conventional wisdom is that drinking together after work allows colleagues to loosen up and share thoughts and opinions that they never would express in the workplace. If an employee misbehaves or says a little too much, it's chalked up to drunkenness, although smart managers mentally make note of everything they hear. The gatherings are generally safety zones, since groups are composed of people who have worked together for years.

But Honda's soirees were different. Soichiro Honda insisted that each week the newly hired and the youngest among the engineers be included in the drinking parties, which could last until the wee hours. Honda, as always, had a strategy. The parties relaxed the young engineers so that they came to regard the company founder as someone they could talk to, not a figurehead. They kept Honda in touch with the thinking of his newest generation of employees. And they gave him yet another opportunity to instill in them the Honda approach to doing business, the Honda Philosophy, which some people in the company refer to as the Honda DNA. It is an approach that has its roots in the earliest days of Honda as an engine company. Above all, Honda wanted his products to have character. "Engineering without personality doesn't have much value," he said. But just as important, Honda wanted his employees to be fully involved in making his company a success.

Although the company's philosophy is rarely discussed in detail outside the company, everyone at Honda around the world, whether it's an autoworker at its plant in Lincoln, Alabama, an engineer in California, or a finance staff member in Tokyo, is schooled in it. At the Lincoln plant, the Honda philosophy is taught in night classes before employees begin their jobs, and family members are encouraged to come along so they will understand Honda's expectations. Many employees carry a laminated flip-open brochure, the size of a credit card, that distills the Honda philosophy into easy-to-remember tenets.

What is the Honda philosophy that has been distilled from the principles that Soichiro Honda set in place for his employees more than 50 years ago? Perhaps there is no more important tenet than the most basic: respect for the individual, which comes from "a fundamental belief in the human being," according to the Honda brochure. It is similar to the precept at Toyota that respect is expressed in three ways. The first is initiative. Employees shouldn't be bound by preconceived ideas, but should think creatively, acting on their own initiative and taking responsibility for the results of their actions. The second is equality, meaning to "recognize, respect and benefit from individual differences." The third tenet is trust, which Honda believes is created by teamwork and sharing knowledge.

In keeping with Soichiro Honda's personal enthusiasm for his craft, his workers and the automobile industry, Honda's philosophy also includes the Three Joys. These are the joy of buying, meaning the pride of ownership in a quality product that exceeds customers' expectations; the joy of selling, in which Honda strives to have good relationships with its customers, and exceed their needs and desires ("It isn't just selling cars to them. We have to take care of them," says Honda's former president, Koichi Amemiya); and the joy of creating, which applies to everyone from engineering to design to manufacturing ("By creating quality products, we experience pride in a job well done," according to Honda's written brochures). Once those Three Joys are realized, the company strives for an overarching joy, "the joy of society," in which Honda makes a contribution to the world at large. But Honda's philosophy also places special requirements on management. The first is to proceed with ambition and youthfulness, seeking out challenges with a "fresh, open-minded passion for learning," according to company literature. Managers should respect sound theories but not be afraid to challenge old habits with new ideas. They should enjoy their work, encourage open communications, consider employees as customers and try to encourage teamwork. Finally, managers must value research. "We should always seek improvements, and never be satisfied with what is," the Honda philosophy concludes.

The Honda philosophy results in an automobile company that is different from any of its competitors. Where other companies hype their advances, Honda simply presents them. "We're a company that avoids the limelight," said Tom Elliott, Honda's senior vice president in charge of U.S. sales. "We don't go out and seek the spotlight." Whereas virtually every other manufacturer in the United States is part of a lobbying group called Alliance of Automobile Manufacturers, Honda is not a member. When other companies battle the government over tighter fuel economy and emissions standards, Honda generally is willing to meet whatever requirements it faces. Company executives know that this unusual focus feeds the impression that Honda is full of hubris, or even arrogance, and that even though it encourages its managers and employees to foster teamwork (the cafeteria at Honda's Research and Development Center in Marysville, Ohio, next to its big factory complex, stays open from 6 A.M. to 11 P.M. so that the 1,000 engineers there can obtain food and refreshment at any time during their long days on the job), it has little interest in being a team player where the rest of the industry is concerned. "Sometimes in Detroit, they say, 'Honda, you are being a good boy to the government,'" said Amemiya, who ran its North American operations as well as serving as company president. But Honda officials simply don't seem to care that much, a trait of which Honda himself would be proud.

Independence is this company's watchword. And even though

Honda would be a valuable merger partner, has been approached numerous times by potential suitors and could reap billions of dollars if it wanted to sell even a small stake, it steadfastly remains on its own. It had one disastrous venture, buying a share of the English carmaker Rover in the 1980s. The move ended in acrimony during the 1990s when BMW bought out Honda's stake. (Rover subsequently turned into a financial drain for the German carmaker.) "I suppose if we got together with another company, [then] it would be a mess by now," Hiroyuki Yoshino, Honda's chief executive until his retirement in mid-2003, said during an interview in Tokyo. He saw a drawback to a merger. It was that uniting corporate cultures was extremely difficult, "unless one company totally controls the other. But if it is that case," said Yoshino, "the company being controlled would be completely demoralized. One plus one does not even equal two."

Whereas at most automobile companies mission statements are crafted by consultants, and the founder's identity is relegated to museum exhibits and history books, Honda's own personality and priorities remain alive at Honda today. Because he died relatively recently, in 1991, there remain a great many people at the company who have vivid memories of him, and Honda's operations bear strong reminders of his presence. Both the Marysville and East Liberty plants in Ohio have plaster casts of his handprints on display—molded on his visits to the factories—that allow a visitor to fit their own hand into them. (He would wear a size small men's glove.) Dan Smith, the East Liberty plant manager, remembers Honda's last visit to Ohio shortly before his death. By then, Honda's operations had expanded to include the Marysville assembly plant, a second assembly plant in East Liberty, an engine plant in Anna, and the gleaming white building that housed its research and development operations. Honda could see it all at his feet as he flew from the Columbus airport to a landing pad near the East Liberty plant. A group of about 20 workers and managers from the factory were on hand to welcome him. They expected that Honda would simply wave to them before hopping into a waiting car. Instead, the diminutive company founder reacted with delighted surprise at the sight of the welcoming party. He bounded from the helicopter, and despite his age and his busy schedule, insisted on shaking hands and speaking with everyone there. (Amemiya remembers another occasion, a meeting of company managers, at which Honda borrowed a towel from a waiter, draped it over his arm and went around the room, taking drink orders.)

The vast Ohio operations, on top of the manufacturing plants and research centers that Honda built in Japan and Europe, are testimony to Honda's love for automobiles that began almost at birth. "Once when I was a kid, I ran after a Ford Model T and held up my nose to the oil that sputtered out onto the ground. I took a whiff and was thrilled by the smell," he recalled. Even so, Honda waited to begin building automobiles until he felt the time was right, pushed only by pending legislation. And at the moment he was ready to enter the United States market in 1972, events had conspired to prove his deliberateness correct.

———————

Both Toyota and Honda were boosted in the 1970s by three things: oil shocks, the institution of fuel economy standards and the tastes of baby boomers. In 1973, Arab nations launched the first of two oil embargoes that sparked soaring gasoline prices and fuel shortages across the country. Lines snaked around gasoline stations, and police caught numerous petty thieves siphoning gasoline from parked cars (the practice soon triggered a run on locking gasoline caps). The following year, the Environmental Protection Agency issued its first Corporate Average Fuel Economy standards governing automobiles, which at the time averaged 14.7 miles per gallon. The EPA directed that automakers had to achieve 20 mpg within a few years, a figure that eventually jumped to 27.5 mpg by 1987. Simultaneously, the agency imposed new regulations on the auto companies for exhaust emissions, demanding that they clean up their cars and reduce the amount of pollutants coming from their tailpipes. Detroit auto companies were paralyzed. Their lineups were chock-a-block with gas guzzlers, long-hooded, large-trunk cars laden with angles, shiny trim and fat tires that promised comfort but could by no stretch of the imagination be called economical. They were dirty, too, spewing carbon monoxide and other dirt into the air with each cough of their tailpipes. Although small cars like the Mustang, the Falcon and the Pontiac GTO had been enormously popular during the 1960s, by the 1970s Detroit's offerings had swelled in size. The Mustang was but one example, going from a nimble, affordable and sporty car at its birth to a heavy, fast and powerful automobile a decade later. Detroit's lineups had almost nothing to offer in the way of smaller cars, and the few they had were afterthoughts.

By contrast, Honda and Toyota's lots were replete with small, fuel-efficient vehicles that met customers' immediate needs for better gas mileage. True, American auto industry executives and car reviewers laughed at Honda's first entry, the Civic, a minicar that seemed little more than a passenger compartment with a roof. The company had to make some significant improvements in size and durability in order to protect the car's reputation. But Toyota, with its Corolla and a lineup that was slowly expanding, provided some decent consumer options. Detroit's Big Three auto companies begged consumers to wait out the crisis. In just a few years, they promised, they would remake their lineups and bring their fuel economy in line with the new government requirements (all the while fighting the new regulations tooth and nail in Congress and in court).

Many customers remained loyal. But others, particularly consumers in their twenties and thirties, did not. They sampled the vehicles that the

Japanese companies offered, and discovered that these small cars were economical and durable. Honda may have been the subject of derision from Detroit, but fans of its motorcycles knew how reliable its bikes had proved to be and became some of the first customers for its cars, including the mid-sized Accord, which was introduced in 1975 as a 1976 model. Californians were among the first to embrace Toyota's vehicles, pleased with their gas mileage, their low-polluting engines and their maneuverability in the state's heavy traffic.

Those early fans became evangelists for the company, convincing friends and neighbors to take a chance on the vehicles. These new buyers were not disappointed. And the cars' quality and affordability resulted in some of the deepest buyer loyalty among any brands in the car business. About two-thirds of Honda owners are repeat customers, while half of Toyota's owners have bought one of its vehicles before.

While Detroit scrambled, the Japanese companies began to see that the United States would be a valuable market. The next step for both Honda and Toyota would be to open factories in the market that had increasingly joined Japan as their most important. Conventional wisdom is that these companies were forced to build plants in the United States by political pressure. According to James Womack, author of *The Machine That Changed the World*, a 1990 book that examined the companies' manufacturing expertise, that was not the case. The Japanese companies saw the United States as a key opportunity to expand automobile sales, and political pressure in the end turned out to be a valuable cover. "They were going to come here all along," Womack said.

Honda beat Toyota to American production by several years, opening first a motorcycle plant in Ohio and then its first car manufacturing plant in Marysville, Ohio, in 1982, before Toyota had begun talking about building vehicles in the United States. But Toyota's own approach was more comprehensive and much more like that of one of the Detroit companies. One of its most important tactics was to populate its American management ranks with scores of talented executives recruited from Detroit companies, especially Chrysler and Ford. Among the most outspoken and enthusiastic managers was Robert McCurry, a savvy former Chrysler executive who ran the company's sales operations from 1984 to 1995. Now 80, McCurry's place in automotive history would have been ensured even if he hadn't gone to Toyota, for he was the man who invented rebates for Chrysler's cars and trucks and came up with the phrase "Buy a car, get a check." But he retired from Chrysler in the late 1970s, after a 28-year career there, frustrated by the company's management tactics. Enticed by a friend to join Toyota's Mid-Atlantic dealership network, he subsequently moved to Los Angeles and was named executive vice president of Toyota Motor Sales USA in 1984. McCurry and Toyota were a match of American sales acumen and quality vehicles. He taught the Japanese, who still sold vehicles one at a time, door-to-door in their home market, how to market their cars on a much broader scale. "The Japanese, once they got here, found out that the American market was much different," McCurry said.

Meanwhile, McCurry was enthusiastic about the way the Japanese executives listened to him and embraced his suggestions, one of the fundamental tenets of TPS. "In Detroit, it was hard to get your voice heard," he said. "As close as I was to a lot of people in Detroit, it was difficult to communicate. People had their eye on the corner office"— meaning a promotion to a top job. McCurry had a powerful platform in Toyota, where he was first to declare that the company was aiming to capture 10 percent of the U.S. market, a mark it achieved in 1997. He argued strenuously that the company should build plants in the United States to get there, and he was also first to push Toyota into the developing market for light trucks, including pickups, minivans and SUVs.

More low-key, but equally critical to Toyota in the United States, is James Press, who began his career at Ford but jumped to Toyota in

1970, where he spent years behind the scenes as a strategist before assuming the top American sales job, which he holds today. Along the way, Press and McCurry recruited more American managers, including Illingworth and Borst, who each ran the company's Toyota and Lexus divisions before going on to even more critical positions. Illingworth, quiet and thoughtful, and Borst, known for his quick quips, have been linchpins behind the scenes of the company's strategy to attract American consumers. Illingworth was a key player in the project that led to the creation of Lexus, while Borst leads Toyota Financial Services, the automaker's powerful lending subsidiary.

McCurry and the other Americans who joined Toyota were eager to do things differently than Detroit had done them. For Illingworth, switching to Toyota meant abandoning a promising career at Chrysler. In 1979, he was general manager for its Cleveland region, the youngest ever to hold the position. Two weeks after he got the job, Chrysler, which was close to bankruptcy and would soon seek a federal bailout, closed the regional office. Illingworth traveled with his staff to the company's headquarters in Highland Park, Michigan, to meet with Iacocca and determine their future. Illingworth sat in meetings for two days, waiting to see Iacocca, wondering what his fate would be.

He got the answer at 7:30 A.M. on the third morning, when Iacocca burst into a conference room, puffing on his trademark cigar and cursing. The situation in Cleveland was symptomatic of all the problems that Chrysler faced, Iacocca said, blaming Chrysler's customers for their lack of faith, its dealers for their ineptness, and the government for dragging its heels on Chrysler's bailout bid. At the end of the tirade, Iacocca leaned across the table, blew out a plume of smoke, and said to Illingworth, "If you guys can't get the job done, I have plenty of guys who can."

It was just the impetus Illingworth needed to go elsewhere, and at McCurry's invitation, he took a job at Toyota. On his first day there, general managers from all over the United States held a meeting in

California, where they sat at a U-shaped table in a Marriott Hotel conference room. Each general manager was advised by Toyota managers what the company hoped for from their region, and given specific instructions on how to achieve their sales goals. The atmosphere was cordial and polite. Said Illingworth, "It was the ballgame. I thought, 'They get it, they understand it and they are driven by the marketplace.'"

With these Americans at the helm, reporting to some of Toyota's smartest Japanese executives, Toyota began implementing a strategy that would, years later, lead to its continuing growth. Its success didn't come quickly. It was simply a step at a time. Among the most significant was its first manufacturing venture in the United States. In 1982, Toyota reached agreement with GM on a joint car-building venture in Fremont, California, that was called New United Motor Manufacturing Inc.—or NUMMI for short. GM was not Toyota's first choice. Two years before, Toyota had approached Ford Motor Co. and offered a similar deal in which it would share production of the mid-sized Camry with Ford at its Twin Cities plant in Minnesota. Ford at the time was mired in a financial crisis almost as deep as the one at Chrysler, and there were real worries that it would not be able to emerge without its own federal bailout. The Toyota venture, though appealing, was too risky for Ford's management to approve. In a decision that echoed all of Ford's past reluctance to tie up with Toyota, it declined the offer, prompting Toyota to turn to GM.

On the surface, the joint venture with GM benefited GM more than it did Toyota. Barely in better financial shape than Ford, GM had suffered badly from its lack of competitive small cars. It had tried developing them on its own, sharing the vehicles among its different divisions as a way to expand their sales, but the vehicles looked too much alike and suffered from terrible quality compared with their Japanese counterparts. Then it tried importing them from lesser Japanese companies, like Suzuki and Isuzu, only to find out that not all Japanese companies were the same when it came to quality. Finally, GM embraced the deal with Toyota as a way to give its customers a vehicle equal to the competition, and perhaps learn some of the secrets that had made Toyota such a strong manufacturer.

In an agreement negotiated by Jack Smith, later to become GM's chief executive and chairman, and Tatsuro Toyoda, a member of the founding family who went on to become president, the companies agreed to share production of the Toyota Corolla. It would be built, under Toyota's supervision, at a factory in Fremont, California, that GM had recently closed. GM's version of the Corolla would be sold by Chevrolet, which solved GM's most immediate need for a small car. Toyota chose not to sell the NUMMI-built Corollas right away, waiting to see if they were as good as those its workers built in Japan. Eventually, in 1988, two years after the first NUMMI Corollas were produced, Toyota did put a NUMMI car into its lineup. It was a limited-edition hatchback called the Corolla FX, and it marked the first time Toyota was able to claim a locally built car. But Toyota, through the venture, had an even more important strategy in mind. It saw the NUMMI plant as a way to find out what it would be like to work with American workers, and help it make up its mind about building its own plant in the United States.

By the time the NUMMI deal got under way, Toyota was late to American production. With Detroit companies demanding that Japanese companies build cars in the United States or risk trade sanctions, Honda, Mazda, Nissan and Mitsubishi had announced joint ventures or built their own plants years before. It seemed that Toyota was being overly conservative, and in fact its executives were very nervous about the NUMMI plant. "There's no question in my mind that NUMMI was the test case," said Dennis Cuneo, senior vice president of Toyota North America. An attorney who helped negotiate the deal between GM and Toyota, Cuneo wound up being the first NUMMI employee, hired personally by Tatsuro Toyoda. "There was quite a bit of dissent in Japan about even doing NUMMI," Cuneo said. "I was told by several people that if NUMMI had not been a success, Toyota would have gone back to building cars only in Japan." That would have meant billions of dollars in North American investment would have never occurred, and Toyota today might be half the size that it is now.

But Toyota's caution paid off, due in part to the efforts of a former assistant plant manager at Ford named Gary Convis, who had spent 18 years in Ford's manufacturing operations. He had been promoted from plant to plant, finally landing a position as a manager in Lorain, Ohio, where Ford built trucks. Having spent so many years at Ford, he had no intention of leaving, and ignored a headhunter's call when he was approached about a job at NUMMI. "I didn't know what it was," except that the job would be in California, said Convis. His wife, however, who commented that "Lorain, Ohio, wasn't California," suggested he call back. He knew nothing about Toyota and had never heard of the Toyota Production System. But Convis was encouraged that Toyota was ready to build cars in the United States.

Abandoning a position at one of the Detroit companies was like stepping off a ledge. And Ford made him an attractive offer to stay. "They said, 'You can write your own ticket. Tell us what you want,'" Convis recalled. "But Toyota said, trust us and join us." He became employee No. 5 at NUMMI. But he spent little time in Fremont, boarding a plane two weeks later for Japan, bound for Toyota City. As he toured Toyota's factories, he was stunned by their efficiency. He watched, amazed, as parts arrived next to the assembly line just before they were needed, illustrating the just-in-time inventory concept, then unknown in Detroit automakers' plants. At Toyota, parts were seamlessly unloaded, and materials handlers scooted off with empty bins to restock them and return again just as fresh supplies were needed. There were no arguments, no phone calls demanding deliveries, no shutting down the assembly line to wait for replenishments, and most important, no need to stock weeks' worth of parts in warehouses out back in case suppliers didn't show up. "What I was seeing was something I had never seen before. It was like poetry. It was like a dance," Convis marveled. "It scared the hell out of me. I wondered, 'How on earth are we going to compete with this?'" He had good reason to be frightened. The workforce in GM's Fremont plant—the labor pool for the joint venture—was known as one of the most difficult in the industry, rife with complaints of drug abuse, absenteeism and a general disinterest in anything but punching a clock. But UAW leaders insisted that GM employ workers from the closed Fremont plant in the NUMMI venture, or it would not give its sanction to the deal. GM could have challenged the union, but it didn't want to risk a confrontation with the UAW, which had struck GM numerous times over its various efforts to streamline its operations. Home from his trip, Convis held a five-hour meeting with Bruce Lee, the UAW official in charge of the plant. He leveled with Lee, telling him that workers' previous behaviors couldn't stand. "The world has changed and it will never be the way it was again," Convis said.

He insisted that workers from the NUMMI plant travel to Japan to work for three weeks alongside their Toyota counterparts, a strategy meant to open their eyes to what was expected of them. Dennis Cuneo was on hand when workers, some of them grizzled veterans with 30 years' experience at GM, boarded a bus for the airport. He was full of trepidation. "I remember watching and thinking, 'How is this going to work? Are they going to survive?'" But the workers came home surprisingly enthusiastic. "I called them converted Catholics," Cuneo said. The workers also discovered that they got the same message when they came home as they had heard in Japan. Both Cuneo and Convis had learned the Toyota Production System, then taught it to others at NUMMI. It was another big change from Detroit at the time, where bosses gave orders and workers were just supposed to comply without explanation. Once production began in 1985, the

NUMMI plant quickly became one of the best within either the Toyota or the GM system, confirming Convis's faith in American workers and reassuring Japanese management about American workers' abilities. It also launched Toyota's journey to eventually building vehicles on its own in the United States.

Toyota opened its first solely owned American factory, in Georgetown, Kentucky, a hamlet that was barely a dot on the map outside Lexington, Kentucky, in 1988. The executive that Toyota sent to run the factory was Fujio Cho, Ohno's acolyte, and Dennis Cuneo's instructor in TPS, who had become one of the company's rising stars. Toyota had taken a deliberately conservative approach with Georgetown, choosing not to build a new vehicle there but to produce the latest version of the mid-sized Camry. Once again, Toyota was proceeding cautiously, hedging its bets. If for some reason it was disappointed by its American plant, it could replace the vehicles built at Georgetown with Camrys produced in Japan. Even so, according to Cuneo, "it was kind of a risky venture for Toyota." It displayed faith not only in American workers but in the Camry, which was selling about 125,000 a year. The new Ford Taurus had raised eyebrows at Toyota, proving that American companies could compete if they really applied themselves. The Georgetown venture, which planned to build at least 200,000 Camrys a year, was Toyota's response.

Cho was determined to make Georgetown successful. His faith in American workers was confirmed quickly. Soon after the Georgetown plant opened, northern Kentucky was paralyzed by a snowstorm that began during the day shift. Cho was not sure that enough workers would make it in for the night shift, so he asked for volunteers to work a double assignment. Virtually the entire shift offered to stay on, and to Cho's surprise nearly all the second shift showed up, as well. Many of those workers drove in hours early because they were afraid they would be late due to the storm.

The episode showed the respect employees had for Cho, according to Sam Heltman, the plant's director of human resources at the time. It was a respect he had cultivated with interest and determination. Though he barely spoke English at the time, Mr. Cho would walk the plant floor each day, talking to its 1,100 workers, using an interpreter when necessary, and listening to their complaints. "He acted as though he had nothing more important to do than to listen to this person and give them his undivided attention," said Heltman. The conversations helped Cho understand the challenges of building vehicles in a foreign market, according to Takahiro Fujimoto, a professor of economics at Tokyo University who has studied Toyota for decades. Despite his background as an attorney, Cho had "a real shop floor knowledge about manufacturing vehicles, much as Dr. Ohno did," said Fujimoto. Cho did more than just walk the plant floor. Every Wednesday night at 8 o'clock, workers and managers gathered to discuss Toyota's philosophy, to go over new manufacturing methods and to allow workers to share their concerns. Initially, there was a significant Japanese presence in the factory. Japanese engineers and staff employees, called "coordinators" in Toyota parlance, sat next to their American counterparts to supervise what the Americans were doing.

Cho promised that as the Americans became more capable, the coordinators would go away, and today there is only a sprinkling of Japanese faces to be seen within the plant's vast complex, which has grown to include two car factories and an engine plant, employing 8,000 people. The performance of the American workers under the Toyota system reassured executives in Japan that they had made the right choice in putting their faith in the United States. "It was absolutely the most exhilarating thing you can think of," said Heltman, who is now in charge of human resources for Toyota Motor Manufacturing in North America. Cho helped Toyota lay the foundation for a series of factories that would eventually become the heart of its strategy in the United States and, indeed, the world.

In much the same way, Honda's operations in Ohio were its stepping-stone on its own particular journey. Both Toyota and Honda proved that American workers could build great cars—on the West Coast and in the American heartland—that American consumers would embrace. They became the nucleus of a new American automobile industry. And whereas they would pursue different paths going forward, Toyota and Honda kept their focus squarely on their compass point: the customer. Marysville, for Honda, and the NUMMI plant and Georgetown, for Toyota, became launching pads for companies determined to serve the needs of American customers. To fulfill their promise, they had to venture out beyond the Accords built at Marysville and the Civics built at East Liberty, the Corollas built at NUMMI and the Camrys built at Georgetown, into new parts of the market. By leveraging those factories, the people working in them and the vision of the companies' founders, they have grown dramatically. Toyota is shaping up to be the Japanese equivalent of a Detroit company—focused only on producing reliable vehicles, profitable operations and consistency throughout its approach. Honda is taking its place as a company that puts engineering before everything, selecting its new ventures very carefully. In the process, they are providing Detroit with more competition than it ever imagined.

CHAPTER FOUR

JOURNEY FROM
THE INSIDE OUT

HONDA IS A COMPANY that charts its own course. It fiercely prizes its independence, and that applies not only to its status as an automobile company, approaching the market without partners, but to the way it develops its automobiles. It keeps control of every step of the engineering, design and manufacturing process, starting with the very first inkling of an idea. Honda's approach is a rare thing in an industry where the creation of a car can seem like shopping at a bazaar. About the only thing a car company really needs to do anymore is dream up a name for its vehicle. Gone are the years when American automobile manufacturers oversaw every phase of their vehicles' features. In the modern automobile industry, automakers can outsource the design of their vehicles to independent studios. They can buy engines from their competitors, including Honda, which sells 1 million engines a year to other companies, including GM. They can contract with suppliers like Lear Corp. to produce entire portions of the car, such as the interior compartments that Lear is designing for GM. And they can even have their automobiles built by somebody else, as the Canadian auto supplier Magna does in Austria for BMW. Honda keeps all of this in-house. Its goal with the vehicles that it creates is to meet the needs of its customers succinctly and squarely on target. It wants to build the best vehicle in every segment in which it competes. Honda was not always able to do this. It had to turn to Isuzu to assemble its first big SUV, the Passport, because it wasn't ready yet to build trucks on its own. But while the Passport filled a space in the market, Honda figured out how to do an SUV—and now has not one, but three.

Honda's single-mindedness leads to very specific vehicles that are aimed primarily at the customers it knows best: its own. Hondas do not appeal to everyone, and for years they have perplexed the Big Three, who couldn't figure out why people were so enamored of such unadulterated cars when they could have something much flashier. But anyone who buys a Honda knows that the secret is that Honda is consistent and knows its business inside and out. Moreover, it keeps reinventing itself. Every new vehicle is an opportunity for improvement and to learn something new. It is a philosophy that has its roots in Japan, and that is spreading to the United States as Honda entrusts its employees here with more responsibility. It is an approach that leads to something reliable, dependable and thoroughly researched, inside and out. In all aspects of Honda, there is an attention to detail that manages to escape Detroit, but that its customers have come to value and expect.

Deep within Honda's vast Research and Development Center in Tochigi, Japan, hidden by an avenue of cherry trees, Honda engineers prepare for their latest crash test as meticulously as doctors map out how they will perform delicate surgery. Nothing is left to chance by the teams of studious men and women, clad in immaculate white coats and trousers, the Honda equivalent of hospital scrubs. The 200 people on staff here have been trained to spot the minutest differences in results each time a vehicle comes barreling down one of the pathways in this building and careens into its target. That happens an average of twice each workday, or about 500 times a year, at what Honda calls its real-world, multidirectional testing center. A pristine white, two-story building an hour north of Tokyo, it is constantly in use, day and night, as one of just two such indoor collision laboratories in the global auto industry. The other sits a continent away in Sweden, where it was built by safety-obsessed automaker Volvo and has since, like its creator, been taken over by Ford. There are no such indoor testing centers in the United States, where, as they have for decades, auto companies perform a number of their crash tests outdoors. This means that weather conditions, darkness and environmental impurities can all play havoc with testing. To be sure, American auto companies have added computerized tests to the mix, crashing vehicles into one another in simulated collisions, and they have indoor testing labs where they can perform some kinds of crashes, such as those in which a car smashes into a fixed barrier. But despite the fact that they dwarf Honda in size, neither GM nor Chrysler has invested in a place like this.

Making Honda's test center even more distinctive is the fact that in Japan, automobile companies don't have to do their own crash tests. They have always relied on data from the Japan Automotive Research Institute, which performs government-required tests for them. Thus, this center is yet another reminder of the fact that here, as elsewhere throughout the company, engineers rule. You see them in virtually every Honda building, whether its Tokyo headquarters or its factories or its design centers, distinguished by those white outfits. Their requirements have become paramount through the years, as Honda has expanded from focusing primarily on automobiles to a full lineup with everything from luxury cars to big SUVs. In the mid-1990s, tired of waiting for data from the government, Honda decided it needed to have its own testing center. In 2000, it opened this place, which can best be described as an engineering heaven. "We are serving the customer even better," said the personable director, Tomiji Sugimoto, a veteran of 25 years as a safety engineer and the prime force behind this showplace. As one walks inside, the first thing that comes to mind is that this would make a truly awesome hockey rink. The testing floor is 40,000 square meters in size and shaped like a fan, with the runways as its spokes and garage doors where each vehicle enters for its test. Here, working 24 hours a day, Honda can crash vehicles at up to 80 kilometers an hour (about 50 mph), from any conceivable position, beginning at 15-degree angles and ranging up to 90 degrees, the equivalent of a head-on crash. It can perform crashes from the side, stage rear-end collisions and, significantly, measure what happens to pedestrians when they are struck by cars. While not so much a major subject in the United States, car–pedestrian collisions are an issue of huge concern in crowded Japan, where 28 percent of all fatal accidents each year involve pedestrians. As if to illustrate the point, a family of dummies, from a babe in arms to a full-grown adult couple, sits in chairs next to the testing area. They are so lifelike that on a day when a visitor didn't get too much sleep, or imbibed too much sake the night before, it's more than easy to mistake them for real live people.

The dummy collection, which marks the second generation of such pedestrian stand-ins, lends a humorous touch to a place where data collection is serious business. A bank of 36 cameras overhead, at the side of each runway and in the floor beneath record 280 types of information. Hanging over the collision point is a control room, staffed by a half-dozen engineers sitting at computer screens, or standing to watch the proceedings. Before each test begins, six engineers fan out around the vehicle or the dummy that is to be the subject of that day's test. Today, a male dummy will be struck by a white HR-V sport utility, a popular Honda vehicle in Japan and similar to the small CR-V sport utility sold in the United States. The test, which is being recorded by a film crew from the Discovery Channel for a documentary on automotive research, touches on both of Honda's biggest concerns: injuries to pedestrians that result from crashes, and the kind of damage that minivans, SUVs and pickups can wreak both on other vehicles and on people. Honda never had good data on the latter in the past, because its lineup focused exclusively on cars. Now, however, it vitally needs the information. Its American lineup has three sizes of SUVs—the luxury Acura MDX and its twin, the Honda Pilot, the Element and the CR-V—plus the big Odyssey minivan. It doesn't build a pickup truck, but it is rumored to be considering one. In fact, Honda has been shipping Chevrolet and Dodge pickups from North America to this site in order to see what happens when they run into another vehicle or into one of Honda's dummies, storing up data it may use in the future.

As the engineers hang the dummy from a cord that descends from the ceiling, a bank of red lights blink in the minutes before the test is to begin, signaling the direction from which the vehicle will be coming. A whistle blows, and a verbal countdown in Japanese from 10 begins. As the numbers get smaller—"*san, ni, ichi, zero*"—the engineers step well away and then the HR-V begins its trek down the runway on a rail beneath the concrete floor. Watching from above in the control room, the group of onlookers, including Sugimoto and the film crewmembers, is quiet. The HR-V reaches 40 kilometers per hour, draws closer and closer, and then slams into the dummy. The impact brings a gasp from the assembled watchers. The dummy's body goes soaring off to the right, landing squarely on a canvas-covered mat, losing a sneaker when it hits the ground. (The engineers and crewmembers had been taking bets on whether the dummy would land on the canvas, and there are some quiet grins as the thunk is heard.) The HR-V comes to a stop, its front end dented and the hood askew. The windshield is cracked and the wiper blade is broken.

The collision is captured on Honda's video cameras, by the Discovery Channel film crew and by still cameras. Within seconds of the completion of the test, the engineers are checking the data that the collision has yielded. Walking over to the front of the HR-V, the center's director, Sugimoto, points out how the body hit the dented front end. First came the thigh, then the hip, he surmises. The dummy was thrown onto the windshield, where its head collided with the glass before the body was tossed aside. The whole episode took less than five seconds. What was different about this test? Well, says Sugimoto, he can't remember a previous test in which a shoe came off. Sugimoto has a long history here, having joined the company in 1977. One of his first assignments was working on airbags, more than a decade before they became commonplace in automobiles. He is bluntly not a fan of the devices. Although an airbag offers protection in a high-speed, head-on crash, when it comes to overall safety, "a seat belt is more effective," Sugimoto declares during a lunch of sandwiches, seafood salad and custard.

Sugimoto said the results of the tests conducted here can already be seen on Honda's vehicles, which are scoring high marks on government crash tests in North America and elsewhere. In one instance, data collected here during a crash between a small Honda Civic and a luxury Acura RL led Honda to make changes to strengthen the front end of the Civic, a vehicle of which Sugimoto is very fond. "The cabin integrity is so nice," he muses.

But he is concerned about the growing popularity of SUVs, from purely a safety standpoint, and he said that even with a facility like this, Honda can't change the facts of physics, which are that something heavier tends to smash something smaller. "It's difficult to control the mass weight itself," Sugimoto says. That won't stop these engineers from their tasks. Already they have set up for another crash test, and repeated calls to his cell phone summon Sugimoto from his hasty lunch. But before he leaves, he offers a prognosis on the dummy damaged in the morning collision. His leg was hurt, and there is an 85 percent chance that he suffered a head injury—or would have, if he were a real person. But, says Sugimoto, smiling, there's only a 15 percent chance that he died. Not bad news at all.

Halfway across the world, in Honda's North American research and development center in Marysville, Ohio, Charlie Baker is sprinting to get to his next meeting. Lanky, with glasses and a quick smile, Baker is the brain of Honda's American engineering operations, having been named vice president here in 2003. In his hands rests the most important vehicle in Honda's American lineup, the mid-sized Accord, which has been the linchpin of Honda's lineup here for the past two decades. Baker delights in giving a visitor a teasing look at the nerve center of this vast facility. He swipes a security card that unlocks a door and unveils a wonder: a room, stretching for nearly a quarter of a mile, that houses Honda's American engineers and product development teams. They each sit at a desk, without dividers or walls, the only private spaces being a row of conference rooms along the farthest end of the building.

Nearly all of the faces are American, with some Japanese colleagues sprinkled among them, men and women who, like their colleagues in Tochigi, wear white trousers and jackets with their names embroidered over the breast pocket. The vastness of this place mirrors that of Tochigi, and it and the Marysville facility are only two of three such centers that Honda has worldwide. The third, just as impressive and even more sprawling, sits in Torrance, California, an hour south of Los Angeles. These three automotive research centers form the nucleus of how Honda brings its vehicles to life for the United States. And engineers from each of them played a role in the development of an automobile that was a milestone for Honda in terms of its influence in the U.S. market—the second-generation Odyssey minivan, which was tailored by Honda to appeal to American families.

More than any other vehicle, the Odyssey exemplifies a strategy that import auto companies are using with great success to torment the companies from Detroit. By offering excellent products, with innovative features and a top pedigree of durability, reliability and quality, the imports are able to attract the most desirable portion of customers in any single market, whether for cars, minivans, SUVs or pickup trucks. "The story here really is one of the domestics losing out because the imports are suddenly competing in areas that were the privy of the domestics, and the imports are doing a wonderful job," said Ron Pinelli, an auto industry analyst with Autodata, based in Woodcliff Lake, New Jersey.

Moreover, these customers become ambassadors for their vehicles, posting enthusiastic missives about them on Internet message boards, telling their friends, family and neighbors about their new automobiles, and prompting them to go out and buy them. In short order, the reputation of the vehicle is made, its profitability generally assured, and Detroit is left, once again, to scramble after customers more attuned to the aspects of a deal than the attributes of the vehicle that the companies are trying to sell. When this strategy is used successfully, an import automobile company can become a leader, selling 100,000 vehicles or so, enough to establish it as a real competitor and sufficient to cover investment, but scarce enough so that customers believe that they own something rare and special.

Within only a few months of its introduction in 1998, the Odyssey had leapfrogged Chrysler's minivans to become the gold standard in family transportation. Only Toyota's Sienna, which was redesigned in 2003, challenged its top rank on quality surveys. Demand for the Odyssey would be expected if Honda had limited its production and kept it deliberately scarce, or if the Odyssey were moderately priced to begin with. But Odyssey starts above

$24,000, much more than Chrysler's cheapest minivans, and fully equipped versions can cost as much as $31,000. Regardless, by 2002 Odyssey was the second-best-selling minivan nameplate, behind the Chrysler vans and ahead of minivans from Ford, GM and Toyota.

To meet the American customers' feverish demand for it, Honda, which originally built the Odyssey on one assembly line at its plant in Alliston, Ontario, built a new factory in record time in Lincoln, Alabama, so that it could expand its supply of Odysseys. The Odyssey is not a niche product but a real volume competitor, selling nearly 200,000 a year, all at a substantial profit and to the enthusiasm of consumers across the country. "Get the Odyssey," declared Tom and Ray Magliozzi, hosts of "Car Talk" on National Public Radio, when a caller one weekend asked which minivan to buy.

Tim Benner had no idea that the Odyssey would turn into the juggernaut that it has become when he set out in 1994 to measure the dimensions of his Orange County, California, garage. Benner, the father of a young daughter, worked as an engineer at Honda R&D in Torrance and had been assigned by Honda on a project that the company considered to be of critical importance: the design for the second generation of its minivan. The first-generation Honda Odyssey had merely been an adaptation of the minivan that Honda sold in Japan, and the flaws were visible at a glance. "The first-generation Odyssey was a home run in Japan. It was not a home run in the States," said Erik Berkman, an executive engineer at the R&D facility in Marysville who joined Benner on the second-generation Odyssey project. In a country where a sliding side door had become mandatory, so that children could hop in and out at will without their parents having to unbuckle themselves and let the kids out, the Odyssey arrived in the United States with four conventional doors. Moreover, the Odyssey was narrow, designed for Japan's crowded streets and small parking places. It had a four-cylinder engine, the same used on the Accord, and lacked the power and maneuverability that a minivan needed to transport families on the highway. Interestingly, the original Odyssey had a feature that would eventually become a Honda trademark: a third row of seats that could be folded flat into the floor, creating more storage space. That was a standard feature on Japanese vans, known for their interior design and flexible use of space, which is at such a premium throughout all aspects of Japanese life. But the fold-flat seat was hardly noticed on the original vehicle, given all the other ways in which it was inferior to other minivans on the American market. Honda was selling only about 25,000 Odysseys a year when Venner was assigned to work under the project's leader, a Japanese Honda engineer named Kunimichi Odagaki, on a vehicle they called PJ—for "personal jet."

Odagaki, now one of Honda's highest-ranking development executives, arrived in the United States speaking only a modest amount of English, but intrigued by the challenge of how the Odyssey could be improved. "I wanted to create an all-new minivan," he said. "I didn't want to eat into Chrysler. I wanted to expand the minivan market." Modest and soft-spoken, with curly dark hair, Odagaki yields enormous power within Honda as what the company calls an LPL, for "large project leader." Though he is virtually unknown outside Honda, within the company he demands such respect that there is talk he may ascend to one of the company's top jobs, perhaps even as chief executive someday. The clout that Odagaki holds makes it even more remarkable that he would spend so much time on the project. In Detroit, it's rare that a chief engineer would make it out of the office, unless for a company conference, let alone spend months on the road researching whether there was a market for a new vehicle. But it is a common practice at Honda, and a reason why its chief engineers carry so much clout. "This is good for the customer," Odagaki explained. "I am always saying this to young engineers at Honda:

'Please do not follow the competitors' cars. Customers' needs and demands are always changing. I want to hear the voice of the customer.'" Adds Berkman: "We don't have layers of protocol and so on. Engineers have to develop their own data. Some people say, 'I don't want to get dirt under my fingernails.' And we say, 'Didn't we explain that to you in the job interview?'"

In more formal terms, Honda's practice is a Japanese term that translates as "go to the spot." That is exactly what Odagaki did, traveling 25,000 miles over six months across the American South and West. Honda's research had determined that the primary market for the kind of minivan that it wanted to create lay in cities and suburbs where new homes, new schools and new shopping malls had sprung up during the past 15 years. Though it welcomed customers from everywhere, its goal was to meet the needs of modern Middle America (or, in reality, upper-middle-class America). It felt the best place to find these people was in states like the Carolinas, Georgia, Tennessee, Kentucky and Ohio, along with California—all places where Odagaki and his engineering team visited. "We wanted to see the situation of usage," said Odagaki, interviewed on a warm afternoon at Honda's research center in Wako, Japan.

The difference between how minivans were used in Japan and their role with American consumers became clear almost immediately. In Japan, he explained, minivans were more like recreational vehicles, used primarily for long trips and for holidays. His first lesson, Odagaki said, was that "in America, minivans are not used for camping" but for everyday commutes. The three engineers—Odagaki from Japan, Berkman from Ohio, and Benner from California—learned a lot of things that any mother might have been able to tell them but seemed even more compelling because they discovered them for themselves. One realization came late at night, when the crew missed their highway exit and had to stop to look at a map. The only way to turn on a light in the old Odyssey was to illuminate the entire passenger compartment, which woke up the dozing engineers in the backseat, much to their displeasure. That taught Odagaki that there should be a separate light for the driver, so that sleeping children would not be disturbed.

Returning to California, the engineers traveled to the elementary school in Benner's neighborhood to watch parents unload their children in the morning and load them up after school. (The research trip got them in trouble more than once. Sitting in the minivan one day, taking pictures and filming with a video recorder, Odagaki and Benner were startled to find a policeman rapping on their window, telling them in no uncertain terms to get moving. "He thought we were going to kidnap the children," Odagaki said.) Their observations resulted in one of the biggest disputes the engineers had with senior Japanese officials over the minivan. When it introduced the original Odyssey, Honda hadn't seen a need to include sliding doors, even though they were a feature of American minivans, and its lack of them was one of the original Odyssey's biggest flaws. But after spending time in America, Odagaki became convinced that the Odyssey should have sliding doors on either side, and that they should be easy to operate. The Japanese engineer saw that it was difficult for both adults and children to yank open their minivan's sliding doors and to shut them afterward. He watched in sympathy as one young father, laden with a baby, tried to open a minivan door with his free hand to let out his other children.

But the minute the engineers proposed not one, but two sliding doors, Honda's manufacturing executives balked. "They said to us, 'Please cancel this,'" said Odagaki. The company didn't know how to build a vehicle with sliding doors, and including the feature would mean time and expense. Moreover, hinged doors were cheaper to engineer and to install than two large sliding doors. It turned into a serious showdown, a rarity inside a company where engineers and managers ordinarily see eye-to-eye. An engineer in Odagaki's position generally carries so much power that even Honda's chief executive, Hiroyuki Yoshino, can't force changes in his designs. "I hear him, but I'm not hearing him," Odagaki joked. Realizing that the engineers and manufacturers had reached a stalemate unsolvable by Honda's usual consensus-building methods, Odagaki knew he would have to draw a line in the sand. "I was very afraid and scared," Odagaki admitted, "but I'm the servant of the customer. I went to my boss's desk and said, 'I've decided we have to do this.'" In the end, he won the battle, based on their research and backed up by the videos and photos that had gotten them momentarily in trouble with the cops.

The engineers won another important battle, too, over giving the Odyssey a six-cylinder engine. Honda had honed its reputation on the reliability and the soundness of its basic four-cylinder engine, which was installed in most of its cars and had been installed on the original Odyssey as well. Sufficient for the Civic and Accord, it did not provide enough power for a bigger vehicle, which Odagaki learned when he took the minivan out on California's freeways. He needed to be able to accelerate from lane to lane, to avoid obstacles and avert the frequent traffic jams that plague Los Angeles traffic. Once he found himself dangerously close to a guardrail, trying to get around a stalled vehicle, and the minivan's wimpy performance convinced him that the new version of the Odyssey had to have more power under the hood. Ultimately it got it, in the form of a 3.5-liter, V-6 engine with 240 horsepower that would power the van from 0 to 60 mph in under eight seconds. It was still fuel-efficient, always a Honda priority, earning 18 mpg in city driving and 25 mpg on the highway.

Odyssey also needed a more powerful appearance. Odagaki was sitting behind the glass in a conference room, listening to the opinions of participants in a focus group that Honda had collected to discuss how buyers felt about minivans. The answer of one man caught his ear. "He said, 'I want a minivan, but my wife doesn't.'" Intrigued, Odagaki asked if he could visit the man's home and speak with his spouse, in keeping with the custom of "going to the spot." The man's wife told him, "I have a career. I don't want to be seen to be a housewife. A minivan is a Mommy-mobile." What part of the minivan? Odagaki asked the woman. All of it, she replied, and after more questions, he realized that to her a Mommy-mobile was a van with a very round shape, like the curvy minivans that Chrysler was selling. "I decided the shape should be much stronger," Odagaki said, insisting that the Odyssey have angular features and slightly squared-off corners.

That coincided with the company's decision that Odyssey should come only with a long wheelbase, a conclusion that set it apart from Detroit vehicles and other minivans offered by Japanese companies. From the outset, Chrysler had focused on the "mini" in minivans, making long-wheelbase versions available primarily on its top-of-the-line Town & Country and on the Dodge Grand Caravan. But Honda couldn't afford to do multiple versions of its minivan, and the concept of so many choices also didn't fit with its focus on hitting its market target squarely in the center. Honda engineers could already tell that short-wheelbase minivans were falling out of favor. Odagaki came to that conclusion when he sat with Benner in the parking lot of a Home Depot store. Odagaki watched, fascinated, as shoppers came out toting two-by-fours and four-by-eight-foot sheets of plywood. To Benner it was an everyday event, but in Japan, Odagaki explained, almost no one spends time on major home improvement projects. Homes are too small, and besides, the country is stocked with skilled craftspeople who arrive promptly and finish the job quickly. "But Americans like to do that," he said, understanding that it was very important to have space in the back of the minivan in order to bring the building supplies home.

He also noticed a number of short-wheelbase minivans in the parking lot that had a cargo carrier strapped to their roofs, or a cart attached to the rear end, to hold all the things that wouldn't fit inside.

It seemed incongruous that someone would spend so much money on a vehicle only to have it fall short of meeting its needs. "Maybe there weren't cowboys in cowboy hats, but there were plenty of real people driving minivans," said Berkman.

That meant the van had to have the fold-down rear seat that had been on the original Odyssey. But the seat would have to be wider, which would be another challenge for engineers in Japan to pull off. The original fold-down seat had only been big enough to hold two people. The engineers wanted the new Odyssey's seat to be able to hold three, meaning it had to be four feet wide. It was another point of resistance, but one which Odagaki and his engineers were able to overcome by using their own experience. On a flight from Japan, Odagaki and the engineers rented a General Motors minivan at Los Angeles International Airport. They were unable to fit all their suitcases in the back, and there wasn't enough seating room for the entire team, some of whom ended up sitting on one another's laps. "It was a unanimous vote" to ask for a wide, fold-down seat, said Berkman, who calls the feature the van's "charm point." "People didn't think we would do that," he said.

In the end, Odagaki said, nothing mattered more than safety, for minivans were primarily family vehicles. He was determined that the Odyssey would be sound enough to win a five-star rating in U.S. government crash tests, because he knew that safety was a determining factor for many family buyers. Odagaki wanted passengers inside to be well protected, so each of the seven seats had headrests, and each seating place was equipped with a three-point seat belt. Every Odyssey, not just the most expensive ones, came equipped with antilock brakes and traction control, as well as a system Honda called EBD, for electronic braking distribution.

———————

All of the features of the Odyssey combined into a package that the auto industry had never seen before. The first glimpse of it came at a Christmas party that Honda threw at the Automotive Hall of Fame in 1997. Dick Colliver, the general manager of the Honda Division, was smiling like a cat that had eaten the canary in one gulp, as he showed off the minivan to a group of Detroit journalists. "We are going to sell a ton of these," Colliver confided, standing at the back of the crowd crawling all over the Odyssey. The proof came within months of the Odyssey's debut in spring 1998. Odagaki, Benner, Berkman and the rest of the team had hit their target. Odyssey was an immediate success, in hot demand among Honda customers and attracting new buyers to the auto company who had heard about the suburban status symbol. Across the country, waiting lists mounted, particularly on the East Coast, where a dealer on Long Island asked for a $500 deposit just to take a test drive. Honda had hedged its bets originally with the new Odyssey, figuring that it would sell about 80,000 a year. But demand was soaring, and clearly Honda would be able to sell twice that many.

The Odyssey's success spurred Honda into a project that it had long been considering but had not found a reason to do: a new American manufacturing plant. As part of its decision to create a new minivan for the American market, Honda decided to produce it in North America. The decision was in keeping with its practice of building vehicles in the same markets as the customers who bought them. Moreover, the bigger Odyssey would have to be built on its own assembly line. Because of its size, and because it was not based on any previous Honda underpinnings, Odyssey could not be built in the same Japanese factory where its predecessor was produced. In any case, Honda was keeping the smaller Odyssey in its lineup, so it had no need or interest in tearing apart its Japanese plant in order to build the new version. It chose to build the Odyssey on a new assembly line at its factory in Alliston, Ontario, north of Toronto, and when Odyssey proved to be so successful, it increased production at Alliston in order to get more vehicles out of the plant while it decided where the new plant should go.

Though Honda had been the first Japanese manufacturer to build an automobile plant in the United States, it had not built one since East Liberty, Ohio, opened in 1989. Since then, Toyota had opened a truck plant in Princeton, Indiana, a move that had been central to its production of the Tundra pickup. The Princeton plant was the first of the second generation of Japanese-owned factories in the United States, and now Honda, too, was ready to expand. Ohio was eager for Honda to build the factory right there, and Honda was deluged with offers from other states as well. But it wanted to go somewhere completely new, because it had new manufacturing ideas that it wanted to try.

A lot had changed since Honda had built both the Marysville and East Liberty factories. For one thing, Honda in the 1980s was still new to the car business. It was feeling its way as an automobile manufacturer. It had never had a Taiichi Ohno, and its factories looked that way. "What Honda wants to be good at is not making cars," said author James Womack. "It's designing and engineering cars with the feel and features that Japanese and American customers are willing to pay a premium for."

To visit one of Honda's factories in Japan, like the giant Suzuka plant near the famous racetrack, is to be taken aback by what Honda is able to accomplish. Suzuka's production lines are situated on three floors of the factory: the body shop downstairs, assembly on the second floor and the paint shop up top. It's a rabbit warren of manufacturing, stuffed in a shoe box. Nonetheless, the plant has an amazing production capacity, building more than 750,000 vehicles a year in more than half a dozen body styles, and the roads outside the plant are a constant buzz of activity, with parts deliveries coming in and finished vehicles heading out to marshaling yards. In the same way, Marysville is no showplace of factory-floor layout. It has undergone significant overhauls at least three times, including the most recent, in 2002, for the introduction of the 2003 Accord. The plant's manufacturing engineers built entirely new assembly lines behind those that were operating, then shifted production over a weekend so that the plant could restart the following Monday without any loss of cars. It was a remarkable feat that Detroit plants wouldn't even attempt to accomplish. Among the Big Three, it's still acceptable to shut a factory for weeks, months or years to change over from production of one type of vehicle to another. Honda, however, simply can't afford to lose the units, because that would mean customers would have to wait longer for their cars.

Honda's decision to build a new factory led to a number of company firsts. It selected a site in Lincoln, Alabama, about 15 miles east of Montgomery, the first time it had ever ventured so far into the American South. The plant would be Honda's first that was solely dedicated to the production of light trucks, starting with the Odyssey, adding the Pilot, and eventually, some auto industry analysts believe, including a pickup truck, once Honda finally decides to build one. Honda decreed that the plant would produce not only vehicles but engines, the first time that it had put both an engine plant and a car plant under the same roof, and it would have a foundry there, too, to make the blocks for the engines. (Though it isn't unusual to have an engine plant and a car plant on the same property, as Toyota does in Georgetown, it is still a rarity in the automobile business to have one big manufacturing plant with both. One of the few factories to do so is the Saturn complex in Spring Hill, Tennessee.) Along with that, Honda decided that the plant in Lincoln would have to be up to speed far faster than it originally planned, because demand for the Odyssey was just too enormous.

That led to a timetable that itself was something of a first for the auto industry, where all manner of hiccups, from the weather to environmental permits, can knock a manufacturing plant off schedule. Even years after it opened, people in the industry are still amazed at how quickly Honda opened the Lincoln factory, particularly given all the risks that the venture involved. Honda announced the $580 million project in May 1999, with an initial completion date set for two years later. It planned to hire 4,300 workers, who would build 150,000 vehicles a year in a plant that had 1.7 million square feet. Honda broke ground for the factory in April 2000. It went into production in November 2001, six months earlier than Honda had first planned. Not only that, but before Honda even finished the plant it announced that it would expand it. By the time the expansion is complete, Honda will have invested $1 billion in the Lincoln plant, which will employ 4,300 workers, cover 2.8 million square feet and produce 300,000 vehicles a year.

The project was a breakthrough assignment for Lincoln's plant manager, Chuck Ernst, a native of Middletown, Ohio, who had begun his manufacturing career working in the steel industry. But Ernst heard positive stories from friends in Ohio who had joined Honda, and he signed on there in 1985 when Honda began hiring staff for an engine plant it planned to build in Anna. He became the second American assigned to the plant, which Honda announced three years after it began building cars in Marysville. When Ernst arrived, Honda didn't even have a trailer parked on the site for the factory, so Ernst and his small staff made do with offices in a house. Ernst, who looks more like a banker than an automobile industry manager, with neat graying hair and fashionable small glasses, spent time in Japan training in the ways of Honda's manufacturing operations and learning to understand the Honda Way. "Honda's corporate culture is made up of a lot of little things," said Ernst.

He loved his job at the engine plant, which built engines not only for the Honda Accord and Civic but also for the Gold Wing motorcycle, Honda's premier touring bike. On the first day of production, he remembered looking at the engines coming off the assembly line and thinking, "Will it start? Of course it will start!" He draws on his engine-building expertise every day at the Lincoln factory, which has emerged within the Honda network of factories as a collaborative effort, drawing from the company's experiences around the world. Walk through the plant and you'll hear a collection of accents, many from the South, of course, but others from Ohio, from Japan and from Canada. The Lincoln plant has relied heavily on its sister plant in Alliston, Ontario, for advice and a road map as it has begun producing the Odyssey. It isn't so much the minivan's size that sets it apart, said Ernst, as the fact that it is not a car, and the production lines here draw a number of visitors from all over Honda's operations to see the company's only dedicated truck plant.

Lincoln has borrowed from elsewhere in Honda in other ways. It was able to keep its investment costs low and speed up its timetable by procuring unused equipment from Honda's factory in Swindon, England. Over came a giant machine used for machining, or polishing, engine blocks, saving the plant $600,000, while from Honda's plant in Wako, Japan, came a big casting machine used to produce the blocks themselves. That saved another $500,000. Meanwhile, its stamping pressures, which make sheet metal parts for the Odyssey, are so productive that they are making extra parts and shipping them up to Honda's plant in Canada.

But along with the savings, Honda is paying an attention to detail inside the Lincoln factory that is remarkable even in a company that is known for the care it takes in building automobiles. One such example is in the stamping plant, where, standing on a catwalk above the plant floor, visitors can watch big metal presses in action. They make a constant thumping sound as they hammer through layers of steel to make roofs, side panels and hoods. Larry Hughes, the stamping plant's manager, knew nothing about this process when he joined Honda at its Alliston plant, but he is here now to train Honda's Alabama workers in the intricacies of making sheet metal parts.

———————

Half a dozen workers, wearing protective goggles and cotton work gloves, stand in anticipation next to a conveyor line at the end of one of the stamping presses, waiting for roofs to be completed. When one appears in front of them, they pore over it, looking for nicks and scratches and any kind of minuscule defect that might cause a customer to complain to their dealer. Every so often, one of the roofs is taken off the conveyor line and walked over to a special inspection area. Here, one of the Honda workers rubs a stone coated with oil across the metal hood, a process that is supposed to expose any flaws within the metal surface itself. "You can pretty much see the deformities," said Gordon Hammond of Talladega, Alabama, demonstrating how he uses the stone, much like an eraser, to see if there is anything amiss. Perhaps 10 to 15 times during an eight-hour shift, Hammond might spot something wrong, and if that happens, the inspector immediately shows the flawed hood to a supervisor. Together, they take action. "We stop the press, and go in and clean out the die [before the press is allowed to resume operations]," said Hammond.

That same care can be seen in the engine plant, whose foundry is quiet, clean and virtually odor free, in contrast to the filthy, noisy and smelly foundries that auto companies have operated since the earliest years of the industry. Soichiro Honda would have a hard time finding anyone to slap here, and he would probably be likely to be pleased by all the care that is being taken with the engine components. Months after the plant began production, the engine plant staff noticed that Alabama's humidity was having an effect on the metal bearings and cylinder parts that were being shipped to the plant. The heat and the stickiness caused them to weep moisture. So engineers decided to store the parts in air-conditioned trailers until they were needed on the assembly line. It was a minor detail, but if an engine were to fail on an Odyssey, Honda would wind up with an unhappy customer and lose a chance for positive word of mouth. Appearances count here, too, even in places owners might not think to look. After each engine is finished, it gets a protective wax coating that takes 45 minutes to cure. It provides an attractive sheen and also protects the engine from wear and tear.

John Penrose, the manager of the plant's paint shop, is even more concerned about the way vehicles look when they leave this plant, because the Odyssey's finish is one of a customer's top priorities. Like the foundry, the place is scrupulously clean. Nearby, a line of workers is inspecting vehicle bodies under bright white lights that, combined with their gleaming uniforms, seem to cast a halo around the minivans. Penrose, a veteran of 20 years at Honda, said he has not yet gotten bored at the company in a range of assignments, from the R&D center at Marysville to three years spent in Japan. "Honda's approach is that they give everyone a chance," said Penrose, who is stocky with blond hair and looks like he'd be right at home running the rowdiest fraternity on campus. "If you take half an interest, they'll let you try." But he points out that Honda's preciseness is not for everyone, and he admits that over the years he's been the subject of calls from headhunters many times. "I know a lot of people who didn't like it. It's not an easy company to work for," Penrose said. Still, after 20 years of the Honda Way, "I'd be a fool to go anywhere else. What I give them, I get back in respect."

Back on the plant floor, the day's production of Odysseys is winding through the assembly line, passing before the eyes of two tour groups—one of senior citizens, the other of high school students—who have come to see the Lincoln plant. The seniors look amazed by the robots and the rest of the technology, while the students are trying hard to be blasé about the field trip, but it's clear that this is a sight that has all of them transfixed. When production is complete, the minivans go through a series of tests, checking their engines, their gauges and tires, before being taken out on a short test drive. Then it is off to a marshaling yard, which sits in the distance beyond the construction site for the new plant. The yard is filled with Odysseys as far as the eye can see, and as fast as they arrive from the factory's back door, they are lined up in order to be driven onto delivery trucks. Every one of them has a customer waiting for it.

And that's no more than the minivan's engineers—Odagaki, Benner and Berkman—could have hoped for when they spent so many miles crisscrossing the United States. Long before the Odyssey went into production in Lincoln, the trio had already gone on to their next engineering projects—Odagaki in charge of the Honda Civic, Benner assigned to the Honda Element and Berkman to work on the Acura CL and TL luxury cars. Another new version of Odyssey was set for the 2005 model year, with even more improvements than the one developed by the three engineers. Even now, however, the Odyssey stands out in their memory as a project that typifies what Honda is all about: coming up with the best vehicle in its market segment, no matter how long it has been dominated by the competition. Said Berkman, "The Odyssey has become a pillar" for Honda and for its determined engineers.

CHAPTER FIVE

HOT DOGS, APPLE PIE AND CAMRY

A VISIT TO TOYOTA'S CHAIRMAN, Hiroshi Okuda, can be an intimidating experience. His office is in Nagoya, Japan, two and a half hours west of Tokyo on the bullet train, and an hour from Toyota City, the sprawling complex of factories, engineering labs and research facilities that is the center of Toyota's global empire. Upon arriving at Toyota's office building, visitors shoot down a ramp to an underground garage, where an assistant to Okuda stands waiting at an entrance near the elevator to greet them and whisk them upstairs and down silent corridors to a conference room, sparsely decorated with ten chairs, with low coffee tables in between and subdued paintings on the walls. Though it is a warm March day, a smartly dressed receptionist brings cups of steaming green tea. Then Okuda's assistant returns, to remind his guests that the chairman has a full schedule. The meeting must start precisely on time and end on time, for he has a meeting afterward in connection with his role in charge of the Keidanren, the Japanese equivalent of the Business Council, a symbolic yet influential group of the country's most important companies. The warning simply adds to the sense of tension, and the room falls silent.

Ten minutes early, Okuda bursts in. Unusually tall and broad-shouldered for a Japanese man, his face breaks into a smile beneath a sweep of jet-black hair, giving him a jaunty look that belies his 69 years. Greeting his visitors in English, he gives a quick command to his assistant. Within minutes the receptionist returns, removing the green tea and replacing it with refreshing glasses of iced tea, and makes yet another trip a bit later to bring orange juice and then ice water. In contrast to the formal atmosphere before he arrived, Okuda is relaxed, loquacious and happy to talk about where he thinks Toyota is headed, particularly in the United States, which in 2001 became its biggest market, outdistancing Japan for the first time. Speaking through an interpreter, but clearly understanding questions asked in English, he stays on for 20 minutes beyond the allotted time for the meeting, clearly enthusiastic about his role in crafting Toyota's future.

The experience is analogous to the situation that Toyota itself is in—encumbered by formality and tradition, yet with executives who see that there is an opportunity to grow if Toyota can change the way it does things, and who are seeking the right pace and strategy for the company to achieve its goals. Though Okuda's title is now mostly ceremonial—in Japanese companies, the chief executive has the greatest day-to-day influence—Okuda was a key driver in Toyota's efforts during the 1990s to position itself for the global growth that is occurring now. It was Okuda who backed Toyota's expansion in American manufacturing, traveling to a farmer's backyard in Princeton, Indiana, for the groundbreaking when Toyota launched its truck plant there. Okuda approved Toyota's push into the light truck market, and he played a key role in the selection of his successor, Fujio Cho, who put into motion the plans that Okuda crafted.

It's tempting to say that what's happening to Toyota is an Americanization process. That's certainly how its efforts have been perceived by the media in the United States and Japan. It's more accurate to say that Toyota is breaking out of the mold of a traditional Japanese company to become the world's first truly global auto company. More than General Motors, Ford or DaimlerChrysler, Toyota has the best opportunity to be a player that meets the needs of consumers around the world, no longer relying on its traditional home market for the vast majority of its sales and revenue, as the Detroit auto companies do. Since 2001, the United States has been Toyota's biggest market, followed by Japan, Europe, Asia and Latin America. While it has yet to make a significant impact in the European market, it has not yet given up. Its cars score top ratings on J.D. Power surveys there, and its plant in France is considered within the company to be its most efficient and advanced.

What's more, Toyota has enormous financial strength from which to launch its plans. It earned an operating profit of $10 billion in 2003, more than the combined profits of the Detroit auto companies during the past 5 years. It has $34 billion in cash and $100 billion in assets, and it is basically able to act as its own bank. Toyota's quest to become the biggest global auto company by 2010 would be unthinkable without its Japanese roots, sunk deep in Toyota City, but it also would be unthinkable without its strength in the United States. In that, Toyota is pulling off something Detroit companies have not yet been able to do—provide itself with both a solid foundation and opportunities for seemingly endless growth for the future.

Until 2003, Toyota was the most Japanese of auto companies. It was governed by a 58-member board of directors, all of them Japanese males, many of whom had responsibility for Toyota's day-to-day operations along with their directors' jobs. The board had no women, no Americans, no Europeans and no one from outside companies. It was quintessentially Japan-centric. The structure was vastly out of sync with the way companies are run in the United States, where directors have oversight over company management but do not play an active role. And it was even at odds with other Japanese companies, particularly Honda, which had only a 25-member board, and Nissan, which was aiming to cut the size of its board to seven members. Throughout 2002, Okuda, Cho and the company's management debated the best structure for the company going forward. Some of Toyota's most conservative managers argued that no change was necessary: Toyota could keep the same structure and keep its power centered in Japan, just give more power to the regional executives. Their view represented a small faction within the company who thought that the American market's dominant role was just temporary. Once Japan rebounded from its decade-long economic slump, they said, it would be Toyota's primary market again. So there was no need to change. A few rebels, particularly those who had spent time working overseas, called for the board system to be completely dismantled and an American-style board created. They wanted to see a complete reorganization of Toyota's management functions to reflect its global reality. "I have a lot of frustration, as a manager who's been here 22 years, that Toyota is not globalized enough," said Illingworth, the executive who left Chrysler for Toyota, subsequently ran Lexus and is now Toyota's senior American strategist.

But Cho resisted efforts for a quick resolution, saying that the right structure would be announced when Toyota was ready. The result, like many things at Toyota, seemed like a modest first step. In March 2003, the company said it would cut its board by about half, to around 30 members. Below them, for the first time, Toyota would create a new layer of managing officers. This group included Americans,

Europeans and executives who were younger than traditional board members, who generally got their appointments in their fifties and sixties. It was not radical change, but it was change. And it will not be the last step Toyota will take on the matter. Its history has shown that when it comes to key developments, it reaches its goals by evolution, not revolution.

There is no better illustration of how Toyota achieves its objectives than the creation and gradual dominance of the Toyota Camry. Just as the Model T symbolized Ford's early history and the K-car the renaissance at Chrysler in the 1980s, the Camry sums up everything that Toyota has become in the United States. "The Camry is literally the straw that stirs the drink for Toyota," said Peter DeLorenzo, editor of Autoextremist.com. "This one car was responsible for convincing a generation of Americans that there was a whole other world of transportation out there. It is transportation that is reliable—meaning *where things just didn't go wrong,* a totally alien notion to American consumers. It changed the American market forever."

Camry is the centerpiece of Toyota's growth and achievement in the United States. While Toyota's focus most recently has been on expanding sales of light trucks, none of it would be possible without the Camry as its linchpin. The Camry has been the best-selling car in the United States since 1997, despite a strong challenge from the Honda Accord. It has become to the car market what the Chevrolet Impala was in the 1960s, what the Ford Taurus was in the 1980s: the indisputable leader. It is the quintessential American family car. Every Camry sold in the United States is built in Georgetown, Kentucky, just north of Lexington, where it rivals Thoroughbreds and bluegrass as the most treasured icon in the state. "If there's such a thing as a politically correct car in central Kentucky, it's a Toyota," said Mike Tewell, a local Toyota dealer. John Stewart, an assembly line manager at the

Georgetown plant, said everyone there sees Toyota as a local company now. That wasn't true when he was growing up. "When I first got hired here, I didn't even know what a Camry was," said Stewart.

But there are millions of other people who did. In the 20 years in which the Camry has been on sale in the United States, Toyota has sold more than 6 million of them, whether sedans, coupes or station wagons. Moreover, more than 5 million of them are still in operation, according to statistics from R. L. Polk & Co. Year after year, Camry gets high ratings from *Consumer Reports*, whose recognition of the car in the 1980s set it on its road to American dominance, despite whatever challenges have been posed by the Accord, the Hyundai Sonata and the Nissan Altima. One reason is its resale value. In 2003, a five-year-old Camry was still worth 52 percent of what a customer paid for it, versus less than 40 percent for a Chevrolet Malibu, according to calculations by Edmunds.com. Camry received an unexpected tribute in February 2003 from one of its rivals, proof how even Detroit companies can't ignore what the Camry has come to symbolize. "Very frankly, Camry is a better product than Taurus today," said Jim O'Connor, head of sales and marketing for Ford. O'Connor's comments, made to journalists at the Chicago Auto Show in 2003, came as it was becoming clear that Ford would lose to Toyota its title as the number-one car-selling brand in the United States.

The 20-year track record doesn't stop Camry from being seen by rival executives and many automotive enthusiasts as a vanilla-flavored car, especially the latest version, introduced in 2002, which struck some critics as particularly bland. Jim Press, chief executive of Toyota Motor Sales, doesn't care. "Do you know what the best-selling flavor of ice cream is? Vanilla," he declared. "It's to our advantage that we're not the flavor of the day. Our course of action is slow and steady growth. We don't shoot up like a rocket and fall back down." But Camry, to Toyota, is more than a single car. It is the foundation of its American product development. Working from the Camry, Toyota's engineers through the years have developed a half-dozen different vehicles—including a coupe, a minivan, a crossover vehicle, and a large family car—that collectively represent 44 percent of Toyota's annual sales in the United States. It is a feat that many auto companies have attempted over the years, only to fall far short of what Toyota achieved. And it began, as things do at Toyota, with a single idea: a car built specifically for North American customers, not for Japanese consumers. Press, the top-ranking American within Toyota's sales operations, was involved in the car's development from the outset. "It was the first car designed by an international car company for the American market. It finally created the awareness that the U.S. market could be self-sustaining with unique products, not just an outlet for excess capacity from Japan," he said.

The concept for Camry took root in the late 1970s, when Toyota saw that its original American customers were starting to need more room than their subcompact Corollas provided. Toyota sold a mid-sized car called the Corona, which had originally gone on sale in Japan in 1964, but it was aimed at Japanese consumers: It was narrow, had a less-powerful engine and was rear-wheel drive. Then in charge of product planning for the United States, Press was emphatic that Toyota needed a car that was akin to American tastes. He argued that it should focus on interior space as well as fuel efficiency, and be equipped with front-wheel drive. He faced stiff opposition. The Corona was a hugely important car to Toyota in Japan. Toyota's middle management thought the idea was ridiculous.

But Press found advocates for the vehicle in two Toyoda family members—Eiji Toyoda, the company's chairman, who had spent much time in the United States during the 1950s, and Tatsuro Toyoda, the automaker's president, who within a few years would launch the NUMMI venture with General Motors. With the backing of the Toyoda family members the project was approved, only to stall on a name. Toyota officials thought the car should simply be called the Corona, even though it would be completely different from the Japanese Corona. The Americans did not want to go that route. They suggested the name Crown, but again, there was already a car called the Crown in Toyota's lineup, an upscale sedan that is still sold today. So a compromise was struck. The planning team took the Japanese word *kanmuri* (pronounced "CAN-murry"), which means "crown," and Americanized it. *Kanmuri* became Camry, which seemed friendly and easy to pronounce, and also gave the marketing team a hook. "We called it the Family Camry," Press recalled. The Camry went on sale in the United States in 1983, a year after the Honda Accord went into production in Marysville, Ohio, and in time to wake up Ford to the challenge that it had to meet with the Taurus.

For the first five years of its life, the Camry was built in Japan and shipped to the United States. Its popularity, plus the experience that Toyota had gained at NUMMI, helped to convince Toyota executives to build their first assembly plant in the United States. And Camry was clearly the ideal vehicle for Toyota to produce there, according to Press. "It was our strength, and it matched the mainstream of the market," he said. "It was a high-volume product that had fairly consistent demand, it wasn't affected by sales trends and it had pretty level production." Because it was a bread-and-butter car, aimed across the breadth of the market, the Camry also didn't experience a big drop in sales when it got to the end of its model run, five years out. That could have been a danger signal for Japanese executives, who were wary of building a car in a brand-new factory only to see interest in it wane after its first couple of years on the market. "It suited itself to being a single product in a single plant. If you can build a lot of the same kind of product, you can reap tons of efficiency. It was the right place for us to start," Press said.

The Camry that Toyota built at the Georgetown plant had been revamped in the fall of 1987, which gave American workers the opportunity to go to Japan and see how it was built before they came back to the United States to begin production in Kentucky in 1988. That in itself was a milestone, but as the Georgetown workers were building their first Camrys, Toyota was already setting out to achieve a breakthrough with the next generation of the Camry, which would be introduced in 1992. The car that was being built in Georgetown was the same as the one that Toyota built in Japan. The next-generation Camry would be vastly different for the American market, both in appearance and under the hood. It owed that, in part, to one of Toyota's other achievements in the American car market: the Lexus luxury division.

As the Camry is to American family cars, so is Lexus to American luxury vehicles. Lexus has been the top-selling luxury brand in the United States for the past two years, surpassing Mercedes-Benz and BMW. If the Camry is vanilla ice cream, Lexus is a cashmere sweater. It is a recognizable symbol of luxury, but not an ostentatious one. It is expensive, but attainable. Lexus cars and SUVs start at around $30,000 and range up to about $70,000, certainly not cheap, but far below the prices of top-level Mercedes, BMW, Porsche or Audi cars. No one would call Lexus vehicles overwhelmingly stylish, yet they are pleasing to the eye and manage to remain contemporary-looking even when they are a few years old. For many American customers, Lexus is just enough luxury, particularly for consumers who have plenty of other ways to spend their money: on houses, antiques, travel, sports and entertainment. Lexus, like the Camry itself, perplexes Detroit. Compared with the classic luxury cars of Motor City history, the Cadillacs with their daunting fins and shining chrome, the Lincolns with their eye-catching opera windows and long hoods, or German performance cars with their guttural engines and stiff, road-hugging handling, Lexus seems practically anonymous. Moreover, there was no Japanese luxury tradition from which Lexus could draw as it came into being. It was created completely from scratch, the one trait that German auto companies to this day insist is Lexus's greatest shortcoming.

But many of the people who own them would not have anything else. To them, the appeal of a Lexus is not only its understated appearance but its interior comfort, the smoothness of its engines, its sense of quiet, its easy handling, and above all, its quality, reliability and resale value. "It's about discipline, consistency, attention to detail, and *really* listening to customers," said Paul Higginbottom, an Atlanta executive who is part of a two-Lexus household. He owns a Lexus GS 400 sedan and his wife has an RX 300 sport wagon. Higginbottom said he could afford to buy any car on the market but was drawn to Lexus because of its overall reputation for quality. "There is a huge swath of people out there who have figured out there's something better," he said.

A key part of the Lexus ownership experience is the way dealers treat their customers. An owner taking a Lexus in for routine maintenance drives into a spotlessly clean reception area, used only for dropping off and picking up cars (the actual repair bays are out of sight). A signboard set next to the door welcomes each day's customer by name, and a lab-coated service technician appears instantly to help the customer out of the car and take the keys. In the showroom, there is a coffee bar with cappuccino and croissants and a waiting room area with leather chairs, newspapers and a TV set tuned to the *Today* show or CNN, depending on the time of day. Customers may read, chat or use a separate booth where they can connect to the Internet. When maintenance is finished, the technician returns, like a doctor after surgery, to kneel next to the customer's chair and explain what tasks were performed and to detail any repairs that were needed. The car appears back in the drop-off area, freshly washed and vacuumed. Customers who can't wait for their vehicles are assigned free loaner cars, and if it's impossible to get to the showroom, a salesperson drives to the owner's home or office to pick up the car being serviced and to leave a loaner.

This pampering is one reason why, for 12 years running, Lexus has been named the top franchise in annual customer satisfaction surveys by J.D. Power & Associates, both for the way customers are treated and the quality of their cars.

It is remarkable to think now of the important events that were occurring when Eiji Toyoda challenged his engineers to build "the finest car in the world." In addition to dominating the Japanese car market, Toyota had just started building the Camry for the American market and was concluding talks with GM on the NUMMI venture, both of which would eventually lead directly to production in Georgetown. As with Camry, Toyoda thought a luxury car would meet the evolving needs of its customers in the United States. It was the logical place to concentrate. Japan had no luxury car market at the time. Luxury car buyers there turned almost exclusively to BMW and Mercedes models. It would be a real stretch for Toyota to try to break into the heavily parochial European luxury car market. "The people who have been buying our cars were moving up in life," he said in an interview with *Fortune* magazine in 1989. "We wanted to meet their heightened needs."

The challenge he posed was high, as well: Toyoda wanted a sedan that could achieve speeds of 150 mph in quiet, comfort and safety, while earning fuel economy that was good enough to escape the American tax on gas guzzlers, which was imposed on foreign luxury cars that earned less than 22.5 mpg. (Still in effect today, the tax is largely borne by the cars in BMW's lineup.) The fact that Americans couldn't legally drive that fast meant nothing, since he thought customers would like to be able to boast about the ability to do so. The task of developing the sedan, which was code-named F (for Flagship) One, fell to a chief engineer named Ichiro Suzuki.

Like the large-project leaders at Honda, chief engineers at Toyota had complete authority over their vehicle projects in a way that Detroit companies simply cannot match. Even though Big Three companies have streamlined their product development operations, they generally assign at least three different executives, from design, engineering and marketing, to each vehicle project. Suzuki had all that authority. "In the Toyota chief engineer system, you really have one mastermind," said Dana Hargitt, executive project manager for the most recent version of the Camry, which was designed in large part at the Toyota Technical Center in Ann Arbor, Michigan. Hargitt, who joined Toyota in 1998 after 20 years at GM, said that a Toyota chief engineer "sees, feels and lives" his assignment. There is nowhere that a Toyota chief engineer can hide and no place to lay blame. "His true success or failure hinges on how the vehicle does in the marketplace," said Hargitt.

Suzuki's first task was to dispatch 20 Toyota designers to the United States, in the tradition called *genchi gembutsu*, or "go to the spot," to gauge what American customers might demand. (Honda engineers followed this same method with the Odyssey.) The engineers found that Toyota would have no chance to attract the blue-hair and toupee crowd that was then buying Cadillacs and Lincolns. Nor would cash-rich yuppies, then at the height of their love affair with BMW, be interested in a vehicle whose status hadn't yet been proven. The heart of the market would come from owners of Toyota vehicles, and others who would have liked to own the best German luxury cars but for either affordability reasons or fears of poor quality just wouldn't buy them. The specific customer was a 43-year-old male earning $100,000 a year. (It would later turn out, however, that Lexus was equally attractive to women buyers. Some of the models in its lineup sell overwhelmingly to women, particularly the RX 330, which people within the industry dubbed "the ladies' SUV.") As they were visiting dealerships and buttonholing customers, Suzuki set out on his first priority: the engine. It was to be an all-new V-8, the first offered in a Japanese car, built on an aluminum engine block, with aluminum valve lifters—the first time an auto company had used aluminum instead of stamped steel. His initial try resulted in a failure. The engine wouldn't achieve high enough fuel economy. So Suzuki tore it apart and started over. Eventually, he achieved the 22.5 mpg standard, and then came the matter of the car's appearance.

Five of the designers remained in California, where Lexus expected to sell most of its cars, and rented a house in Laguna Beach, not too far from Toyota's sales headquarters in Torrance. They crafted three scale models of what a luxury sedan could look like and took them back to Japan. Executives turned them down—and kept turning down design ideas for the next 18 months. One of the reasons was that Toyota faced a real challenge in designing a vehicle that looked expensive. It couldn't copy Mercedes or BMW, yet it had to look enough like them to get buyers interested in paying a premium over a Toyota. There were plenty of complaints that the resulting car did look like a Mercedes E-Class of the day (before Mercedes switched to the distinct round headlights that are the car's trademark now). But Toyota insisted that there were enough differences that they looked unique and would offer something different for the U.S. market. The most notable difference was the vehicle's interior. Its dashboard was free of clutter, and its console, with polished wood and flawless leather, looked beautiful. Lexus's simplicity was a refreshing contrast to American cars at the time, which were stuffed with digital readouts, complicated trip computers and voices that announced, "The door is ajar." There would be no such gimmicks in the Toyota luxury sedan.

While this was going on, Toyota officials in the United States were in the dark. They did not get official word that the project was under way until 1987, four years after its birth. One reason was that Toyota didn't want its existing dealers to clamor too soon for the car, nor did it want to award showrooms to them automatically. It wanted a separate network of dealers, who would be required to abide by strict customer service standards in order to get around the reputation Toyota dealers had—and in some cases still have—for being disdainful of potential customers. That is not to say that Toyota's dealers are not a key part of its success. They play a critical role in the way the company learns about its customers. Information from dealers can get back to Toyota's sales operations in Torrance, California, with speed. It means the company can spot problems with its vehicles much faster and can also tell which vehicles are selling best, allowing it to make adjustments quickly on its assembly lines.

Dealers also are a primary research tool for Toyota, letting the company know what customers are asking for. And they keep the company primed with a constant demand for vehicles, since more than half of Toyota buyers are repeat customers. "Our dealers are our Israeli fighter pilots," said Denny Clements, Lexus's general manager. Still, executives have fumed in frustration because of the difficulty some consumers have reported in getting Toyota dealers to pay attention to them. The rationale has always been that Toyotas sell themselves, meaning that salespeople don't need to work as hard to explain their features, and that if a particular customer doesn't buy a car, there will be one coming along soon who will. Such tactics are an Achilles' heel for the company that it is constantly addressing.

Toyota didn't want to risk such treatment for luxury car buyers as it was developing Lexus. Dealers would have to invest $3 million to $4 million in new luxury showrooms, apart from their existing Toyota operations, and they were going to have to treat customers better than they had ever treated them in the past. Toyota wanted its buyers to be cosseted and coaxed, not intimidated. Once dealers were in the luxury car project, Toyota's American operation was clued in. Rather than assign it to one of its veteran executives, the company hired Jim Perkins, a GM executive, to take charge, and named Illingworth as his assistant.

From the moment he found out about the luxury car project, Illingworth was skeptical. "I didn't know what it was," said Illingworth, who was then the corporate manager of special projects. "I thought, 'How can you build a franchise with one car?'" He voiced his misgivings to Yuki Togo, an effervescent Japanese executive who was in charge of Toyota's U.S. sales operations. Togo, who knew about Eiji Toyoda's dedication to the luxury car program, told Illingworth to set his reservations aside. "At no time are you ever to have any questions about whether this will be successful," said Togo. He showed Illingworth the resignation letter he had written to Toyoda, which was tucked in his suit coat pocket. "He said he would resign at any minute if it failed," Illingworth said. But he did not expect that to happen. "'We will back you 100 percent,'" Illingworth said Togo told him. "And they did."

There were still many hurdles to overcome, including the name. Nobody knew what to call the luxury sedan, and it didn't make sense to give it a name beginning with C, like Camry or Corolla, because the idea was to make the new division distinct. In came Lippincott & Margolies, a New York consulting firm that had come up with corporate monikers like Allegis, the title of the short-lived arrangement of travel companies that included United Airlines. The firm recommended a series of ideas, including Verona, Calibre and Chaparel, as well as Lexus. That became the first choice, because it sounded a little bit like luxury and could be conveyed with a capital L logo. (Toyota executives chose it despite the fact that words beginning with an L are hard for the Japanese to pronounce.) But the choice turned into a fiasco that almost threatened to stall Lexus before its debut. In December 1988, as the division was about to unveil its first car at the Detroit Auto Show the following month, Toyota was sued by Mead Data Central, owner of the Lexis-Nexis data retrieval service. It obtained a court injunction and Toyota frantically searched for a replacement, selecting the name Luxor, which would have used the same capital L logo. But before it had to make the change, a judge threw out the suit, saying that the two companies were sufficiently different to keep customers from confusing the two entities. With that crisis over, another ensued: Perkins quit Toyota to return to GM, where he was named Chevrolet general manager. The task of launching the car would be up to Illingworth.

All of the attention up until then had been on the big sedan, which Toyota decided to call the LS 400. But when it came time to unveil the Lexus lineup in Detroit, the LS arrived with a smaller sibling, the ES 250. Illingworth's nervousness about an entirely new franchise selling just one car, and the emergence of Honda's Acura luxury brand in 1985, prompted Toyota to add another vehicle to the Lexus lineup. As a placeholder, it took the 1988 Camry and transformed it into a Lexus, primarily with wood-grain trim and leather seats and a higher price. If there were doubts that Toyota could build a luxury sedan, there was even more skepticism about the ES 250. Who would pay $22,000 for a tarted-up Camry, critics said, when they could get the Toyota version for only $13,500? Moreover, wouldn't the transformed Camry suffer by comparison with the all-new LS 400? Toyota was sensitive to the criticism, and almost as soon as the ES 250 arrived, it promised that there would be a replacement in the near future. But the ES 250 played two roles. It gave dealers a lower-priced alternative to the $35,000 LS 400, putting the Lexus cars within the reach of more customers. And it gave Toyota some practice on experimenting with the Camry, which would prove to be valuable down the line. The experience had a tremendous impact on the development of the 1992 Camry, which became known, to Toyota's delight, as a mini-Lexus.

The project got under way even as the first of the prior-generation Camrys were being built at Georgetown. The original Camry had been designed to provide more space to buyers who had outgrown the Corolla. Now it was time for the next-generation Camry to grow, too. The end result ranks as one of the most gracious, comfortable cars that Toyota ever built, particularly so because of what it learned with Lexus. The advertising theme, "They just couldn't leave well enough alone," seemed apt. The Camry shared a list of elements with its Lexus sibling, which was renamed the ES 300 for 1992, starting with an aluminum V-

6 engine (optional on the Camry) and size. Both cars grew in length and width. Each used the same material for the firewall between the engine and the passenger compartment; each had the same sound-deadening fabric; and each used similar supports beneath the engine, to give it steadiness and smoothness while accelerating.

Where such features might be too expensive to offer on the Camry alone, Toyota was able to swing it because it was leveraging them across two models. The primary difference between the two was a unique, slightly stiffer suspension on the ES 300, which added 200 pounds to its weight and gave it more of a performance car feel. The ES also had standard antilock brakes, which were optional on the Camry. But the differences were minute, and to many people, the Camry seemed like a steal. Even if buyers didn't upgrade to the V-6, the Camry had a nice, basic 145-horsepower, 2.2-liter four-cylinder engine that was as peppy as many of the V-6 engines that were offered by Detroit. And the car was pretty, with its slightly rounded roof and its soft lines, reminiscent of those on the LS 400. Though it became one of the car's hallmarks, the design was not what Toyota engineers in Japan had originally planned for the car.

When Robert McCurry, executive vice president of the American sales operations, traveled to Japan for a styling review in 1989, he found a Camry that looked a lot like its predecessor, only bigger. "It was conservative, Japanese styling, what Japanese cars looked like at the time," he said. After the efforts Toyota had gone through with Lexus, McCurry was displeased, and he brought the Japanese engineers a list of what he wanted in the car—namely, a sleeker, more modern appearance and more interior room. The Lexus had been designed completely with Americans' taste in mind; the Camry had to be, too, McCurry argued. To the engineers' credit, they came up with a new design within a few weeks, McCurry said. "They realized it and acknowledged it," he said. The 1992

Camry was the kind of car that Detroit by all rights should have been able to build—a luxurious sedan whose $15,000 starting price was within the reach of most consumers.

But Camry ended up doing far more for Toyota than just serving as a mid-sized car. By 1994, when Toyota introduced a two-door Camry coupe, Okuda had become the company's chief executive, and he was bent on expanding production in the United States. There was a good reason: the appreciation of the yen. Its value had soared against the dollar, biting into the profits of every Japanese company that depended on the United States for sales. The exchange rate, which had been as high as 160 yen to the dollar in 1992, ultimately reached 85 to the dollar in 1995. The difference cost Japanese companies as much as $2,000 in profits per vehicle. Detroit auto companies were gleeful as they watched their Japanese competitors raise prices above those for many competing Detroit automobiles. As a result, Japan's share of the American market, which had been 35 percent during the early 1980s, fell to just 22 percent in 1994. The situation led to declarations that the Japanese threat was over, that the competition had been put in its proper place and the Detroit companies could relax. Their focus was already shifting to the light truck market, which was red hot thanks to the popularity of vehicles like the Ford Explorer, the Jeep Grand Cherokee and even the Chevrolet Blazer, which was finally available in a four-door version that year, prompting a flock of GM executives, including the CEO, Jack Smith, to take them home as their company cars instead of big Cadillac sedans.

But the demise of the yen turned out to be a blessing in disguise for the Japanese companies, and ultimately a benefit to American customers. It forced the import companies to look more seriously at the American market as a production source. Shifting market trends made them get serious about light trucks, which they had only skirted in their emphasis on cars, and it forced them to leverage all their resources to fill out their lineups. The idea of platform sharing, as it is called in the industry, wasn't a new one. Over the years, carmakers around the world have tried all kinds of ways to take a basic chassis and transform it into something else. The practice flourished in the 1980s, when Chrysler introduced its K-cars, which proved the base for its original minivans, while GM rolled out whole families of cars that were shared among its various divisions, such as the small J-cars, the compact X-cars and the mid-sized A-cars. They were supposed to share components under the hood and look different on the outside.

Instead, they ended up being different underneath, because the companies' various purchasing divisions didn't coordinate when it came to buying parts, and too much alike on the outside, despite various attempts to differentiate the cars with headlights and hood ornaments and chrome (what the industry calls "jewelry"). GM was stung by a famous commercial for Lincoln in which a waiting customer fumes because a valet parking attendant can't tell the different Oldsmobiles, Buicks and Pontiacs apart. To really get the idea of platform sharing right, vehicles have to look different on the outside, drive differently and have different interiors, but have as many common components as possible underneath. That's easier now than it was in the 1980s owing to advancements in computer-aided design, and with the high costs of developing vehicles, even more important. Auto companies spend an average of $1 billion on each platform, including the revisions needed in factories to build the new vehicles. Something as simple as a stamping die, used to make a hood, can cost as much as $500,000. A single day's delay in a vehicle development program adds $1 million in cost. The burden is on companies to keep costs as tightly in line as possible, and that is one of the hardest tasks a manufacturer faces, because there are so many ways that projects can drift.

Faced with the burden of the strong yen, Toyota set its manufacturing experts, product planners and engineers off to see what they could yield from the basic four-door Camry. In his office in Torrance,

Toyota's chief of advance product planning, Chris Hostetter, began jotting down ideas and sending researchers off to see how consumers would react to them and to find that if they had any requests. One of the first reactions was: Build us a decent minivan. Toyota had sold the bulbous Previa for a number of years, and it got high quality ratings, but the Japanese-built minivan was just plain odd compared with the versatility of Chrysler's minivans. It was narrow, had rear-wheel drive and was hard to steer. It also had an underpowered, mid-mounted engine under the front seat. Moreover, it was expensive. Its reputation had been sullied when Detroit auto companies filed suit against Toyota and Mazda in 1992 before the Federal Trade Commission, charging that the Japanese companies were selling their minivans for less than they charged in Japan. The dumping suit seemed frivolous, in view of the fact that American companies controlled 94 percent of minivan sales in the United States and that the Previa was among Toyota's worst-selling products. Though the Japanese companies won their case, it was clear that if Toyota wanted to compete in the minivan market it needed a more appropriate vehicle. Hostetter doesn't agree with the criticism but understands why Previa had to go. "It was a beautiful vehicle that didn't fit the core of what Americans wanted," he said.

What customers wanted, the research showed, was a front-wheel-drive minivan with a V-6 engine. The end result was the Sienna, built from the Camry chassis and produced at the Georgetown assembly plant. Though it wasn't the first U.S.-built minivan from a Japanese company—Nissan built the Quest in Avon Lake, Ohio, in a joint-venture plant with Ford—it was the first time that a Japanese company had built a minivan on the same assembly line with its cars—in contrast to Detroit automakers, who still dedicate whole plants to them. Toyota plant manager Mike Da Prile turned to an old friend, Dennis Pawley, the executive vice president of manufacturing at Chrysler, for help. Years before the pair had worked together at GM, with a third

colleague, Gary Cowger, now president of GM's North American operations. During the 1990s, Pawley had begun crafting the Chrysler
Operating System, a manufacturing process that he based on TPS, and
Da Prile had allowed Pawley's manufacturing engineers to do research
at Georgetown. (One of the creators of the Chrysler system, Jamie
Bonini, would end up joining Toyota in 2003, at its Princeton, Indiana, truck plant.)

In return, Pawley let engineers and manufacturing staffers from
Toyota come up to Chrysler's minivan plant in Windsor, Ontario.
There they learned how to install the big pieces of carpet that Toyota's
minivans would require, which were far larger than the carpet in a
Camry. They also got ideas on how to assemble parts in the rear of a
minivan, which was longer than one of the Toyota sedans, and they
came up with a way to install the roof insulation, called the headliner,
that stretched the length of the vehicle. Then the Toyota experts
refined the processes, to the point where there were only eight spots,
out of more than 200 tasks along the assembly line, that were significantly different from the way they built the Camry. One place was the
door assembly area, since the Sienna had sliding doors on either side.
Unlike Honda, where the idea of two sliding doors had sparked a
showdown between project leader Odagaki and his boss, Toyota executives accepted the idea right away because it was a feature on the
Chrysler vans, according to Hostetter.

By the time the Sienna went into production, the Georgetown
plant had already doubled in size and added another vehicle to its
lineup: the full-sized Avalon sedan. It was the biggest car that any
Japanese company built in the United States, and it was in direct
response to requests from Camry owners who wanted to be able to
transport five people comfortably, instead of the four that could fit
with ease into a Camry. Here, McCurry played a personal role in the
car's development. As with the Camry, he wasn't happy with the first
effort that Japanese engineers showed him. The burly executive pulled

open the driver's-side door, hopped inside, put the seat back as far as he could go and pointed to the steering wheel. "I want four more inches between my legs and the seat," he said.

Moreover, McCurry declared the car's trunk too small, dictating that it had to fit four sets of golf clubs, a frequent selling point for Lincolns and Cadillacs. Upon his return to Japan, McCurry got his wish: The engineers had stacked four bags of clubs next to the car, eager to show him that they would fit inside. Avalon came available only with the V-6 engine, another McCurry request. At $25,000 it was more expensive than a Camry, but a little cheaper, and certainly roomier, than the luxury ES 300. Avalon brought up inevitable comparisons to what Alfred P. Sloan had envisioned, generations before, when he laid out identities for GM's division. Sloan had famously declared that GM should sell "a car for every purse and purpose" and encourage its customers to trade up the scale of its divisions as they became more successful. If the Camry was Toyota's Chevrolet, then the Avalon, it was said, would have made an ideal Buick. Hostetter disagreed. "It was never meant to be our Buick," he said. "It was just meant to satisfy the needs of our buyers for more space and a larger sedan." Avalon is a low-profile car, selling about 90,000 vehicles a year, but each turns a profit for the company and allows its dealers to compete in more segments of the market. In typical fashion, Toyota signaled in 2003 that it was about to get more serious in the minivan market when it began building a new version of the Sienna at its truck plant in Princeton, taking a page from Honda by introducing a much bigger, plusher minivan that from the rear looks like an SUV, not a Mommy-mobile. The latest Sienna is the result of a 50,000-mile journey by Toyota's engineers across the United States, and an extensive research effort in which not just parents, but children, were asked for their input. The minivan, as a result, had features like a fold-down third rear seat that splits in two, allowing room for both an extra passenger and that person's gear. Sienna was an instant success: Within days of going on sale in March 2003, it had spawned waiting lists of seven to 10 weeks. Its desireability soared when *Consumer Reports* named it the country's best minivan, ahead of the aging Odyssey. Moving the minivan from Georgetown to Princeton gave Toyota more room to build more Camrys. That marked another manufacturing feat. It meant that Toyota could build minivans and pickup trucks on the same assembly line—even though one is based on a car frame and the other on a truck frame—something still undoable for its competitors from Detroit.

Still, a minivan and a family sedan are hardly groundbreaking vehicles. They are simply ways for Toyota to keep pace. Two other derivatives of the Camry—the Lexus RX 300 and the Toyota Highlander—were far more significant to Toyota. The RX, which went on sale in 1998, and the Highlander, which followed in 2001, were Toyota's first entries in a market that would explode in the next few years: crossover vehicles, or sport wagons. In essence, these are sport utilities that are built on a car chassis instead of the rigid truck frames from which sport utilities used to be built. Lately, Detroit companies are claiming that they invented this new segment of the market—Chrysler with its Pacifica crossover, which debuted in spring 2003, and Ford, which is developing the Freestyle, whose debut date still lies ahead. GM has its own on the way, and analysts are predicting that the sport wagon market will mushroom in coming years as consumers give up bulky truck-based SUVs and shift into the more maneuverable crossovers. But they are years behind Toyota, which introduced the second generation RX in 2003, called the RX 330, and plans another version of the Highlander in the near future. The RX was Lexus's third light truck product to be introduced within two years, before either GM or Ford had been able to get luxury trucks onto the market (the Lincoln Navigator and Cadillac Escalade hit the market in 1998).

The idea of a Lexus light truck had been a revolutionary one. It first came up in 1991, when Illingworth, the Lexus general manager, traveled to Nagoya, Japan, with McCurry to see the next-generation version of the Land Cruiser SUV. The daunting Land Cruiser, a true monster of a sport utility, had been around since 1951, when it was introduced as the Toyota Jeep, and was a perennial if modestly selling member of the Toyota lineup. Looking at the future vehicle, McCurry suddenly grabbed Illingworth's arm and said, "You need that in the Lexus division." Illingworth was stunned by the concept, since none of Lexus's competitors had even conceived of a luxury sport utility. It was years before Acura introduced the MDX, or Infiniti the QX4. Neither Mercedes nor BMW had talked about their luxury sport utilities. The only thing close to one was a Range Rover, priced thousands of dollars above what a Lexus cost. "I said, 'Bob, you're nuts,'" Illingworth recalled. "But he could see that was where the market was heading. One of the curious things to me about Toyota is how we do make those right decisions when others don't."

McCurry said he had an instinct that baby boom consumers, already beginning to buy Ford Explorers in big numbers, were going to want to go plusher someday in sport utilities. In 1996, Lexus turned the Land Cruiser into the LX 450, its most expensive offering to date, costing close to $60,000. It introduced an updated version in 1998, called the LX 470, and introduced it at the same time as the RX 300. Though the crossover vehicle was an unfamiliar animal on the American market, Hostetter could see a need for it emerging as early as 1993. He noticed that baby-boom–era buyers were returning their Land Cruiser and 4Runner sport utilities and pickup trucks after their leases expired, and not taking home new ones. The company's surveys showed that these customers had the highest dissatisfaction of any of Toyota's owners, unhappy with the vehicles' fuel economy, rough handling and size. Although Toyota had introduced a Camry station wagon, these buyers weren't interested because they had been shuttled around in station wagons as children and thought them to be passé. Hostetter started tinkering with the idea of an SUV that had the handling characteristics of a car but the room and functionality of one of the bigger vehicles. "I had dreamed about it for a long time," Hostetter said. It was a market that Toyota didn't want to ignore, because these were wealthy customers who were willing to spend significant amounts of money on their vehicles.

In Japan, Toyota's engineers were thinking along the same lines. In 1994, the company introduced the RAV4, a small sport utility vehicle based on the Corolla platform, and by 1998 the RX 300, sold as the Harrier in Japan, was ready. The RX has turned out to be one of the most popular vehicles in the Lexus lineup, a key reason why Lexus pushed past Mercedes and BMW in 2001 to become the country's best-selling luxury brand. Lexus's performance comes in the face of the toughest competition it has seen to date. Along with the German brands, both Cadillac and Lincoln are trying to stage comebacks. Cadillac's effort has gotten the most attention, pegged to a growing lineup of edgy, macho-looking vehicles such as the Escalade sport utility, the CTS sedan and the XLR two-seater, all with the same angular front end. GM has been relentless in keeping Cadillac's profile high, and Cadillac has scored well on J.D. Power surveys, coming in second to Lexus in 2003 in customer satisfaction. Denny Clements, the Lexus general manager, says he's impressed with GM's determination. "They get high marks. I'm excited for them. It's still a hell of a name," Clements said. But he isn't worried. Cadillac's efforts have had no effect on Lexus's sales, he said, sitting in his office in Torrance. "Someday they will be a competitor. Right now, I don't see it."

Almost fifteen years after Lexus was created, it is still appealing mainly to customers who own imports rather than buyers who own Detroit products. It has an enviable mix of repeat customers, who represent 60 percent of its owners, and new customers. Lately, Lexus has been branching out beyond its original reputation as a producer of high-quality, serene automobiles. It has added the GX 470 sport utility, as well as the IS 300, which is aimed at younger customers who might otherwise buy BMW's 3-series or an Audi. And Lexus scored an undeniable hit in 2001 when it added the SC 430 coupe to its lineup. For the first few months it was on sale, the SC 430 was the hottest car around. Fast and low-slung, it was sexier and more chic than any Lexus coupe had been before. Across the country, dealers were commanding $10,000 premiums above the car's $60,000 sticker price, and SC 430s became a car of choice for celebrities, athletes and trendsetters. Unlike the usual Lexus audience, 66 percent of buyers for the SC 430 were first-time Lexus owners, earning an average income of $270,000. Dealers clamored for more, and Clements knew that Lexus could have easily sold twice as many SC 430s. But it did not increase the supply, for fear of diluting the car's appeal. Clements, who began his career at Ford in the 1970s, had seen too many instances of auto companies flooding the market as soon as they had something successful. "I'm not going to mess that up," said Clements, a tall, broad-shouldered man who resembles Homeland Security Secretary Tom Ridge. "Sometimes it's very difficult not to say, 'Let's just crank it up.' But you've got to pay attention and have discipline." With the luxury market flooded, from a resurgent Cadillac to an aggressive BMW and all manner of other competitors, Clements does not take Lexus's luxury car leadership position lightly. "When you're the most successful, you're the most vulnerable," he said.

Another company might sit back, stick to the formula that led to its achievement and simply defend its turf. Not Lexus. In the surprise fashion that the brand added trucks to its lineup in the mid-1990s, it is about to shift into another category: hybrid-electric vehicles, which are powered by both gasoline engines and electric motors. At the Detroit Auto Show in January 2003, Lexus showed off a hybrid-electric version of the RX that Clements thinks could be as important to the Lexus lineup as the original LS 400 was to the creation of the brand in 1989. The hybrid called the 400 H, which is due to go on sale in early 2005, is a sharp contrast to the small hybrid-electric vehicles that consumers are most familiar with, such as the Toyota Prius, the Honda Civic and the original Honda hybrid, the Insight.

———————

No other luxury car brand has even whispered about adding a hybrid-electric vehicle to its lineup, because the cars simply seem at odds with the statement that luxury vehicles make. But Clements sees it otherwise. "For Lexus, this is a real statement about technology," Clements said. "We're saying that you don't have to sacrifice perform-ance to be environmentally friendly." His face lights up when he talks about the 400 H's potential. "It's huge. We think nobody knows how good this vehicle is," he said. With its combination Lexus engine and 650-volt electric motor, it will go from 0 to 30 mph "right now" and 0 to 60 mph "incredibly fast," Clements said. Moreover, it will earn 38–40 mpg in city driving, twice what the gasoline-powered RX 330 achieves.

But will Lexus customers be interested? Bob Lutz at GM doesn't think so, dubbing this hybrid and all of Toyota's other environmental efforts a PR campaign. Detroit auto companies delight in statistics that show Toyota's fuel economy has dropped in recent years because it has added more SUVs to its lineups, even as it promotes the Prius hybrid. But Clements is convinced his well-heeled customers will want a hybrid too. "This is not a decision anyone took for the hell of it," he said. He believes the 400 H will appeal to the same kind of cus-tomers who were willing to take a chance on Lexus in the first place. The 400 H, like the Camry, like all vehicles across Toyota's lineup, is meant to be a statement from Toyota of what it can offer its cus-tomers, said Press. "We are there so that we can fulfill our mission from each car individually, instead of making all kinds of trade-offs," he said. "If you're driven by the customer, you know that they want good quality and value. They want to get on the freeway and feel their car go when they push the throttle down."

Press says he's frustrated by critics who deride the Camry as uninspired, a particular criticism of the latest version of the car, introduced in fall 2001. Though it remained the country's best-selling car into 2003, Camry has suffered in comparison to the 2003 Accord, whose ride is stiffer than Camry's and closer to that of a Volkswagen Passat. Some customers have complained that the Camry, which cost the company 25 percent less to develop than previous cars, is less Lexus-like these days than its predecessors and that the company cut some corners. Dana Hargitt, who took charge of the American side of the Camry's development, is naturally sensitive to that, contending that the Camry is a smoother car with more room inside than Accord, whose ride he considers to be harsh.

Press draws another analogy. "It's like a classic suit versus an Italian suit," he explained. "You might buy the Italian suit and it might look great when you buy it, but you take it out three years later, and it looks old-fashioned." Likewise, Press said, the Camry meets customers' needs but doesn't overreach. "The core Camry customer really doesn't care if they can corner at 80 or 90 mph—they corner at 60 or 70 mph," he said. He sees a parallel between Toyota and classic retailing brands like L.L. Bean and Lands' End, whose catalogue offerings evolve to reflect trends that take hold among consumers. These retailers add Capri pants and thong sandals as they sense their customers want them, but they never abandon the bathing suits, parkas and hunting gear that comprise the core of their catalogues. Like them, Toyota feels comfortable broadening its line to include vehicles like the Lexus SC 430, or its upcoming lineup of Scion automobiles, aimed at the industry's youngest and hippest consumers. But it will never abandon its basic mission, which the Camry represents. "That's us. America, the mass of us, that's us," Press said. "As the lifestyles and needs of the customers move, the Camry will move with them. It's a brand. It's a van, it's an SUV, it's a sporty car, a sedan, a luxury car. The name Camry will always be there. It may not always be the volume vehicle that it's been, but it will be there."

Press claims he is delighted to see his competitors spice up their lineups with all types of flavors, from the speedy Accord to the trendy Altima, hoping to end Camry's dominance. He just wants them to remember one thing: "Our strength is that we make a *ton* of vanilla," he said.

CHAPTER SIX

THE CHALLENGER

WHEN CARLOS GHOSN APPEARS at a Nissan news conference, he's almost always alone on stage, in front of a plain screen bearing the Nissan logo. Occasionally, a new vehicle shares the spotlight. But whatever car or truck the company is promoting that day generally takes second billing, for clearly Ghosn is the show. With his hawklike face and dark, sweeping eyebrows, Ghosn (pronounced "GO-nn") is the mastermind of Nissan's aspirations for the future, which are already taking root just four years after Ghosn arrived in Japan from the French automaker Renault to rescue the torpid company. His task seemed impossible, for Nissan in 1999 was deluged with debt, its operations an organizational mess plagued by interlocking holdings in suppliers, who themselves were struggling, its culture lethargic. Moreover, Nissan's lineup was confused, with both mundane cars and halfhearted attempts at bold styling on vehicles whose reliability and quality clearly lagged that of Toyota and Honda. Nissan seemed destined to be constantly overshadowed by its competition. What's more, few people outside of Europe had ever heard of Ghosn, whose name, which is of Lebanese origin, was constantly mispronounced. But Ghosn, as it turned out, was not to be underestimated.

His comeback plan has been marked by two elements: a flood of aggressively styled cars, trucks, minivans and SUVs that are intended to give Nissan a definable niche in the auto market, and a financial strategy aimed at restoring record profitability. Both have come about with breathtaking speed and resounding success. The cars, plus the company's dramatically improved financial performance and Ghosn's bold personality, have made him a celebrity in the automotive world, especially in Japan. Wherever he goes now in Japan, whether Tokyo Disneyland with his family, or a company event, he attracts a sea of admirers. Some approach bearing copies of his autobiography, *Renaissance*, which remained atop the best-seller list in Japan for more than a year. Others bring the Japanese comic books, called *manga*, that dramatically depict Ghosn's life story. His reputation for relentless work has prompted the Japanese press to dub him 7-Eleven (after the 24-hour convenience stores). Journalists flock to hear his utterances. The news conference held by Nissan in the spring of 2002 to announce the completion of its recovery plan was typical: Ghosn stood by himself before an auditorium crowded with Japanese, American and French journalists and even a television crew from Lebanon, his parents' home country. It is the kind of notoriety that some car executives have basked in and taken pains to cultivate, sometimes to the detriment of the job at hand. But Ghosn keeps his intense focus. Supremely confident, some might say to the point of arrogance, he is not a man known for wasting words or for entertaining small ambitions.

Having stabilized the company, Ghosn's next goal is to return Nissan to the upper tier of Japanese manufacturers, making it the equal once again of Toyota and Honda. That might be daunting enough, given the benchmark that those two companies have set for quality, reliability and durability. But long-term, Ghosn's reach is even more formidable. He wants Nissan and its French partner and savior, Renault, to become one of the world's top-ranking automobile companies, not only in reputation but also in size. He wants Renault and Nissan combined to sell 8 million vehicles a year worldwide by the year 2010, which would make it twice as big as the combined companies were when they began their alliance in 1999—and a rival in size to Toyota and General Motors. While he admits such a goal is audacious, he refuses to say it is out of reach. "I don't think about stumbling," Ghosn said in an interview in his office in one of Nissan's two headquarters buildings in the Ginza section of Tokyo. "This is not something that I consider. I simply don't give it too much thought. The only thing I'm saying is, judge us on the performance that we are delivering."

When Ghosn arrived at Nissan in spring 1999, the automotive giant was drowning after a 10-year decline coinciding with the downfall in Japan's economy. Despite having turned in some of the industry's most distinctive designs over the years, most notably the Z sports car, and having created a global manufacturing empire that stretched from Japan to Europe to the United States, Nissan was saddled with $22 billion in debt and a hopelessly tangled bureaucracy. Though Nissan was the first of the major automakers to begin production in Japan in 1933, it had lately been eclipsed by its far younger and spunkier competitor, Honda, which pushed past it to become the second-biggest automaker in Japan. The best and brightest graduates of Japan's universities, who used to choose Nissan because its design-focused culture was far less rigid than Toyota's manufacturing-based approach, were passing the company by. Nissan had been reputed to be in play by the summer of 1998, and speculation was rife within the company that a takeover was looming. "We all got it second- or thirdhand," recalled Jed Connelly, senior vice president in charge of Nissan's U.S. sales operations. "We heard DaimlerChrysler, we heard Ford."

In fact, DaimlerChrysler was the company's most serious suitor, but the negotiations fell apart in March 1999, after German executives had spent months vetting the company as the potential player in Asia that would broaden the newly created auto giant beyond the United States and Europe. The rejection was not a surprise to Nissan, but it was a slap in the face for DaimlerChrysler's creator, Juergen Schrempp. He had argued heatedly in favor of acquiring a stake in Nissan in the face of opposition from every other company board member, particularly the American officials who had so willingly combined forces with Schrempp less than a year before. Finally giving in to the wall of resistance, Schrempp flew to Japan himself to deliver the bad news, a sign of respect that helped Nissan save face. DaimlerChrysler ultimately turned to Mitsubishi Motor Corp. as its Japanese partner, which also had deep financial problems that were time-consuming, and ultimately proved as extensive as those at Nissan. (After Nissan's turnaround had been achieved, the joke around Tokyo was that DaimlerChrysler had chosen the wrong sick Japanese auto company as its partner.)

Fortunately for Nissan, a second suitor was already waiting at the door when DaimlerChrysler walked away—Renault. It was Ghosn who began bugging fellow managers as early as summer 1998 to consider a bid for the struggling Japanese company. But he met with resistance, because mergers were a touchy subject at Renault. It had made a deal to combine forces with the Swedish auto company Volvo in 1992, only to see the arrangement drown in red tape and political outcry in both France and Sweden. Renault's quiet but focused chief executive, Louis Schweitzer, still hungered for a partnership that would help Renault grow beyond Europe. Pushed by Ghosn, he held negotiations with Nissan even though it looked as if Nissan's discussions with Daimler-Chrysler would culminate in a deal with the German company. Within weeks of the collapse of the DaimlerChrysler talks, Schweitzer was able to reach an agreement with Nissan on a deal in which Renault would contribute $5.4 billion in cash to help shore up the Japanese auto company's finances and provide management talent to run the place. Ghosn was named as Nissan's president and second in command in April 1999, shortly after his forty-fifth birthday. The deal came as a complete shock to Connelly and other Nissan executives in the United States. "Renault was not on our radar screen, because they had not been in the United States for a long period of time," Connelly said. Renault, in fact, had stopped selling cars in the United States in the early 1990s, after it sold its stake in American Motors Corp. to Chrysler in 1986, a deal that had also sparked opposition within Chrysler's management ranks. (In fact, that deal sent Chrysler into a tailspin that pushed it close to bankruptcy in 1989 for the second time in a decade, forcing then-CEO Lee Iacocca to implement his own recovery plan.)

Ghosn had arrived at Renault in 1996. He had come over from the tire maker Michelin, joining Renault as the highest-ranking executive ever to be brought on from outside the auto company's generally closed ranks. As unusual as that situation was, so was Ghosn's background. Truly a product of a global society, Ghosn was born in Brazil in March 1954 to Lebanese parents. His mother, Rose, had dual Brazilian and French citizenship and his father, Jorge, also held a Brazilian passport. When he was 11, his mother moved with her brood of four children back to Lebanon, a not-unusual situation among the families of Lebanese men who moved abroad to advance their business interests. His father remained in Brazil, where he ran an airline consulting business. But he made frequent trips back to Lebanon to visit the still-growing Ghosn family (Carlos's parents had two more children despite their distance). Ghosn gained a reputation as something of a scamp in Catholic school, where he loved to pull pranks on his fellow students and was frequently called on the carpet by the priests. He was an undeniable car buff, too. The comic book that tells his life story depicts an 11-year-old Ghosn, blindfolded and with his back to the road. A playmate asks him to identify an oncoming car by sound alone. "Cadillac Eldorado," he declares. "Bingo!" says his friend.

Cars were part of his fascination with America, something that many youngsters in Europe and the Middle East shared at the time. And when it came time for college, he considered MIT, and in fact traveled to the United States in 1976 to tour the country during the bicentennial year. But Ghosn ended up in Paris, at the topflight École Polytechnique, and subsequently advanced to the École des Mines for a master's degree and the preliminary work on a doctorate. It was here that he crossed paths with François Michelin, scion of the family-held tire company. The company had expanded its operations in Brazil, where it operated two rubber plantations, and executives were looking for French-trained engineers who spoke Portuguese.

Tipped off about Ghosn by a friend of his sister's, Michelin himself took Ghosn under his wing, promising him an eventual assignment in Brazil if he would take charge of a factory in France. Ghosn agreed. There Ghosn, at age 26, supervised 700 workers; back in Brazil, he tested out some of the efficiency ideas that would eventually mark his reputation. Within three years, Michelin's South American operations were among the company's most profitable, and in 1988, Ghosn, then 34, was promoted to run Michelin's North American operations, based in Greenville, South Carolina. Among his first encounters was with a company executive named James C. Morton, who oversaw a variety of functions, including the selection of sites for Michelin plants. When Ghosn arrived, the first thing people commented upon was his youth, Morton said. Within weeks, that was replaced by a buzz about his relentless energy. "He always demanded a level of respect, and he controlled the situation. I'm seven years his senior, and after a while, I never even thought about [the age difference]," said Morton.

Ghosn's duties in the United States included supervising production at Michelin's factories, whose costs he attacked with the same fervor he had shown in Brazil. Then, in 1990, he oversaw Michelin's acquisition of Uniroyal-Goodrich, a merger that took painstaking months to complete and still more time to integrate the companies' factories. But Ghosn relished the assignment and developed a deep fondness for Greenville, where he still owns the home in which he and his wife, Rita, also of Lebanese descent, lived with their four children. They made dozens of friends in the area—Rita frequently cooked Lebanese food for company gatherings—and might have stayed in the United States much longer. But Ghosn, after finally completing the merger, was told in 1996 to return to Michelin's French headquarters. By this point, Ghosn was open to alternatives elsewhere in the auto industry, preferably at a major manufacturer instead of a supplier. When a headhunter called to ask whether he'd consider a job at Renault, he was receptive. He eventually accepted the No. 2 position.

As at Michelin, it did not take long for Ghosn to make an impression. Under the studious Louis Schweitzer, Renault's sales and market share had grown thanks to a lineup of vehicles such as the small, spunky Twingo (its name a combination of twist and tango) and the Megane sedan. They were aimed at Europe's burgeoning group of Generation X first-time car buyers. But the company's costs had soared, and the government, meanwhile, was in the process of selling off its shares in what had been a partially state-owned company. In 1996, Renault faced a $1 billion loss, its first loss in 10 years. Upon arriving, Ghosn immediately set off through Renault's automotive and parts plants, combing through its manufacturing processes and delivery systems for ways to save money. He declared he wanted savings of 20 billion francs over the next three years (the equivalent of nearly $3 billion, a large sum at what was a medium-sized player).

The proposal included the unthinkable: Renault would close its manufacturing plant in Vilvoorde, Belgium, resulting in the loss of 3,500 jobs. The action enraged Belgian workers, who immediately went out on a wildcat strike, flooding the streets around the factory and picketing Renault's offices. The French company was accused of making the Belgians pay for cuts it would not make in its home country, and Ghosn was dubbed "Le Cost Killer." The furor eventually died down, and the pain of the cutbacks was offset by the profits that Renault posted in 1997 and 1998. At the same time, Renault scored a huge hit with the Megane Scenic, the first of Europe's mini-minivans, which Ghosn touted as proof that Renault could spin its car platforms into other vehicles. Scenic was years ahead of its competition and had attracted 300,000 buyers before GM introduced its own version, the Opel Zafira. Ford executives, incredibly, doubted that the category would bear fruit. Despite the urging of its designers, Ford originally chose not to join the fray (a much-regretted mistake: the category now has sales of 1 million vehicles a year in Europe). The successes at Renault gave Ghosn substantial clout inside Renault, enough that Schweitzer was convinced to gamble on a stake in Nissan at his recommendation. As the Nissan deal was taking shape in the spring of 1999, Ghosn seemed like the logical person to send to Japan. The stakes, however, were bigger than any challenge he had faced in the past.

By 1999, Nissan was a mess, saddled with debt and a shaky future. Before World War II, it had been Japan's premier auto company, beating Toyota to the market in 1933. It was faster to rebound after the war than Toyota, and it still held on to a sizable share of the Japanese market well into the 1990s. But Japan's lingering economic downturn and Nissan's own culture kept it mired in the past. As auto companies developed in prewar Japan, they, like other major business organizations, became involved in a system called *zaibatsu* that created extremely close-knit operations between the participants. Similar situations grew up in the shipping, banking and other industries. In essence, the *zaibatsu* were the result of Japan's efforts to keep out foreign competition and to ensure that companies supported one another's prosperity. When Japan came under American authority after World War II, the *zaibatsu* were officially abolished, but the Japanese companies got around that by establishing a similar method of doing business called *keiretsu*. On paper, these were merely long-term business relationships, the result of an effort to ensure the famous quality standards that Japanese auto companies were known for. The *keiretsu* were framed as the equivalent of family members.

But the system evolved to include cross-ownership ties in which the companies bought stock in one another and had a vested interest in one another's success. It worked beautifully in the case of Toyota, which drove its suppliers to achieve the same cost savings and quality measurements that it expected of itself. But when discipline faltered, the arrangement could be a stranglehold. As auto companies poured money into their suppliers to ensure that they used the best technology, or subsequently propped them up in poor economic times, the *keiretsu* became as enmeshed as the *zaibatsu* had been. Where an American auto company might simply walk away and look for a cheaper source of parts, Japanese auto companies felt beholden to their suppliers, especially because of the emphasis placed in Japan on purchasing locally made parts. But this could backfire, because the auto companies sometimes were forced to pay whatever prices the suppliers demanded, rather than searching out cheaper sources elsewhere. Thus, a system that was supposed to be beneficial could in fact greatly hinder a parent company lacking the chutzpah to challenge the arrangement. And indeed, this was the case at Nissan.

By 1999, Nissan held an interest in 1,394 different companies, including an ownership stake in one of its competitors, Fuji Heavy Industries, the owner of Isuzu. Further, Nissan owned 50 percent of its car dealerships and was burdened with their costs in a slipping market.

Not surprisingly, in the 10 years leading up to Ghosn's arrival, Nissan had been profitable in just one year. Its Japanese market share, which had been one-quarter of the market at the start of the 1990s, slipped to just 17 percent by 1999. In the United States, it had dropped from its perennial place as the second-best seller of Japanese vehicles to third, behind Toyota and Honda, and for a time it was even in danger of slipping to fourth place behind Mazda. The company had tried several times to right its sagging operations, most notably with a turnaround plan begun in 1997, but with little success. "Morale was very uncertain," said Jed Connelly, Nissan's senior vice president for sales and marketing. The hurdles were enormous, and the stakes for Renault were equally high, because the $5.4 billion that it had invested in Nissan was about all the money it had to spend on any kind of acquisition. Should Nissan fail to improve and pay back the investment, both auto companies could find themselves in a downward spiral.

Looking back now, the swiftness with which Ghosn moved seems incredible. Within five months of his arrival in June 1999, Ghosn had outlined the tenets of the Nissan Recovery Plan. Within a year, Nissan was profitable again. And within two years after that, Ghosn had achieved all the goals he had set for the company, a year ahead of schedule, and had moved on to the second phase of his turnaround plan, which he dubbed Nissan 180. None of it appeared easy at the time, and certainly Ghosn arrived under a microscope. Although Japanese companies had headed out around the world during the previous two decades on an international buying spree, that rarely happened in reverse. In the auto industry, only Ford, which had management control of Mazda, had sent a foreign executive to run the place. At the same time, there were basic operational questions: Ghosn spoke French, English, Portuguese and Arabic, but he did not speak Japanese, and cross-cultural management teams in Japan were an unknown quantity. How would he manage—literally and figuratively? And even more important, how would he sweep away the stu-

por that had settled over Nissan's operations? Over the years, its executives had become used to their dire situation, he discovered. There
was a sluggishness around the place that he found disheartening and
that had to be immediately addressed. "You're in a company that has
been through a decline for 10 years. So the sense of urgency's been
lost," Ghosn said. He woke them up with a bang.

In contrast to the Japanese management style in which executives
spoke to executives, managers to managers, and so on down the hierar-
chy, Ghosn showed up everywhere in Nissan's operations worldwide.
He would take 12-hour trips to facilities in the United States or Europe,
spend a few hours in conference rooms with employees of all levels,
then get on a plane for another trip. He encouraged everyone in the
organization to speak up; he asked some questions, but mostly he listened. At his first meeting at Nissan's sales operations in Carson, California, Ghosn arrived alone, without an entourage, to find that the
organization had no five-year sales plan. Instead of asking the managers
to prepare one for him to review on a future trip, or telling them to hire
a consultant to help them draft a proposal, Ghosn sent out for pizza
and legal pads. He paid for the pizza and spent the next hours in the
room with the executives, kicking ideas around until the plan was
sketched out. "He was no-nonsense. He was probing. He wanted
answers. He drilled down," Connelly said. "He had so much know-how
and insight. It was one-on-five, and it was not a fair fight."

In another instance, when a manager at the Nissan Technical Center
in Farmington Hills, Michigan, told him that he had wanted to make
a change that could save the company thousands of dollars but did
not have the authority, Ghosn replied, "There! You have the authority! I give you the authority!" Connelly said the executives were shell-
shocked, at first, by Ghosn's direct approach, which was such a sharp
contrast with the polite but noncommittal answers they had always

received from Nissan's Japanese executives. Connelly's anxiety must have showed, because at the end of his first visit Ghosn took him aside. "Don't worry," Ghosn told him soothingly. "It will be easier than you think."

By the end of his global listening tour, Ghosn had come up with a series of elegantly simple, although incredibly challenging, goals. The first, and seemingly the most difficult, was his vow to return Nissan to profitability within one year. And to demonstrate his seriousness, Ghosn said he and the management team would quit if they failed to achieve an operating profit. "This was the most important objective, and the most difficult one, but it was the cornerstone," Ghosn said. "If the NRP was to have any chance to succeed, we had to do it." Behind that, Ghosn issued another directive that sent shock waves through Japanese society: He would break up Nissan's *keiretsu* and cut by half the 1,000 parts suppliers with which Nissan did business, eventually dropping the figure to just 400. On top of that, another shock: Nissan would eliminate 21,000 jobs worldwide, 16,000 of them in Japan.

A few years before, the company had rattled Japan when it had closed a single assembly plant. Ghosn planned to close three, leaving Nissan with just four plants in Japan, half the number it had at the beginning of the 1990s. The reasoning was simple: Nissan's capacity utilization rate, which measured its plants' productivity, was only 50 percent. By contrast, when factories in the United States were running on constant overtime during the 1990s, there were months when Ford achieved a capacity utilization rate of 110 percent. Auto companies, to achieve minimal profitability, had to run their plants at least at a 75 percent rate, and higher if they had high overhead. Ghosn could see no alternative to the plant closings.

As part of the plan, Ghosn also said that Nissan would combine its product development operations with those of Renault—no surprise, since the idea had been talked about from the first day of the merger. He said the company would reduce the number of car platforms from 22 to 15, greatly simplifying the tasks that its engineers would face in developing new vehicles, but also stretching their ability to share underpinnings while making the vehicles on which they were set distinctive. The most ambitious directive from Ghosn, however, was not the series of cutbacks, which he hoped would save the company ¥1 trillion. It was his vow to roll out a wave of new vehicles for Japan, the United States, Europe and elsewhere that would establish a new image for Nissan as a company that was focused on styling and performance, as well as match the quality of the best global companies. As Nissan was cutting back, Ghosn wanted to aggressively grow. And the United States, the world's most ruthlessly competitive market, would be the most important component of this attack.

Nissan's image in the United States had always been one of a company that stressed design but also seemed to hedge its bets. Nissan boasted one of the most colorful and quirky designers in the car business, Gerald Hirshberg, who for a time in the 1990s was featured in the company's ads talking about the importance of smart car design. And the company had seemed to be trying to make its vehicles stand out. Its mid-sized Altima sedan, introduced in 1993, certainly had a more interesting appearance than both the Toyota Camry and the Honda Accord, but it had never really broken through to their level of quality. The Maxima was a cult car, a performance sedan of near-luxury quality for a decent price, with a fast engine and good handling.

And, of course, there was the legendary Z sports car, which Nissan had retired in 1996 when the price climbed above $45,000. But there had never been a coherent approach to pulling it all together. The same was true for Nissan's luxury division, Infiniti. It had started out in 1989 on the same footing as Lexus, offering affordable luxury vehicles with high quality, but while Lexus kept growing and adding to its lineup, Infiniti never seemed to really carve out a niche. Models came and went, with little impact on the market—"committee cars," Womack called them, which bore little of the stamp of the brand or the personality of their designers. Infiniti, more than its competitors, was forced to resort to discount lease deals and other incentives to lure customers, many of whom chose Infiniti for the deals rather than the vehicles themselves. By the time Ghosn got there, Infiniti was somehow forgotten—a situation that he vowed to fix as he overhauled Nissan's product lineup. For to Ghosn, the financial success story was only a part of Nissan's recovery plan. It had to be based on new vehicles. So, he declared, Nissan would roll out 22 new or overhauled vehicles by 2004—with more planned for later in the decade. They would speak for Nissan in a better way than he could.

The first of the new models was announced literally as Renault and Nissan were cutting their deal: the return of the Z sports car. But when Nissan originally decided to revive the Z, its designers had thoughts of a retro-designed vehicle whose appearance echoed the lines of the trademark Z cars, with a long, low hood and rounded passenger compartment. Ghosn, seeing the design, feared that it would appeal only to the aging fans of the first generations of the Z. As a father of four, he was attuned to the fact that his children had tastes far different from his and Rita's. And he felt that the next Z needed to be a car that Generation X and Generation Y buyers after them would find appealing, even if the car sold primarily to baby boomers. He also wanted it to be affordable, and he pressed the designers to keep the car's price tag close to $25,000, rather than drift higher, as the old Z had done.

By the time Nissan's design team had finished with the 350 Z, as it was called, it looked significantly different from the first concept cars Nissan had put on display at various auto shows. It was small and low-slung, and it looked fast. Elements of the old Z were there—in its long hood and sloping rear roof—but even without knowing the car's legacy, a buyer who had never seen the old Z might still be intrigued. The Z was an instant hit, outselling the venerable Chevrolet Corvette in its first months on the market in 2003, and it began to pop up on roads in wealthy parts of California and the South, where buyers were most attuned to the newest thing on the market. Nissan didn't stop with the Z, either. It used the car as the platform for its Infiniti FX sport utility, a fast, powerful vehicle that stunned the luxury car market when it appeared in early 2003 and threatened to overshadow the Porsche Cayenne SUV, which had been years in development and had received an inordinate amount of hype.

But while Nissan thrived on the attention that the Z generated, no company could stake its future on a niche model such as a sports car. Luckily for Ghosn, work had already begun before he arrived on a new version of the Altima sedan. Introduced in fall 2002, the Altima typified exactly what Ghosn was looking for: a distinct personality in a car that was aimed at a multitude of customers. It was peppier than either the Camry or the Accord, although not as quiet or smooth. The Altima was definitely something to get used to for drivers more accustomed to the Accord's ease of acceleration or the Camry's solid feel. Punch the accelerator, and the Altima instantly responded, occasionally to the driver's surprise. Its exterior design boasted the bold, chiseled front grille with the round Nissan emblem that was becoming the identifiable Nissan look. Its interior was more like a sports car than a family sedan, although there was plenty of space and it boasted a huge trunk. Nissan had planned to sell only about 125,000 a year, but by early 2003 the Altima was selling more strongly than Nissan had anticipated and the company was scrambling to find ways to build more. The solution came as Nissan took on the biggest challenge that the company had ever faced in the United States—the full-sized Titan pickup truck.

Over the years, Nissan had sold small pickups that were popular with California surfers and other young buyers, and more recently had pushed into the mid-sized market with the Frontier. But it held off on a full-sized truck, even as Toyota dipped its toe into the pickup market in 1992 with the modest T-100, then followed up in 1999 with the bigger Tundra. By the late 1990s, it had become clear that in order to have the full lineup of vehicles that could expand Nissan's reach, it simply had to have a pickup. On a trip to the United States in July 1999, Connelly brought together a group of 15 dealers to meet with Ghosn. Instead of the speech that Connelly expected Ghosn to give them, Ghosn peppered the dealers with questions. "He asked them, 'What do you like? What don't you like? What don't you have?'" Connelly recalled. And the overwhelming answer was a full-sized pickup truck. The dealers, and Connelly, too, saw the vehicle as "an important sign that Nissan was committed to the U.S. market."

But Ghosn did not commit to the project right away. For one thing, he was focusing on how best to use Nissan's limited assets. For another, he knew that a pickup had to be produced in a new factory. Nissan's plant in Smyrna, Tennessee, was full to bursting with product, and although workers there were among the most productive in the industry, the company simply couldn't load them down with another vehicle. There was not one decision to be made, but two. Connelly, after the dealer meeting, had no idea how long Ghosn would take to make up his mind, given that he still had to finalize the company's revitalization plan. He expected that the truck might take years to come to fruition. But as soon as Ghosn put the pieces of the recovery plan together, he began thinking about the pickup truck project—and called in an old friend to help.

Not long after Ghosn's announcement at Nissan, he and Rita made a trip back to Greenville to check on their house and to see Jim Morton and his wife, Susan, with whom they had stayed in touch after Ghosn left Michelin. The Mortons had just spent a year renovating their home, and were excitedly showing the Ghosns around the vast new kitchen and expanded living room. As Susan Morton prepared lunch, Ghosn casually asked Morton if he'd consider leaving Michelin and joining him at Nissan's operations in California as senior vice president in charge of finance and administration. Morton thought his wife wasn't listening, but she was, and her first question was "Would we have to sell the house?" Morton recalled. They eventually did, because Morton accepted a job with wide-ranging responsibilities, one of which was to select the site for Nissan's new truck plant.

Years before, Morton had been to Mississippi to look at possible locations for a Michelin tire factory. State officials had shown him a variety of sites, but the factory eventually went elsewhere. But Mississippi still had plenty of land for companies to choose from. And, having come in second or third repeatedly over the years when other companies chose states for their factories, Mississippi's governor, Ronnie Musgrove, was determined to land the Nissan plant. Morton joined Ghosn and Emil Hassan, senior vice president in charge of Nissan's U.S. manufacturing operations, at a meeting at the governor's mansion to discuss the $1 billion project, which would be the biggest single manufacturing complex ever to be built in the state. Mississippi was one of only four states that Nissan considered. And from the moment the project was put on the table, Nissan took just six months to choose a site—far less than the 12 to 18 months that most companies require as they consider locations for factories and sift through various packages of incentives. The governor was so eager for the project that he gave Ghosn a cell phone, preprogrammed to speed-dial the governor's number, and asked him to call when he had made up his mind. Early on a morning in November 2000, the phone rang from Tokyo with the news that Mississippi had won this time. Said Morton, "It is about as fast as I've ever seen anything come together."

The overwhelming reception that Ghosn and the Titan received when the truck was introduced at the Detroit Auto Show in January

2003 eased the nerves of a lot of people at Nissan. Among the most relieved was the young design team that had worked on it at Nissan Design America in La Jolla, California. Known as NDA, the Nissan design facility is a workplace that is as much Zen as an office building. It is built into a hill, and could easily be mistaken for an architectural firm rather than a car company office, albeit one whose partners favor the Z 350 sports car, if the row of cars parked out front is an indication of their preferences. The low white building is decorated with manicured flower beds, a courtyard in the middle and pools inside the front door. But the decor pales in excitement by comparison with the work going on here. The place pulses with creativity. The staff of American, Japanese and European designers, of all ages, jogs through here in jeans and khakis, shirts and turtlenecks. The only people wearing suits and ties are clearly outsiders.

The group that took charge of the Titan was headed by Diane Allen, who, like many of the designers on Nissan's staff, didn't own a pickup truck and had little knowledge that she could bring to the project. Their lack of understanding drove the Nissan designers to hunt down pickup truck owners across southern California, Texas and elsewhere. They interviewed them about the way they used their trucks and observed them in action, watching them secure cargo with bungee cords and struggle to juggle children and gear inside the truck's passenger compartment. Inside the Red Studio at Nissan Design America (the studios are named by colors), these owners' pictures are taped to a big display, called a design concept board, that's meant to express what the designers hope to accomplish. Atop the board is a list of priorities culled from watching the truck owners and asking them what they wanted in a truck. The answers sum up how the Titan turned out.

First, it had to be "a true Alpha truck" meant for "living large." Second, its exterior had to be bold and assertive. Third, the interior needed to emphasize roominess and thoughtful innovation. Fourth came superior quality. Fifth, it had to express Nissan's identity as a maker of vehicles with performance and personality. The conclusions came not from a research report conducted by the marketing department, Allen explained, but from the designers themselves. "We took out the middleman," she said. "It's why we're unique at Nissan. This is us experiencing what the truck had to be." As they spoke to the owners, the Nissan designers found that the potential market for the truck was quickly emerging. Many of the owners they met with had a Big Three pickup as well as a BMW or Lexus parked in the garage, a clear sign they'd be open to owning a pickup from an import company, said Nicholas Backlund, the truck's design manager. "They just didn't have another choice," he said. Moreover, Nissan's research showed that 13 percent of Frontier owners were defecting to Big Three pickups, since Nissan had nothing to offer them.

A few years before, Nissan had shown at the Detroit Auto Show a pickup concept vehicle called Gobi, which Allen had designed. It had an exciting, radical design, but it seemed far-fetched next to the classic pickups that Detroit companies sold. "It might as well have been a truck with wings," recalled Backlund. The experience taught the designers that "there is an envelope for acceptability with a pickup," Allen said. Added Backlund, "The question that we had to deal with was: How do we become authentic? We didn't want to be a sumo wrestler in a cowboy hat." The answer, they concluded, lay in size. There could be no fudging, as Toyota had done first with T-100 and with Tundra. The Nissan pickup had to be every bit as big as a Detroit product, which posed a problem for the designers. The truck was the biggest vehicle that Nissan had ever developed. When it came time to build a life-size, mockup version honed from a block of design clay, "it wouldn't fit on our milling machine," Allen said. That problem was surmounted with new equipment.

Then came the issue of its appearance. Having been stung by reaction to the Gobi, the design team wasn't sure how far to reach. So seven different versions were designed, from conservative to eye-popping. The list was narrowed to four, then two. At the same time that the truck was under development, the designers were working on the next-generation Quest minivan and two SUVs—one for Nissan, the other for Infiniti—that would be built alongside the truck at the plant in Canton, Mississippi. Two quarter-size tabletop models of each vehicle were sent to Japan for examination by Ghosn and Shiro Nakamura, Nissan's chief designer, whom Ghosn had recruited from Isuzu in 1999. (Nakamura's hiring had been another shock at the company, where designers had long ruled the roost, especially since Isuzu had never been known for its vehicles' appearance. But Ghosn said he wanted a new approach from someone who had no preconceived notions of what Nissan should be.) Since the four designs would be manufactured together, Ghosn and Nakamura had to select them all at once.

The truck, to be built in Canton, had to be selected first. Of the designs sent to Japan, one version was polished, a bit conservative, and could have blended right in with the rest of the truck market. The other was bolder, gutsier, and was the slightly unpolished work of Giovanny Arroba, a 23-year-old designer fresh out of the Art Center School of Design in Pasadena, California, the automotive design world's premier training academy, who had joined Nissan only a few months before. The truck was his first major project, and Allen and the other designers found a number of problems with his design, code-named G, which would have to be addressed down the road. Regardless, Arroba, who has shoulder-length dark hair and a quiet manner, said he'd relished the experience. "I love the challenge of this much sheet metal," he said.

Having seen the designs, Ghosn, Nakamura and an entourage flew to San Diego to meet the team and hear their arguments in favor of each version. On a sunny day, Ghosn and the others examined scale models of the trucks out in a courtyard. Then he looked at the team and said, "Okay, if you believe it, G is picked. Let's do it." Allen said that was the moment when he was convinced that the Titan really could have an impact on the truck market. "There's so much complacency among the domestics and it was so delicious to have Ghosn buy into it," she said of the winning design. "As soon as Ghosn blessed it, the sea opened up." Ghosn's choice was also resonant for another reason. It's routine in Detroit for auto companies to show versions of their future vehicles to consumers for their reaction. These sessions, called clinics, are supposed to gauge whether consumers would be likely to buy the vehicle. Frequently, changes are made in the vehicle's appearance as a result of the feedback, sometimes slowing down the development process and adding cost to the project. Nissan, however, had abolished these clinics a few years earlier, for just that reason. "One of the biggest choke holds was that in these clinics people say, 'Do away with this' when they don't really understand what we are trying to do," Backlund said. On a project as vital as the pickup, the company might have been justified in holding clinics, given the stakes. But, said Backlund, "Nissan walked the walk and talked the talk on this project. This was a statement of faith."

Even so, Nissan is deliberately cautious with its sales estimates for the pickup. At the Detroit show, Connelly predicted 100,000 sales a year; on the surface this is hardly a threat to the Big Three, which sell more than 2.3 million pickups a year. But clearly the company sees more potential than that. Down the road, it would like to hold at least 5 percent of the pickup market, meaning a minimum of 125,000 vehicles. "The truck market is huge," said Jack Collins, Nissan's U.S. vice president of product planning. And there's more opportunity if Nissan can achieve the kind of loyalty rates that Toyota and Honda manage. Only about 25–30 percent of Nissan customers are repeat buyers, versus 50 percent at Toyota and about 65 percent at Honda. "Our plan to be a bigger company depends on getting into segments like a full-sized truck," Collins said. But Nissan officials know that unlike Toyota with its pickups or Honda with the Odyssey, Nissan is not going to get a chance to build a starter truck, not with the fierce competition at hand in the market. "Nobody can hide today. But that's healthy," said Connelly. "It's like playing 21 with your cards face up." Nowhere is the gamble bigger than the one that Nissan is taking in Canton, Mississippi, where the pickup went into production in 2003.

The factory, Nissan's second in the United States, sits squarely beside Interstate 55, two and a half hours south of Graceland and just 15 miles outside Jackson, the state capital. It sprawls along Nissan Parkway, all white except for a soaring archway, tiled in red, at the main entrance, and the name "Nissan" in red block letters out front. Inside lies a truly risky endeavor. In this brand-new plant, Nissan is building four brand-new vehicles—Titan, the Quest minivan, and the Nissan and Infiniti SUVs—with a brand-new workforce, most of which has never seen the inside of an automobile plant. And even before the plant built its first pickup or minivan, Nissan announced plans for a second factory here; it will build the Altima sedan, providing the company with a way to meet demand for the car, but also giving Nissan a complex that builds cars, trucks, minivans and SUVs, all on the same grounds. It's a situation fraught with peril, but one that Nissan is attacking with Ghosn's characteristic confidence.

Nobody in the industry questions Nissan's American manufacturing expertise. Even as Nissan's factories in Japan were operating half-full, its plant in Smyrna, Tennessee, outside Nashville, was repeatedly ranked as the most efficient factory in the United States in the annual survey by Harbour & Associates, a Troy, Michigan, consulting firm. In size, Smyrna is reminiscent of the big auto plants of Detroit's glory days, sprawling with long rows of assembly lines where workers toil away on the Altima, Xterra, Maxima and Frontier. Years before its competitors boasted of their ability to do so, Nissan was building cars, pickups and SUVs in one plant, thanks to an assembly system that it called IBAS, or intelligent body assembly system. As the sheet metal pieces came into the welding area, the IBAS system detected which type of vehicle was being made and changed its welding apparatus, which encased the side of the vehicle, so that the robots could perform their tasks. The system looks big and clumsy now compared with the lithe operations at Toyota and Honda, but it did the job, and a smaller version of IBAS has been installed inside the Canton plant to build the trucks, SUVs and minivans. The system isn't the only innovation here.

Nissan is relying heavily on modular assembly, in which entire pieces of the vehicle, such as the instrument panel, arrive at the assembly line prebuilt. It leaves responsibility for assembling the components up to suppliers, who deliver each module as it is needed on the assembly line. Modular assembly thus cuts out steps in the assembly process, meaning the factory can assemble vehicles more quickly, with fewer tasks for workers to perform and, in some parts of the plant, fewer workers. Modular assembly has been tried with varying degrees of success throughout the auto industry in recent years, almost always outside the United States, because of strong opposition to it by the United Auto Workers. GM, in fact, had to scrap plans to assemble a future family of small cars with modular assembly techniques, because of the UAW's outrage at the potential loss of jobs and influence in the production process. But Emil Hassan, in charge of Nissan's manufacturing operations in the United States, said modular assembly is vital for the Canton factory to accomplish what Nissan is setting out to do. "The ones who do it love it. The ones who can't envy those that do," Hassan said. It is a change that would not have been possible had Ghosn not taken on Nissan's *keiretsu* system when he arrived at the company. "The biggest impact that Carlos Ghosn made was walking away from the past," said Hassan. "It's a paradigm shift for Nissan."

Joining the company was an enormous shift for the Canton plant's vice president of manufacturing, David Boyer, who ultimately bears responsibility for the project's success or failure. Scooting around the factory in a yellow golf cart on a gray February afternoon, Boyer stops numerous times to solve problems on the assembly line and to lead a visitor through machinery and up catwalks. He grew up in western Pennsylvania, where he was "one of those kids who knew every model, every year and every make of every car," Boyer recalled. That obsession took him to a job at Ford, where he started as a supervisor trainee in the company's Dearborn, Michigan, iron foundry, and ultimately to Ford's Lima, Ohio, engine plant, where he became a supervisor. But the job he wanted as a plant manager eluded him, and he knew it would take years for him to achieve it, perhaps only by the end of his career. Instead, Boyer joined an automotive supplier and then came to Nissan in Smyrna. When Ghosn approved the truck plant, Hassan appointed Boyer in charge of the project. He knows the stakes involved, he said, as traffic whizzed by on I-55, visible through the windows on the western end of the plant. "The whole company is dependent on this. It's a tremendous investment," he said.

Boyer doesn't sense any conflict between his roots in the industry and the job he has attained working for a Japanese auto company rescued by a French investor. "What's a Japanese car? What's an American car? Parts of every vehicle come from all over the world," Boyer declared. "It's a global industry." And for Boyer, it's a personal dream he never thought he'd achieve when he was at Ford. "It's the opportunity of a lifetime, to go from being a little kid and loving cars to starting a new plant." No matter how daunting the challenge, Boyer said, he knows the company is in good hands. "Everybody believes in Mr. Ghosn," he said.

As big as Nissan's challenge is in Canton, Ghosn has even grander ambitions for the future. As he stood in front of the news conference in Tokyo in May 2002, Ghosn had achieved all of the goals in the Nissan Recovery Plan. "The Nissan Recovery Plan is over," he told the audience. In one year, Nissan had returned to profitability. He had slashed the company's debt below $10 billion. Nissan now dealt with just 400 suppliers, a number of them new to the company, such as Delphi Corp., the world's biggest parts supplier, spun off from General Motors in 1999. There was little fuss made about the plants that Nissan had closed, in part because Japan's desolate economy had forced many companies to take similar actions. But there had been enormous fuss made about Ghosn's success, and more was in store as he laid out the next road map for the company. It was called Nissan 180. The name was meant to visualize not only the direction Nissan has taken from its darkest days, but a plan for moving forward.

The "1" in the plan stands for 1 million additional sales per year that Ghosn wants Nissan to achieve in 2004 compared with 2001, bringing the company to roughly 6 million sales per year worldwide, 40 percent higher than when Ghosn arrived. The "8" is an 8 percent annual profit margin, which Nissan actually achieved in 2001 and exceeded in fiscal 2002, when it earned more than a 10 percent operating margin on its vehicles. That was in the same league as Toyota and Honda, and just below what BMW achieved. By comparison, GM's operating margin in 2002 was 3.7 percent. The "0" stands for zero automotive debt, something that no one could have envisioned when Ghosn arrived, but that occurred in May 2003, causing murmurs of disbelief from Nissan's debt-laden competitors, who questioned whether Nissan's original crisis was truly as deep as Ghosn had depicted it. (Asked about that, he simply laughed.) It is the 1 million additional sales goal that has caught the most attention in the press, particularly because the United States is responsible for about one-third of that increase, or 300,000 more sales per year. Asked which companies Nissan planned to target to take the sales away, Ghosn replied, "I don't care. From anybody." The comment struck some as flip, which Ghosn later acknowledged was a valid reaction. "As long as I say it, it has not a lot of credibility. I think we'll just have to demonstrate it," said Ghosn. "We just have to show it by facts and show it by performance, and I hope now that everybody is convinced that Nissan is out of the hospital." Of that, there is no question. But as 2005 approaches, Ghosn will not be spending so much time tending to Nissan's needs.

As Ghosn was unveiling the 180 plan, Renault announced that Ghosn would become chief executive of both Nissan and Renault when Louis Schweitzer, the architect of the alliance, retires in 2005. Ghosn expects to return to Paris then, where he will attempt to run both companies, jumping over to Tokyo as necessary. He will also spend significant time in the United States, for Ghosn said in 2004 that he was taking charge of Nissan's North American operations as well, rather than assign it to another executive.

Ghosn faces the same doubts over whether his management structure will work as he did with the recovery plan, and as he does now with his Nissan 180 plan. And Ghosn has no illusions over what he will attempt to do. "This is the challenge of our industry. You know that. You have to watch it extremely carefully. You have to be always with your eyes on the ball, and make sure that at no moment you've been caught by complacency or been distracted by anything. And I'm going to tell you, we're going to have a lot of temptation in the future," Ghosn said. Womack, for one, is skeptical that Nissan has really made progress. "They've just gone through the Ford Taurus phase of their crisis," he said, drawing a parallel between Ford in the 1980s and Nissan today. Regardless, Nissan is now in the spotlight as one of the industry's hottest players. In the overabundant way that the industry loves to congratulate its winners, Ghosn himself has been deluged with awards, magazine cover stories and Man of the Year designations from all corners of the globe. (In May 2003, Mississippi Senator Trent Lott dubbed Ghosn a "rock star in the automotive industry" on the day the Canton plant officially opened for business.) Yet beyond the attention, Ghosn faced obstacles. Sales of the Titan, the Armada SUV and the Quest minivan all were disappointing in early 2004. Their quality also was below the industry's average on a report from J.D. Power and Associates that was published that spring. The issues did not sink the company, as some detractors hoped. But they threatened to occupy Ghosn's time as he shifted to running the two companies. They were yet one more reason why he was not stopping to bask in adulation and honors.

Significantly, none of the plaques are on view in his office in the Ginza, and despite the behind-the-scenes sniping at him from his various competitors, Ghosn shows no sign of allowing his determination to flag. If it does, and Nissan stumbles, he knows where to lay the blame: squarely on himself. Because as Ghosn stands alone as the symbol of Nissan, he recognizes that he will have to shoulder the burden if it does not succeed. He will have none of the blame-laying that Detroit executives resort to when the competition proves too fierce. "I'm telling you that always whenever there is a decline, a major reason of decline is yourself," he said in a moment of introspection. "Always, always. I mean, look at this industry. It's never competitive pressure. It's never the economic environment. It's never the weakness of et ceteras. It's always yourself." Not that he expects to fail, for, he confides, "I deliver."

CHAPTER SEVEN

NIBBLING FROM THE BOTTOM AND THE TOP

BMW AND HYUNDAI start at completely opposite ends of the automotive spectrum. One is a venerable maker of German luxury cars that holds an unmatched position in the car market for its breathtakingly fast performance automobiles. The other is an upstart from Korea, earning its reputation for selling bargain cars, accompanied by a generous warranty. But BMW and Hyundai have one very important trait in common. They each want more. BMW, at the top of the automotive market, and Hyundai, at the bottom, are both gunning to expand their presence in the United States during this decade, fueled by vehicles they build, or plan to build, at plants in the United States. As a starting point, they share a confidence that Detroit's auto companies have never been able to achieve. They know exactly who they are. BMW and Hyundai have carefully defined brand images, a clear understanding of why people buy their cars, and strong-willed executives who tune out the criticism and complaints of competing companies to focus on their goals. Both dominate markets where Detroit cannot figure out how to successfully compete, despite numerous attempts and failures. BMW and Hyundai each knows its expansion plans are a gamble, but each knows that it must gamble in order to grow. Importantly, each company knows what it is like to falter, for both companies soared in the late 1980s, only to fall ignominiously during the 1990s. They have both gotten back on their feet, and like Carlos Ghosn at Nissan, they do not plan to stumble again.

BMW and Hyundai, along with other import companies, represent a force that has weakened Detroit during the past decade. With the exception of Toyota and its expansive lineup, none of the import companies has designs on meeting Detroit head-on in every segment where it competes. They don't have to. They can be successful by fixing their targets and taking away markets, one by one. They are doing this by introducing more models, of all types, while Detroit shifts from one extreme to the other, unable to balance its approach in order to meet the competition coming at it from all corners.

Look at what happened to the U.S. car market in the five model years between 1998 and 2002. In 1998, the Detroit companies clearly had more for customers to choose from. According to Edmunds.com, they sold 75 different car nameplates, of all sizes and varieties, from entry level to luxury. They sold 52 different light truck nameplates, including minivans, SUVs and pickup trucks. Import companies lagged far behind. In 1998, they sold 63 different car nameplates and just 27 truck nameplates. In those years, GM, Ford and Chrysler were simultaneously swept by the notion that Americans wanted more light trucks. They rushed to build them, giving short shrift, in the process, to their car lineups. Detroit companies' single-mindedness was like an airplane tipping to one side as all the passengers shift across the aisle to peer out the windows at the sights below. By 2002, the Detroit companies had 74 different truck nameplates on the market, while their car nameplates had dropped to 56. It was almost in inverse proportion to the car and truck mix that they'd had on sale five years earlier, and nowhere was it more striking than among SUVs. In 1998, there were just 12 different Detroit models of sport utilities. By 2002, there were 29.

Import companies jumped into the truck market as well. But significantly, they did not abandon cars to do so. In fact, the variety of both kinds of vehicles had swelled. Five years later, import companies had 88 different car nameplates—now well beyond the number offered by Detroit—on the market, and 49 truck nameplates. In other words, they didn't pick a single lane, like Detroit did. They picked all of them. BMW and Hyundai are just two examples of how import companies managed to keep their dual focus. In 1996, BMW sold only four different nameplates. By 2002, it had eight vehicles in its lineup, including the X5 sport utility. Hyundai, in 1996, had three vehicles in its lineup. By 2002, it had six, including a sport utility called the Santa Fe. For their relatively small size, the 100 percent increase for each was phenomenal. And for both companies, it was only a beginning.

———————

Hyundai Motor Co. sells fewer vehicles per year in the United States than the number of Camrys sold by Toyota, or the Accords sold by Honda. But Hyundai has everybody in the auto industry on edge, the Japanese nameplates included, because it is having as much influence on the cheaper end of the market as BMW is having on the more prestigious end. Finbarr O'Neill, its American chief executive until 2003, put in place a set of sweeping ideas for Hyundai's lineup that were paying off handsomely by 2004, even though O'Neill had left to become head of Mitsubishi's struggling American operations. Of medium height, stocky, with dark hair and a seemingly reserved manner, O'Neill possesses a dry wit and the ability to get across a pointed quip that can be as startling as his clear ambition for Korea's biggest car company. In 2002, Hyundai had its best year in history, selling just over 360,000 cars in the United States, and it might have sold more if it had fully used the manufacturing capacity at its Korean factories. That alone was remarkable, given that poor quality and a limited lineup had caused its sales to fall to less than one-quarter of that number in 1998. But O'Neill was not satisfied. By 2005, he wanted Hyundai to sell 500,000 vehicles a year in the United States. And O'Neill was aiming for Hyundai's U.S. sales to approach 1 million vehicles by 2010, which would make it bigger than Mitsubishi or Mazda, and roughly the same size as Nissan. That would be more than 10 times what Hyundai sold in the United States in 1998, the year O'Neill was promoted from behind the scenes to take charge of the floundering auto company.

O'Neill, who laid out his ambitions for the first time during an interview on a sultry September 2002 afternoon, admitted that Hyundai's expansion would take some doing. For one thing, Hyundai might need to build another manufacturing plant beyond the factory that is under construction outside Montgomery, Alabama. And O'Neill knew Hyundai would have to expand its truck lineup to include more sport utility vehicles beyond just the Santa Fe. But he felt it was time to lay his sales targets right out on the table so that everyone could see them and get used to the idea that his company was planning to grow aggressively over the coming years by expanding beyond the assumptions that everyone had about it. And even before he gets there, the conventional view of Hyundai as simply a seller of low-priced automobiles, whose buyers can't afford anything else, is beginning to change.

In the course of just a few months during late 2002 and early 2003, Hyundai was paid two of the highest and most unexpected compliments it had ever received. On a Monday in late October 2002, General Motors called a handful of journalists to alert them that one of its veteran executives, William Lovejoy, had announced his retirement and was willing to talk to them in a brief telephone conference call. Talking to Lovejoy, who had never lost his broad East Coast accent during all his years in Detroit, was always a treat because he had a knack for saying the unexpected. Since Lovejoy was in charge of GM's sales operations, it was natural, after the pleasantries were over, to ask him about GM's chances of meeting the 29 percent market share goal that it had set for 2002. GM had been blasting the market all year with zero percent financing and hefty incentives in its bid to gain momentum. It had spotted a rare opportunity presented by weakness at Ford, which seemed unable to get out of a lingering slump. And by all rights, GM could have expected to steal a sizable chunk of Ford's market share, which seemed ripe for the picking. It would wind up losing 1.5 percentage points in 2002, a virtual hemorrhage given that auto companies fight hard over every tenth of a point. But to GM's dismay, cars and trucks from import nameplates had a banner 2002. They were managing to post sales increases and gain market share without having to meet the GM deals. Though the incentives had helped GM's sales remain strong into the summer, GM's sales had begun lagging in the fall, and analysts were seeing evidence in the slower sales rate that the incentives were losing their steam.

Lovejoy reminded the journalists that the 29 percent goal was a "stretch" target, something that the company designed as a rallying point but that nobody realistically thought could be achieved. GM sets such targets almost every year, generally keeping them under wraps so as not to overstress their importance. However, GM took no such pains in 2002 to keep the target a secret. Lapel pins bearing the number 29 had popped up among GM executives' ranks that summer like dandelions after a rainstorm, and the word around Detroit was that the chief executive, Rick Wagoner, had a pin that read 30, because he wanted the company to stretch even more. Lovejoy, however, seemed bent on dampening expectations. "I'm not going to make a prediction, but 29 percent is going to be a stretch to get there," he said. Then Lovejoy added, joking, "If the competition would just play a little fairer, we could do it." Everyone laughed, and the matter might have been dropped if Lovejoy had simply left it right there. But later on in the news conference, Lovejoy was asked who wasn't playing fair. Instead of ducking the question, he answered it in his typical blunt fashion. The problem lay with Korean automakers, Lovejoy said, especially the largest player, Hyundai. Its lineup of increasingly respectable if bland cars and sport utilities, and its 10-year, 100,000-mile warranty, gave consumers confidence in its vehicles. Such a combination was "difficult for us to match," said Lovejoy. "It's one of the reasons they came out of nowhere to pick up three, four points of share."

In that moment, on that October day, the world's largest auto company went public with what people in Detroit had been saying behind the scenes for months: Hyundai was something to worry about. Further proof of the danger that Hyundai posed came a few months later, when *Consumer Reports* magazine, a bible for educated, quality-conscious customers, came out with its April 2003 issue, which contained its annual car-buying guide. Hyundai had made a "striking turnaround" during the past 10 years, the magazine's quality survey showed. In 2002, Hyundai ranked with the best Japanese auto companies for the first time, just behind Toyota and tied with Honda, and well ahead of the automakers from Detroit. Hyundai could no longer be ignored by anyone, especially the companies from Japan, whose buyers were already attuned to buying import nameplates, and who would be the most likely to check out Hyundai's vehicles as an alternative when they were out shopping. Said Nissan's Carlos Ghosn, "Worried, I would not say. But we are watching them very closely."

The best view of Hyundai's future can be seen in a pair of new buildings, one completed in fall 2003, the other due to be completed by 2004. The first sits on a street corner a few miles from Hyundai's American headquarters. It is the $25 million California Design and Technical Center that Hyundai shares with its sister company, Kia, which it acquired in 1998. The design center houses 150 designers, engineers and others involved in creating cars for the two Korean brands. They had been squashed into Hyundai's headquarters building in Fountain Valley, a modern, low-rise building that sits sheltered off Interstate 405 about an hour south of Los Angeles. The headquarters building, while fine for a sales operation, doesn't have the facilities that the designers need. But the new building does, including an outdoor courtyard so that designers can gauge how their dreams look in the sun, revolving turntables big enough to hold the largest vehicles in the industry, so that a car can be examined from every angle, and a whole host of computer-aided technology linked to Hyundai's engineering centers in Korea and in Ann Arbor, Michigan. Along with the design center, Hyundai is building a $1 billion assembly plant outside Montgomery, where it will produce Santa Fe sport utilities, the Sonata mid-sized car and vehicles that it isn't talking about yet. The design center and the plant are the last two pieces in an 18-year effort to vault Hyundai into the ranks of major automobile companies selling cars in the United States. All this is similar to what Japanese auto companies did when they arrived in America, but with a sharp difference: It is happening much, much faster than it did for Toyota, Honda or Nissan. They kept a low profile while they grew. Hyundai is not so reticent and not nearly so patient. Whereas it took Toyota 10 years to sell 100,000 cars a year, Hyundai reached that mark in its first seven months on the market in the United States. But staying consistent was another matter.

By 2003, Hyundai was actually on its second try at getting a foothold in the U.S. car market. It had roared off to a fast start when it reached the American car market in 1986, less than a decade after the company was founded in Korea. Hyundai is part of the far-flung

Hyundai business empire, called a *chaebol*, whose creator, the industrialist Chung Ju-Yung, made billions by turning Hyundai into the world's largest shipping company. Chung was born in 1915, the oldest son in a Korean peasant family. At 18, he left home for Seoul, where he worked in a myriad of jobs, building railroads, working on docks and training as a bookkeeper. His first venture opened in 1938, when he started his own rice store. That lasted only a year. Chung was forced to close his business by Japanese forces, who had occupied Korea at the start of World War II. As with Toyota, the American military helped Chung get on his feet after the war. He went into the truck repair business, fixing vehicles for the U.S. armed forces. After the Korean War, he saw shipbuilding as a ticket to success and managed to convince a customer to pay him tens of millions of dollars for a vessel, although he had yet to build his first ship. With his empire up and running in the 1960s, Chung decided Koreans should someday have the opportunity to purchase locally made vehicles rather than imports from Japan, whose auto industry was performing with vigor. In 1967, he founded the Hyundai Motor Co., and a year later he signed a licensing agreement with Ford to sell its automobiles in Korea. The deal gave Hyundai access to Ford's vehicles, which it studied with an eye to building its own. Six years later, Hyundai showed its first car, the Pony, a subcompact that had been designed for it by the Giugaro studios in Turin, Italy, among the finest automotive designers in the world. Soon after, Hyundai began building what would be the world's largest automotive manufacturing complex, in Ulsan, Korea, with three automobile assembly plants employing more than 10,000. At that time, Hyundai had no demonstrable need for that much capacity in Korea, where the automobile market was still developing. But Chung had another strategy. He launched what would turn out to be an aggressive campaign to sell its cars outside Korea. By the early 1980s, Hyundai was exporting to Guatemala, El Salvador and Canada. The United States would soon be next.

Flush with cash and prosperity from a booming economy and the then-soaring stock market, American consumers in the 1980s were willing to buy just about anything, especially when it was cheap. They bought the Yugo in droves despite its shoddy reputation, and when Hyundai turned up in 1985, selling the small Excel, they flocked to its cars, too. Hyundai's lineup turned out to be better than that of its competitor from behind the Iron Curtain, although it trailed the best Japanese cars. That didn't seem to matter at first. Fueled by the small Excel, the compact Elantra and the mid-sized Sonata, Hyundai's U.S. sales jumped above 180,000 a year by the early 1990s. Detroit companies paid little notice. They had long ago given up on the low-price end of the market, ceding it to the Japanese, or else making halfhearted attempts to compete with cars such as the Ford Escort and the Chevrolet Chevette. If the foreign companies wanted to focus on small cars, Detroit reasoned, that was no threat, since it was almost impossible to make a profit on them anyway.

As if to prove Detroit right, the excitement over Hyundai burned itself out quickly, first and foremost because of its cars' quality problems. Even when those were addressed, Hyundai's banal lineup and its lack of SUVs, whose popularity mushroomed as the 1990s went on, combined to dampen interest. Hyundai tried to combat its image as a bare-bones maker of small, medium and large vehicles by showing concept vehicles at the world's auto shows and introducing niche models like the Tiburon coupe. But by 1998, Hyundai's sales in the United States had plummeted to only 90,000 a year, and the betting was on as to how long it would last. Dealers were defecting in droves, with more than 100 closing up their franchises. Hyundai, which in 1998 had bought its Korean competitor, Kia, was staggering under the complexity of combining the two companies. It was on the verge of pulling out of the American market when O'Neill became its U.S. president, vowing a turnaround. He ordered a series of immediate changes, the most important of which became Hyundai's trademark: the 10-year, 100,000-mile warranty, among the most generous ever offered in the industry. It was meant to assure consumers that dealers would handle any significant problems, and to give them confidence in the brand. "It addresses the emotional need for reassurance," O'Neill said. And it was truly canny marketing. "Let's face it," said Jim Hall, vice president of AutoPacific Group, an industry consulting firm, "one of the things that put them on the map was the warranty." Moreover, the potential expense was actually not that great. For one thing, Hyundai had been working on its quality for several years, so when the warranty became available, its cars' defect levels had diminished. For another, the warranty was available only to the original owner of the vehicle, meaning that by the time any real issues cropped up five or six years down the road, the car had most likely been sold or traded in.

The warranty bought time and attracted attention, while O'Neill set off behind the scenes to convince Hyundai's Korean management to give the American organization better vehicles. He sensed a true opportunity for Hyundai—namely, as a producer of inexpensive vehicles of decent quality—and he wanted to aggressively explore it. He could see that Toyota, Honda and Nissan, as well as the companies from Detroit, were losing interest in selling cars at the bottom end of the market. The rush to SUVs and other light trucks had sent the average price of an automobile soaring close to $20,000, double what a vehicle had cost only a decade before. That meant a number of customers, working families on budgets and young singles just starting out, would be unable to afford new cars. Their only option would be used vehicles, and O'Neill thought there should be an alternative for them. In spotting his opening, O'Neill was using many of the lessons that he had learned at Toyota, where he had begun his automotive career in the 1970s. But his path to the industry was unusual, to say the least.

O'Neill was born in Cookstown, Northern Ireland, 50 miles west of Belfast, in 1952, and was raised in a primitive stone farmhouse. At age 10, he immigrated with his mother and three of his brothers to the

Bronx, where his father worked as a bus driver. "Northern Ireland hadn't recovered from the depression of World War II, and it was rural and conservative," O'Neill recalled, his voice carrying a trace of an Irish lilt. "I can tell you it was culture shock, moving to the Bronx." And lively. His parents had three more children, two girls and a boy, after they reunited. O'Neill was sent to Catholic schools, including St. Nicholas Tolentine High School, where he thought about becoming an engineer and studied calculus and chemistry. But he learned that "just because you have good SAT scores in math doesn't make you an engineer." Instead, upon being accepted at Columbia University, he chose to study political science, an interest fueled by heated discussions at home around the dinner table. His interests led him to law school at Fordham in New York, where a classmate was Charles Carberry, a former U.S. assistant attorney who made his reputation helping prosecutor Rudolph Giuliani chase down insider traders. "One thing about Finn, he's very responsible," Carberry said about his friend. "You always know where you stand with him." Graduating from Fordham, O'Neill spent seven years at Skadden Arps Slate Meagher & Flom, a prestigious New York firm, where he specialized in antitrust work.

He might never have wound up in the automobile industry except for a desire to travel. Having spent his entire life in the city, O'Neill wanted to find a job elsewhere. One evening in 1983, he was running his finger down the classified ad column in the *Wall Street Journal* and he spotted a notice placed by Toyota's U.S. sales operations, based in Torrance, California. The distant location intrigued him. "It was like the Saul Steinberg cartoon of New York and the rest of the world," O'Neill recalled. "I didn't know from Torrance, California, but I sent my résumé in." Toyota hired him to run its litigation department, and he spent the next two years there, before receiving an offer from a market newcomer. Hyundai had not yet announced its plans to enter the United States, and thus O'Neill got into the operation on the ground floor. "Before there was a Hyundai, there was a Finbarr," he quipped. "I didn't know if Hyundai could sell one car. But I was young enough that I could take the risk. And it was an interesting ride." The founding group was so small that "we could hold our weekly management meetings at a Chinese restaurant and all fit at one table," said Jack Collins, the Nissan product development executive who joined Hyundai at the same time O'Neill did. But with the arrival of the Excel and the rest of Hyundai's lineup, the company took off like a skyrocket. And just like fireworks, Hyundai's American success exploded and quickly faded. It tried during the mid-1990s to respond with incentives, loading its already inexpensive vehicles with deep discounts that brought prices below $10,000. But customers stayed away, dealers began to defect and Jay Leno was using Hyundai as a subject for jokes on *The Tonight Show* almost every evening. Hyundai's Korean management had been supportive throughout the crisis, continuing to invest money in new vehicles, but it realized dramatic change was necessary. "The company had to take stock in ourselves. We needed a reason for being. We had to come to grips with the question of whether we could survive in this market, selling only 91,000 cars a year," O'Neill said. "The experience had kind of a crystallizing effect. When you look over the edge of the precipice, you refine what you need to do."

Hyundai's first tactic for fighting back was its warranty. Its second tactic was to figure out what it could offer the car market that nobody else was offering. The answer came in a single word: value. In the automobile industry, *value* is often a code word for cheap, and certainly in Detroit's eyes, that's what Hyundai cars are. While the average price of a vehicle built by GM, Ford and Chrysler now costs more than $25,000, Hyundai's cars start at less than $10,000 for the Excel. Its vehicles generally are priced at about $2,000 less than their counterparts from Japan, and the price gap gets even more impressive as Hyundai cars go up in size. Hyundai's top-of-the-line XG 350 sedan costs only $25,000, even though it competes with BMW and Lexus models that cost $10,000 more, making the XG 350 one of the real bargains on the car market. Since all of Hyundai's U.S.-market vehicles are built in Korea and then shipped, executives from around the auto industry, not just from Detroit, have been quick to pin Hyundai's price advantage on the weak Korean currency, the won. They also blame government policies that they say deliberately keep the prices of Korean goods low.

But Hyundai vehicles, no matter how cheap, would not appeal to customers if they were dismal. Hyundai learned that lesson in the 1990s. O'Neill contends that the company's strength lies not only in its vehicles' prices or the warranty, but also in the fact that they are solidly built and offer a lot for the money, which, he says, is the very definition of the word *value*. In defining Hyundai, O'Neill likes to look at the retailing business. In Detroit, people scoff and say that Hyundai is the industry's equivalent of Wal-Mart, or maybe Sam's Club, where customers don't even get shopping bags in which to lug their purchases home. O'Neill prefers to compare his company to Target, which has taken the discount department store and turned it into a haven for style, albeit at an affordable price. Another analogy is with the airline business. If the Detroit companies are the big players, like American and United and Northwest, then Hyundai is Southwest Airlines, scrappy, fun, giving customers something for their money at an undeniable bargain price. O'Neill sees a lot of parallels with the people who shop at Target and fly Southwest. This isn't the kind of buyer that Detroit has tried to attract with flash and sheet metal, he says. The Hyundai customer, O'Neill says, is most likely somebody who doesn't care very much about cars. It's extraordinary to hear the chief executive of a car company talk about his customers this way: O'Neill defines who buys Hyundais with a candor that most CEOs lack. But O'Neill knows exactly who is buying Hyundais: "salt-of-the-earth people," he calls them.

"There is a whole market of people who have a quiet confidence about life," he explained during a conversation in his office in

Hyundai's Fountain Valley, California, headquarters that took place before he left for Mitsubishi. "They have a certain sense of satisfaction about how things fit in and enable their lives. A car is just a part of that." Hyundai buyers simply don't respond to the kind of tactics that Detroit has always tried to employ with its customers: playing on their emotions, playing on their sense of excitement, making them lust after new vehicles and what they represent, making them crave them in a primal way. O'Neill, for his part, simply doesn't buy into the traditional definition of "emotion" that shapes the way Detroit sees the world. His buyers are not making their decisions based on that, because a Hyundai customer, male or female, does not express his or her personality primarily through automobiles. "They have other outlets for that," O'Neill says of his buyers. "They have a sense of what life is about. They are connected with their families. It's not the automobile, it's their lifestyles that make their statements. The car, for them, is not sex appeal or the genius of great designers," said O'Neill. That might sound as if Hyundai customers view automobiles as toasters or television sets, and it's a prospect that would send chills down the backs of Detroit's executives. But in fact, O'Neill believes that the Hyundai buyer has more in common with the state of mind of the typical American consumer today than with the mythical, passion-driven buyer that Detroit has traditionally chased. He believes that is a reason why Americans have embraced Toyota and Honda with growing enthusiasm over the past 25 years.

To O'Neill, there is a kind of emotion other than just a superficial sexiness. He completely rejects the thought of "gotta have it" automobiles, the approach that GM, under its product czar, Robert Lutz, is applying to its product lineup. That has a "very short shelf life. It's based on visceral reactions," said O'Neill. "The question that has to be answered is, 'Has it got legs?' A car has to resonate with buyers. It has to meet a real need." Now that Toyota and Honda have broadened their lineups, gone up in price, and in essence abandoned the market for inexpensive cars, Hyundai has hustled right in to fill the gap. But O'Neill knows that he cannot sell toasters forever, no matter how good they are. For buyers' tastes evolve and their expectations grow as well. Rather than offer Hyundai as a step-up brand to them, O'Neill is counting on Hyundai to broaden its lineup as well, in its own way. Through the rest of the decade, he foresees adding more SUVs to the mix, along with a minivan and a crossover vehicle, which would compete in the same category as the Toyota Highlander. He also is thinking about how Hyundai and Kia will mesh their lineups. Through 2003, the two companies maintained separate sales operations, and that's expected to remain the case in the United States for some time to come. However, Hyundais and Kias are going to share the same platforms, or underpinnings, and that presents a challenge in making them look and drive differently from each other. Differentiation is key, because right now the two brands compete head-on in a number of areas.

The trick will be to aim Hyundai and Kia at slightly different customers, instead of fighting for the same consumers. One idea would be to have Kia develop sportier vehicles and limited-edition niche models, like two-seater sports cars and coupes, leaving Hyundai to be a more traditional parent company. It will all have to be sorted out. O'Neill, seeing the market in his unusual way, knows that the rest of the auto industry is just waiting for Hyundai to slip up. In the spring of 2003, when Hyundai's sales rose by only single-digit levels instead of by the leaps that they grew in previous years, there was a sense of *Schadenfreude* among the Detroit companies that perhaps Hyundai's moment of buzz had passed. O'Neill saw it as more of a pause after some very strenuous years. But he says, "We don't have a lot of forgiveness. If we miss the market, it will impact our ability to introduce world-class products." So precision is the key—not trying to be what any other company is in the marketplace. Only, says O'Neill, to be what Hyundai is.

O'Neill's legacy has already borne fruit at Hyundai. In 2004,

Hyundai leapt past all of Detroit's carmakers, all the European brands and most Japanese brands to score some of the highest marks on J.D. Power and Associates' initial quality study. The performance left Detroit companies in shock, and startled Toyota, whose Toyota brand was beaten by Hyundai even through Lexus kept its lead. It was further indication that despite Detroit's disdain, O'Neill had gotten the job done.

———————

The Mini Cooper came to life as a certifiably hot car. In the spring of 2003, more than a year after it went on sale in the United States, Mini dealers still had waiting lists for the car. It wasn't so much the Mini's cost—a decked-out version could be had for $24,000—as the fact that it was rare. Only 25,000 are supposed to be sold each year, but it was clear from the outset that there were far more potential buyers than available supply. The Mini's success was striking given that it was almost impossible for the U.S. market as a whole to have any fond memories of the car, since only 20,000 had ever been sold in the United States during the decades that the original car was on the market. But by the end of the first year of the revived car, more Minis had been sold in the United States than ever had been in its history. The Mini was a gamble that had clearly paid off for Bayerische Motoren Werke AG, otherwise known as BMW, the German auto company that acquired the British brand when it bought England's venerable carmaker Rover in the 1990s. BMW had since sold off Rover, which had been a financial disaster, but it held on to Mini and transformed it into a modern car with every electronic comfort and safety feature that a buyer could want, combined with nostalgia for the swinging sixties.

Nobody was more delighted at the Mini's success than Helmut Panke, BMW's chief executive, who had been one of its strongest champions. Outwardly, Panke seems gaunt, stern, the epitome of a

Teutonic executive. But underneath, he bubbles with enthusiasm for automobiles like a young boy. In August 2002, a few months after the car had gone on sale, Panke confided that he often took a Mini Cooper home on weekends to drive around the foothills of the Bavarian Alps near BMW's Munich headquarters. Given that Panke could have his choice of any vehicle in BMW's august lineup, it surprised both BMW's engineers and passersby that the lanky chief executive would be seen in a Mini rather than one of BMW's performance cars. But, said Panke, the reaction was always the same—smiles, none broader than his own, and for good reason.

Although the Mini is sold separately from BMW, with its own Web site and its own dealers, the car is a key element of BMW's strategy to expand its sales in the United States during the rest of this decade. BMW's goal is to sell 300,000 luxury cars a year in the United States—which would vault it past Lexus as the country's top-selling luxury brand—and for its sales to approach 1.5 million a year worldwide. Both seem well within reach, for with the addition of the Mini, BMW sold about 260,000 cars in the United States in 2002, while its global sales were above 1 million vehicles. On its trek, BMW has already pushed past Mercedes-Benz, which dominated the U.S. luxury car market during the mid- to late 1990s, to grab second place behind Lexus.

But Panke's target isn't simply volume. If his strategy of adding vehicles to both the bottom and the top of BMW's lineup pays off, BMW would evolve beyond its traditional role as a specialty maker of expensive cars appealing only to wealthy customers and those consumed with passion for the road. It has designs on a much broader market, in which consumers of all ages and incomes would find what they wanted in BMW showrooms. Mini was a key element in executing that strategy. And to Panke, Mini's remarkable debut year was proof that his strategy was sound. Consumers ranging in age from 20 to 90 were coming into show-rooms to take them home, and an astounding 80 percent of them were new to BMW, he said. Someone had even traded a huge Hummer H2 sport utility, considered the other car of the moment in the automotive world, for a Mini, which appeared as a convertible in 2004. There could be no better endorsement of how well it was working, Panke said.

But there is lots of disagreement in the auto industry about whether BMW is headed in the right direction. To purists, BMW's expansion into unknown territory was at odds with everything it stood for in the automobile industry. BMW may not appeal to every-one, but there is no clearer definition from any car company of what it stands for: the ultimate driving machine, as its slogan maintains. BMWs have their own distinctive ride and handling. The acceleration is like that of a private jet, swift and smooth. The driver feels the road and has control of the car. It is not the quiet comfort of a Lexus, or the dominance of a Mercedes-Benz. A BMW has real driving character backed by almost 90 years of heritage in performance cars, racing, motorcycles and airplane engines. And it appeals to customers who tend to know a lot about cars. Panke calls them "connoisseurs" rather than customers. One of them is Joe Hammell, who works in technol-ogy sales in suburban Atlanta. A lifelong car buff whose father owned a succession of Pontiacs, Hammell has never owned an American car, starting with a Volkswagen Golf and working his way up to a BMW 530i, which he purchased in 2002. His belief in the superiority of import nameplates runs so deep that he insists on them during his business travels. "In my profile at Hertz, it says 'anything but a Tau-rus,'" Hammell said. He actually resisted buying a BMW because there are so many these days in his upscale neighborhood. "Everyone in Atlanta has a 5-series, either silver, white or black. They're like Chevro-lets down here," Hammell said. But he chose the BMW simply because "it's the best car out there for the money. American cars can go fast, but they can't turn or stop [the way a BMW can]," Hammell said.

The company that became BMW was founded in Munich in 1913 by an entrepreneur named Karl Rapp, who turned his bicycle factory into a plant producing aircraft engines. He couldn't get them to stop vibrating, so he dropped his own design and acquired a license to build Austro-Daimler aircraft engines. Just down the road from Rapp was a fellow entrepreneur, Gustav Otto, who had a small aircraft factory. The two combined their operations in 1916, just in time for World War I, the first time that airplanes were used in combat. They kept separate names for the engine and aircraft companies, but in 1922, the pair officially formed BMW. The legacy of the aircraft engine company lives on in BMW's famous blue and white logo, which is meant to represent an airplane propeller. Throughout the 1920s, BMW focused on aircraft engines and its motorcycles, capitalizing on a growing craze in Europe for motorcycle racing, and in the process pushing well past 100 miles an hour—a stunning accomplishment given that the average automobile at the time could barely climb above 35 mph. But in 1928, the company bought a car factory in Eisenach, in eastern Germany. Along with it came a license to build a small car named the Dixi, which BMW displayed at the Berlin Motor Show. BMW moved further into cars, and in 1936 it introduced the first of the automobiles that would prove to be the building blocks of its performance heritage: the 328 roadster.

It snapped up racing titles before World War II, including the famed Mille Miglia race through Italy, and is considered to be one of the most influential sports cars in industry history, both for its speed and its aerodynamic shape. Almost every two-seater built since owes something to the styling of the 328, which had a long hood, sported low-slung seats set close to the road, and simply looked fast. The war intervened, and with automobile production stopped, BMW focused again on aviation, producing some of the world's first jet engines. Pro-

hibited by Allied occupying forces from resuming production immediately after the war, and with its Munich factory destroyed in bomb-
ing raids, BMW did not reintroduce motorcycles until 1949 and did
not return to the car market until 1951.

The 1950s brought some memorable vehicles, like the little Isetta, a
car that had a front door that swung open where the hood normally
would be, as well as larger sedans. But the 1950s almost spelled BMW's
doom. Out of cash, the company was considering a merger with
Daimler-Benz in 1959 when its largest shareholder, Herbert Quandt,
intervened to purchase control, beginning a new era for the company.

The Quandt family is often likened to the Ford family for the
active role that it continues to play in BMW's operations. But there are
a number of significant differences. The Quandts can buy and sell the
Fords many times over. The family, which now consists of Herbert
Quandt's widow, Johanna, her daughter, Suzanne, and her son, Stefan, is estimated to be worth at least $35 billion, as against roughly $8
billion or so for the third, fourth and fifth generations of Fords combined. The Quandts, moreover, are extremely secretive. Johanna
Quandt, who was Herbert's secretary before their marriage, secludes
herself in a villa outside Frankfurt. Though Suzanne and her brother,
Stefan, have board seats and a deep interest in the company, they
almost never discuss BMW affairs. Neither one would dream of taking
management control of their auto company, as Bill Ford did, or utter-
ing pronouncements about the way it is run. The Quandts' views generally are communicated through a family spokesman, who in recent
years has stuck to a single line: BMW is not for sale. That is important,
because BMW is one of the few auto companies in the world that is
not involved in joint-ownership agreements—the other being Honda.
And it is not lost on anybody in the industry that both BMW and
Honda earned their reputations first as motorcycle companies, or that

there was a personal involvement in both companies, from Honda at Honda and the Quandts at BMW. The Quandts' confidence in BMW is a key reason why the company was able to grow and prosper throughout the last 30 years of the twentieth century.

Most Americans, except perhaps avid car enthusiasts, weren't aware of BMW until it brought out its 3-series cars in 1975. It was a breakthrough for BMW, which saw an opportunity to expand its sales around the world with a smaller version of its performance cars. Thanks to the shock of the 1973 Arab oil embargo, people who wouldn't have considered owning a small luxury car up until then now were open to the idea. Many were willing to sacrifice size as long as they got some performance in return. The 3-series came to the United States in 1977, and by 1978 it was a recognized hit, raising BMW's global profile. In 1974, BMW sold only 184,000 cars worldwide. In 1978, thanks to Americans' embrace of the 3-series, BMW's sales around the world topped 320,000. It owed its success to a new category of American consumers that were emerging in the post-Vietnam era—the young urban professional, or yuppie.

With the explosion in the high-tech sector, the go-go stock market and a general sense of wealth that swept the country during the early years of the Reagan administration, yuppies seemed to be everywhere, spending their money in a deluge of conspicuous consumption. BMW fit right into their needs for status and excitement. There were no Cadillacs or Lincolns that could compete. Both companies still had lineups laden with either large cars that simply had no chic, or downsized cars that lacked the integrity, handling and character of the German models. Though Mercedes had been selling its cars in the United States for decades, it was perceived as dull by the most fashionable young consumers. BMW, by contrast, was fast, small and cool. "The 1980s yuppies didn't want to be seen as the stodgy executive who drives a Mercedes, they wanted to be seen as the rapidly rising, dynamic go-getter who drives a much hipper Bimmer," said Karl Brauer of Edmunds.com.

BMW set a U.S. sales record in 1986, and with the addition of the mid-sized 5-series and the intimidating 7-series to its lineup, it looked as if its success would be unstoppable. But it didn't last.

By the late 1980s, BMW faced serious competition for the first time, not only from Mercedes but from the Japanese luxury brands. It argued that it had heritage, something that Lexus, Infiniti and Acura lacked. But the Japanese cars' quality was far better than the German cars', and their prices were lower. "When you had a 3-series that cost nearly $30,000 in 1989 and a new, rear-drive, V-8-powered Lexus sedan available for the same amount, it was hard to deny the fact that BMWs were basically overpriced," Brauer said. BMW struggled to keep pace, with a management that was divided over which direction to take: stay German and pure and risk seeing the U.S. market slip away from their grasp, or take some of the same actions the Japanese did— namely, improve quality, keep prices reasonable and explore more-efficient ways of production. BMW decided to take the latter course. And one of the key people who pushed it in that direction was Panke.

In a company dominated by the industry's most talented automotive engineers, who spend their entire careers at the Munich company, Panke is an anomaly. He is, in fact, a nuclear engineer who came to the auto company in 1982 from the German branch of McKinsey & Co., the global consulting firm. As head of corporate planning in the late 1980s and early 1990s, Panke could see that BMW's fate would be tied up with the United States. And to really compete, he felt it needed to join other import auto companies in building a plant there. Panke himself set off across the American South, talking to people at churches and truck stops, asking about the quality of the schools and whether there was a good work ethic. He became enamored of South Carolina, particularly the Spartanburg-Greenville area, where Michelin had built its headquarters and where Carlos Ghosn lived. There was friendliness about the place, and a willingness on the part of the South Carolina government to play ball with incentives and other training money that the company was seeking. Panke convinced BMW's aristocratic chief executive, Eberhard von Kuhnheim, to select a site near Greer, South Carolina, for the factory. He got more than a plant out of the deal—Von Kuhnheim placed Panke in charge of BMW's American sales operations at the same time.

Working from BMW's headquarters in Montvale, New Jersey, Panke became convinced that the auto company needed to get into the market for SUVs. But if building a plant in the United States was a risk, an SUV was almost heresy to many company loyalists. Unlike Mercedes, which had produced the hulking Gelandeswagen sport utility, as well as commercial vans and even taxicabs, BMW had never strayed from its mission to produce performance cars. Moreover, there was little demand in Europe for SUVs, for they were too big, too difficult to park and too inefficient. But Panke believed that the auto company was losing customers in the United States because it did not have one. Just as Nissan found that its owners were purchasing Detroit's pickup trucks, and Honda discovered that its owners were buying Chrysler minivans, Panke's research showed that one in four BMW owners had an SUV in their garage, most often a Jeep Grand Cherokee or a Ford Explorer. He knew there would be an opportunity and pushed BMW management to go there. The result was the X5, perhaps the most controversial vehicle that BMW had ever introduced.

Despite the uproar over the vehicle, the X5 struck an immediate chord with BMW owners, nailing two characteristics that defined BMW: speed and the distinctive BMW kidney-shaped style. Nobody would mistake the X5 for anything but a BMW.

Bringing out the X5 proved nothing was out of bounds for Panke. And he is proving it over and over again, taking assumptions about BMW and smashing them. Since becoming chief executive in 2002, he has set the auto industry on its ear with what he is doing with the BMW lineup. The best example is the BMW 7-series sedan, BMW's flagship sedan and one of its most prestigious vehicles, which it completely overhauled for the 2003 model year. While it is just as fast and smooth at 90 mph as BMWs before it, the 7-series has caused intense debate, both for the way the vehicle looks and for the way it operates. For one thing, it has no key. It has only an ignition fob, like the small remote-control device that unlocks car doors and trunk lids that many vehicles now come with. There is a slot on the dashboard where a driver inserts this fob. Then, stepping on the brake pedal, the driver starts the car by pushing a button (shades of the starter buttons that were a feature of automobiles in the industry's early years). Don't look for a standard-size gearshift lever on the steering wheel, or a shifter on the console between the seats. Instead, there is a tiny lever that has to be carefully toggled back and forth, from park, into reverse, neutral and drive. There also are no controls for the sound system, buttons for the navigation system, or dials for the heating and air-conditioning beyond one for the fan. All that is controlled by a big matte aluminum dial between the seats that is pushed, twisted and turned according to a complicated series of instructions found in the thick owner's manual. (The only simple thing is opening the gas compartment to refill the tank. It doesn't require a lever in the floor or a key to unlock. The driver only has to press gently on the little door for it to pop open.)

All of this technology is grouped together under a heading called "iDrive," which BMW contends results in an all-electronic car, more sophisticated and more robust than any vehicle ever before. What it's resulted in is confusion, frustration and jokes. "iDrive?" said a headline in *Road & Track* magazine. "No, you drive while I fiddle with the controller." There are even Post-it notes for valet parking attendants, with instructions on how to start the thing, although by spring 2003 valets in Beverly Hills, used to wealthy buyers owning the latest thing, simply shrugged when a motorist drove up in a $70,000 7-series. "We get a lot of those," said the attendant outside the Fairmont Miramar on Wilshire Boulevard in Santa Monica (although the blasé attitude didn't keep the attendant from misplacing the key fob, later setting off a frantic search through the hotel's key rack for it). The technology might be enough of a jolt, but along with iDrive, BMW substantially restyled the 7-series, giving it a rear end that looked lumpy compared with the tautness of past BMW posteriors. All this combined to make people wonder if BMW had begun creating cars for itself and forgetting what customers would be comfortable driving.

Asked about it at the 2003 Detroit Auto Show, Panke likened the change in the looks of the 7-series to the way the National Basketball League has evolved during the past 20 years. Think about players like Bill Bradley or Larry Bird, and compare them with the way Michael Jordan moved on the court, Panke suggested. Why should cars look the same as they used to? "Design is nothing static," he said. "It is an organic growth. We're shaping the future by making design statements as a corporate philosophy." The cars that BMW designed for 2005 "would not look like the eighties. And nor would they look like 2002. This is a bold shift. We are moving away from the design direction of the previous 7-series," Panke said.

The executive who oversees BMW's design staff is an American, Chris Bangle, who has become one of the industry's most talked-about figures, both for his results and for his attitude. Bangle is from Wausau, Wisconsin, a town that was founded by logging barons and has since become best known as the home of the big insurance company. Bangle hasn't lost his midwestern accent, although his conversation is dotted with German and he is married to a Swiss woman. What he has gained is an audacity that is as much American as anything else—and in which Panke takes delight. Bangle, born in 1956, is basically imposing his own sense of style on a company whose cars, from the 1970s through the present day, are basically all in the same mode: sporty, expensive, heavy and daunting. He is known for both getting emotional about cars and confounding the people who sit, puzzled, listening to him expound.

At a dinner in Detroit sponsored by BMW in 2002, he drew on visions of draping cloth on nude forms in classical sculpture to talk about the Z4 roadster that BMW had just added to its lineup, taking its place alongside the 7-series as yet another one of BMW's nonsymmetrical cars. "That nude, now with the revealing and energizing aspect of a tissue of cloth, is the Z4," he said, as later captured by Danny Hakim in a front-page article in the *New York Times.* "To me, that's as big a jump in terms of aesthetic value systems as there was between an Eve before the fall—when she was innocent and pure, and the sexiness that she had was an animalistic pureness that radiated out of her—and an Eve after the fall who discovered and was aware of the surface of her body, could use clothes and the drapery of form, a slit here, an opening there, to bring a new kind of erotic sensuality. Same woman, two different aspects."

That Panke has entrusted BMW's designs to so eccentric a character is one thing. But Bangle's influence, and that of Panke, is going to be felt at BMW throughout the rest of the decade, and it is going to tell the story of whether Panke can truly achieve the expansion that he wants the German brand to realize. There are already wisps of warnings that it may not be as smooth as the way the German cars shift gears. Heeding the complaints that the 7-series was ungainly, BMW embarked on a modest redesign of the rear end. Meanwhile, the next cars in Panke's stable began arriving in 2003—a new version of the 5-series, plus the X3 sport utility, a smaller cousin of the X-5. The X3 is assembled for it by Magna Steyr, the Canadian-based automotive supplier, at its plant outside Graz, Austria. "We wanted to be fast to the market without building another plant," said Panke. On the horizon is a new version of the 6-series coupe, and then comes the real gamble: the BMW 1-series.

Due out in the middle of the decade, the 1-series, as much as Mini, will show whether BMW can indeed go downscale as well as up into the stratosphere of automobiles. BMW has never sold a 1-series in the United States, and analysts wonder if it should try. It will have to start at around $20,000, given that the 3-series starts at $28,000. Would there be a customer for a $20,000 BMW? And who would that customer be? What would the 1-series do to the sales of the 3-series and the rest of the BMW lineup? How would people who paid $70,000 for a 7-series feel about seeing a car that cheap in the same showroom? Those are questions that people throughout the auto industry are pondering. For, at that price, the BMW 1-series would compete against the breadth of the auto market, from Hyundai on up. Consumers might face a choice between paying $20,000 for a Toyota Camry or $20,000 for a BMW.

"Can you really imagine a small, relatively low-priced BMW? To make it work, everything has to be exactly right, exactly in the right place, and with a bit of brio thrown in," said James Womack. Panke, sitting forward in the August 2002 interview, thinks he can get it right, even at a low price. "A BMW is a BMW," Panke said. It has specific driving characteristics. A specific road feel. A way of handling that is nothing like that of any other car. If Honda owners—or Toyota owners or Buick owners, for that matter—are not already customers for BMW cars, it isn't likely that they can be lured in on price alone. They have to have the aptitude for BMW's cars before they walk into the showroom.

Brauer, for one, sees some wisdom in BMW's approach. With gasoline prices climbing above $2 a gallon across the country, and $3 at some stations in California, there might be an interest in a smaller BMW, without the gas-guzzling habits of its bigger siblings. It made sense for German, Japanese and Korean companies to expand their lineups, he said, because it was clear that Detroit's rush to light trucks had left it vulnerable to its competition. "BMW is still a relatively small, family-owned company, and the family obviously still loves cars and wants to either do it right or not do it at all," Brauer said. "As long as they retain that philosophy and continue to offer solid vehicles in terms of style, interiors and driving pleasure, they will continue to be successful." Womack, however, offers an opposing view. "Don't you eventually start selling cars to folks with no dough and no class that the aspiring don't want to be associated with? I'd be very careful."

For his part, Joe Hammell, the Atlanta 5-series owner, isn't fazed by the prospect of a cheaper Bimmer. He doesn't want to drive anything else, particularly what GM and Ford have to offer. "There's nothing out there from Detroit that we would buy today," he said. "I have always hoped that there would be an American auto that I would want to buy." He's checked out pretty much everything—sat in the latest cars from Cadillac at the Atlanta Auto Show, and driven the Jaguars and Volvos that Ford sells along with Lincolns when he rents cars from Hertz. None sway him away from BMW. Neither does his desire to support the American auto industry. "When given the option to buy the best car for our dollar, the free market in our country has allowed us to have probably the greatest amount of choices in the world," Hammell said. "We are a patriotic people, but for too long Detroit didn't keep up with the rest of the world. Maybe as I get older, Cadillac would have something that I or my wife would consider. But right now, I don't see that happening."

Which is just what Panke, for one, is glad to hear.

CHAPTER EIGHT

DETROIT SOUTH

IT IS POSSIBLE to drive onto the grounds of Ford's sprawling Rouge complex in Dearborn, Michigan, and not have a single guard ask why you are there. Not far from the Detroit city limits, the Rouge was the centerpiece of automobile and auto parts production for decades during the last century, the furnace that fueled Ford's engine of commerce. Its towering steel mill and its assembly lines were captured by photographers like Charles Sheeler and artists such as Diego Rivera, turning the 100,000 men and women who once toiled here into iconic images of the might that Detroit displayed. This is where the famed Battle of the Overpass took place, marking the bloody 1930s showdown between organizers of the fledgling United Auto

Workers union and thugs hired by Ford to keep them out. Thousands of tourists each year flocked to gape from catwalks at the open furnaces and assembly lines beneath their feet.

There is still production going on at the Rouge, of steel and parts and cars, and in 2003 Ford proudly renovated its automobile plant here to create an environmentally friendly factory with a sprawling roof garden and a new visitors' center. But for the most part, the Rouge is abandoned now, its empty brick buildings sitting silent, a sad reminder of the economic power that once was housed here. All around the property are smokestacks, some active, most not, reaching up to the sky like fingers gesturing in despair. On a cold winter day, the winds whip around this factory with biting intensity, adding a particular sense of foreboding to the scene. The Rouge is a powerful reminder of what Detroit once looked like and the erosion that the industry has experienced. While many auto factories elsewhere in the city have been closed and torn down, and executives work from gleaming office towers with underground garages and tight security, the Rouge is the American automobile industry's roots. No matter how Detroit tries to focus on newer factories and production techniques, this is where it came from, and it cannot escape its past.

In Alabama during the winter, a drive west on Interstate 20/59 can be a nerve-racking event for an out-of-towner. Big semi trucks roar by, producing their own brand of wind shear, and there is almost nothing to see except stands of pine trees lining the road. So it's a surprise when, all of a sudden, the Mercedes-Benz manufacturing operation looms up right next to the interstate just outside Vance. Its buildings are gleaming white. Its assembly plant seems to stretch forever to the horizon. Next door, a modern, glass-walled visitors' center sits glittering under the night sky. Atop the building is a replica of the famous Mercedes three-pointed star, slowly revolving, unmistakable even by drivers who are zipping by apace with the truckers. It is a smaller version of the daunting Mercedes logo that revolves day and night atop the company's headquarters in Mohringen, Germany, just outside

Stuttgart. That one serves as a beacon for pilots landing at the Stuttgart airport across the roadway there. This one serves to put the world on notice that Mercedes picked Alabama, as unlike Detroit as a place could be, as the site of its $300 million factory. It is impossible to miss either this factory or the emergence of Alabama as a key player in the new American automobile industry, what many call "Detroit South."

When import auto companies first built their plants in the United States, they stayed surprisingly close to where Detroit companies had located their factories. It is one of the biggest frustrations of the United Auto Workers union that it has been unable to organize workers at a single one of these "transplant" factories, even though in some cases the facilities are right in GM, Ford and Chrysler's backyard. Toyota's plant in Georgetown is just an hour from Ford's big truck plant in Louisville, while GM's Bowling Green plant, home to the Corvette, is not far away. Honda's plants in Marysville and East Liberty, Ohio, have GM, Ford and Chrysler plants within a few hours' drive. There are a number of Big Three factories in Indiana, home to the Toyota plant in Princeton. And Nissan's plant in Smyrna, Tennessee, which was the farthest south of the first round of factories, sits only an hour from the Saturn plant in Spring Hill, where workers are UAW members working under a special con- tract. Though the UAW has accused the employers of preselecting work- ers who were anti-union, or intimidating those who tried to organize the plants, it can't blame those factories' location for the fact that it hasn't convinced them to join up.

It's a different story with the second wave of factories, beginning with BMW in South Carolina and continuing even deeper into the South, with Mercedes and other companies picking up the charge. These are right-to-work states, and even UAW officials acknowledge that their message is a tough sell, legally and culturally. Still, it would be one thing if these plants were small and their impact on their com- munities a modest thing. But the plants have had the effect of chang- ing the landscape in the Deep South, literally and figuratively. The impact has been greatest in Alabama, where, given the state's history, no one could have predicted what has transpired there in the past 10 years.

Inside a packed auditorium at the Civil Rights Institute, on the outskirts of downtown Birmingham, Alabama, visitors sit quietly, watching a slide show that serves as an introduction to the city's history. Black-and-white photographs depict how Birmingham's population exploded after the Civil War to rival that of Atlanta, two and a half hours to the east. The steel industry provided profits for city fathers and jobs for the city's burgeoning black community, which by the turn of the century made up one-third of the city's population. The smell of sulfur was the smell of success, and the steel and textile mills that also mushroomed around Birmingham helped the city prosper. Birmingham became known as the Magic City and, alternatively, the City of Churches, for the 700 different houses of worship within its city limits. But none of this could camouflage the fact that Birmingham was the most segregated city in the South. Strict lines, both legal and by custom, were drawn between its white and black populations. The Ku Klux Klan was a constant and brutal presence, lynching and terrorizing those who it felt needed to be taught a lesson. As the slide show ends, visitors are given a stark reminder of just what Birmingham had become best known for. The screen rises into the ceiling to reveal the entrance to the museum's comprehensive exhibits on the black community's struggle for equal rights. There, in front of the group, stand two water fountains: one, in pristine working condition, labeled for Whites, the other, broken and rusty, for Coloreds.

The sight prompts gasps and murmurs from those who have seen such things only in books, and it brings tears to the eyes of those who were alive when this was the norm in Birmingham. For segregation remained in force here until well into the 1960s, despite presidential decrees, the brave efforts of the Freedom Riders, countless demonstrations in the park that sits just across from the redbrick institute, and above all, the struggles of the late Dr. Martin Luther King, Jr., whose

Birmingham jail cell is replicated here, and whose "I Have a Dream" speech plays on a continuous loop in a room devoted to his historic address in Washington, D.C. Even after integration eventually took hold and the barriers came down, a number of people here feared that Birmingham would be forever restrained by its past and unable to play a role in the resurgent South. But finally, 50 years after the Supreme Court's ruling in the *Brown* vs. *Board of Education* case, Birmingham has managed to rise above those roots in a fashion that leaders of the civil rights movement might never have envisioned. And it owes its renaissance largely to automobiles.

Today, Birmingham has become the de facto capital for a growing number of car manufacturers, parts suppliers and other businesses that flocked to the Deep South during the late 1990s and early this decade. Birmingham's small airport, easy to negotiate, bustles with arriving executives from Japan, Germany and Korea, engineers laden with schematics and designers toting portfolios. Manufacturers are taking full advantage of a southern workforce eager for the kind of well-paying, challenging jobs that these companies offer, and local and state officials willing to offer packages of incentives to win their investments. Given how grateful any state would be to secure just one automobile plant, Alabama's success has been truly astounding. Of the five automobile assembly plants that were up for grabs in recent years, Alabama landed three, along with an engine plant built by Toyota. Since 1993, when Mercedes announced it would build its plant in Vance, 35 miles west of Birmingham, Alabama's automobile industry has swelled to include 19,500 people directly employed by the various auto factories, including the Honda plant in Lincoln, 20 miles east of Birmingham, and the Toyota engine plant in Huntsville, directly north. More jobs will be added when the Hyundai plant, under construction to the south, in Montgomery, opens in 2005. Collectively, the state's automotive employers have an annual payroll of $3 billion. Another 33,800 people work at automotive components and other companies tied to the industry, while 96,200 jobs have been derived indirectly, from hotels, restaurants and other businesses that have sprung up as a result of the investments. There is a spillover effect, too, because one of the plants Alabama missed out on, a Nissan truck plant, sits only three hours to the west, in Canton, Mississippi, which means some companies based in Alabama and some based in Tennessee are serving both states. And Alabama officials believe the wave of investment is far from over. They predict that at least three more automobile factories, possibly from Japan's Mitsubishi and Korea's Kia, plus another Toyota plant, will be up for grabs in the next few years. If Alabama's officials have anything to say about it, at least one if not more of them will end up in the state.

Alabama's position as the home of Detroit South is a sharp contrast to its dilemma of only 20 years ago, when its economy was deteriorating and its unemployment rate was skyrocketing. The steel and textile mills that had fueled the state's growth were closing, and the state's agriculture and timber industries were hardly strong enough to take up the slack. Even though Alabama was a right-to-work state, with some of the lowest average wages in the country, it had to plead with manufacturers to keep their business. In 1982, General Motors threatened to shut one of the plants in its Harrison Radiator division that sat outside Tuscaloosa. The factory was losing $1.5 million a year, executives at the company told a visiting delegation of state officials who flew to Detroit in an effort to save the factory. As a result, GM had no future product to put in the factory, spelling its inevitable doom. But the state refused to let GM proceed without a fight. Malcolm Portera, now the chancellor of the state university system, was then a business professor at the University of Alabama. Asked by the state's governor for advice, Portera proposed that Alabama be allowed to suggest ways to help the plant save money and figure out a product that could be built there. GM said it could make no promises, but it told the state to make its best case. After analyzing the factory and other manufacturers in the radiator business, Portera managed to find savings of $2.2 million a year, and GM agreed to spare the factory. It remains in operation as part of Delphi Corp., the world's largest auto parts supplier, which GM spun off in 1999.

The experience convinced state officials that there was a future for manufacturing in Alabama. But they were far from alone, particularly in the South. Neighboring states had the same idea—most notably Tennessee, which managed to snag two of the most heavily sought-after factories of the 1980s, the Nissan factory in Smyrna and, in one of the most publicized incentive battles in industry history, the Saturn plant in Spring Hill, outside Nashville. Alabama officials had been among more than 4,000 state, city and community leaders who had descended on GM chief executive Roger B. Smith in his office in the GM Building in Detroit in an effort to win the factory, each promising all manner of special tax breaks, road improvements and other deals. The deals actually had little bearing on GM's decision. GM liked the Spring Hill area for its land and its central location. All the efforts to woo the company had been flattering but completely unnecessary, as it turned out. But the decisions by GM and Nissan to go to Tennessee made Alabama's movers and shakers even more determined to win the state an automobile factory. There was another prize to be had, and this one would ultimately begin Alabama's journey to automotive leadership.

Almost nothing of importance happens in Alabama without the knowledge and involvement of David Bronner. He good-naturedly bristles at suggestions that he is Alabama's version of Don Corleone, but it's in the best interests of anybody planning to do business in the state to drive down to Montgomery, the state's capital, and pay him their respects. And plenty of important people have, including Nissan's Carlos Ghosn, who walked the streets of Montgomery with Bronner one evening, puffing on cigars, and DaimlerChrysler chief executive Juergen Schrempp, who flew in from Stuttgart to lounge on one of Bronner's office couches and talk about cars. Bronner, 54, is a cheerful man with twinkling eyes and reddish blond hair who surprisingly is not a southerner but hails from Minnesota. He holds court in a memorabilia-lined office at one of the buildings in Montgomery that is owned by the Retirement Systems of Alabama, the $25 billion pension fund that he has run for 25 years. The buildings built by the RSA are easy to spot in this otherwise easygoing southern city, the state's capital. The RSA buildings are skyscrapers built with green roofs, standing straight at attention like soldiers amid the historic antebellum structures.

These days, Bronner is best known as the chief investor in US Airways, the nation's seventh-largest airline, which he rescued from bankruptcy in 2003 with a relatively minor investment of $240 million. That deal gave him 70 percent voting control of the airline, the chairmanship and the right to select eight of the airline's 15 board seats. When unions balked at granting the concessions the airline said it needed to stay afloat, Bronner threatened to withdraw his investment and force the airline into liquidation. "What's their alternative? We'll Chapter 7 it, and it will be gone," he said. The unions buckled under not long after, and Bronner's place in airline history was cemented. More recently, when the airline stalled in its efforts to win another set of concessions, Bronner told the airline's CEO it was time to go and installed a hand-picked replacement. But years before his investment in US Airways, Bronner—"Doc" to his friends, in joshing reference to his Ph.D.—played a direct role in bringing both the Mercedes and Hyundai factories to Alabama, drawing on the assets of his pension fund to help clinch the deals.

Alabama's efforts to land a major automobile manufacturing plant actually began in Detroit, at the 1988 auto show. State development officials had gone up to see the new cars and trucks, and to visit auto industry leaders. In the course of their conversations, they got wind of rumors that Daimler-Benz, which owned Mercedes, was investigating a "North American project." Taking that to mean a car plant, the development staffers began a search for someone who could help them get a foot in the door. For years the quest seemed fruitless, until, in December 1992, they made contact with a German lobbyist in Washington, D.C. The lobbyist said he would take some information home with him over Christmas and deliver it to Daimler's headquarters. The development office whipped together a booklet, in English and badly translated German, with red and black covers, providing data about Alabama and photos of the state. A few weeks later, the state had a new governor, Jim Folsom, and a new development director, Billy Joe Camp, both of whom sat up in excitement when they were briefed on the possibility of landing a Mercedes plant.

One of their first calls was to Bronner, to get a businessman's point of view on how to proceed. He told them to act fast and to be relentless in their pursuit. Within weeks, the state officials and Bronner were on a plane to Stuttgart for an initial meeting with some mid-level Daimler officials. They didn't realize it at the time, but they would get to know that city well over the coming months. The Germans were cordial, but no promises were made, and the Alabamans flew home. But the Germans had been impressed by the Alabamans' resourcefulness and their determination, and after some visits to the state by the Daimler site-selection team, the Alabamans were invited back to Germany. This time they got to see Mercedes's chief executive, Helmut Werner, whose office was deep in Mercedes's manufacturing complex in Unterterkheim, outside Stuttgart. They brought with them an elaborate presentation, printed, in the days before PowerPoint files, on big poster boards that they had to carry onto the plane for fear that they might be damaged if they were checked into the baggage hold. By this point, the Alabamans knew that they weren't alone in their quest for the plant, which was widely rumored to be for Mercedes's first SUV. North Carolina wanted it badly, too, as did Nebraska—as unlikely a candidate as there could be for an auto factory. But somebody in Nebraska knew Henry Kissinger, who got on the phone to Stuttgart and asked Daimler to send someone to look at the site the state was trying to peddle.

Andreas Renschler, a lanky, boyish manufacturing expert whom Mercedes had tapped to run the factory, flew over to take a look. The

Alabamans, alarmed that Renschler was headed to a rival state, invited him to come to their state, too, and went to pick him up in an Alabama Power Company plane. However, the utility company had a no-smoking policy on its aircraft—anyone who allowed it to be violated could be fired—and Renschler was a chain smoker. The chief executive of the utility, clued in to how important the trip had become, told the development team, "Buy or steal an ashtray and let him smoke." On the flight to Nebraska, the team could see the devastation that had been wreaked on the midwestern plains by widespread flooding during the spring of 1993. There was water everywhere, and the sight was sobering. Renschler was waiting at the airport when the plane arrived, and he jogged up the steps, ducking his head to get in the door of the plane. As he settled into his seat, one of the Alabamans asked him how the visit to Nebraska had gone. "They're very nice people," Renschler replied. Then he paused and, without cracking a smile, said, "We are in the car business, not the boat business."

Back in Alabama, the team flew Renschler over the site in Vance, alongside I-20/59, where they hoped the plant would be built. Renschler, looking down from the plane, saw the rolling hills surrounding Birmingham, with the city nestled in a valley below, and remarked that it reminded him of the topography that surrounded Stuttgart. He returned to Germany on a Friday. On the following Sunday, the Alabama team received a heads-up from Germany: An even more important visitor was coming from overseas. His code name was Ernest. "This will be the most important visit you will have. If Renschler was Jesus, this is God," the Alabamans were told.

On Monday, Dieter Zetsche stepped off a plane at the Birmingham airport's private aviation terminal. Then in charge of Mercedes's passenger car division, he would make the recommendation to Daimler's board on the plant's location. The Alabamans helicoptered him over the location, and then landed nearby. Four-wheel-drive vehicles waited to cart Zetsche around, but he wanted to walk the site. The Alabamans could hear him saying, "I can see the paint shop over there. Here is where final assembly will go." It seemed as if Zetsche was selling himself.

But first the Alabama team had to make one more trip to Stuttgart, in September 1993, when the Daimler board would select the winner. Their fiercest rival, North Carolina, was still in the hunt, and the Carolinians were supremely confident. News reports had claimed that Daimler had already picked that state, and the Alabama delegation, including Governor Folsom and Camp, didn't know what to believe. The two delegations were supposed to stay in the Intercontinental Hotel in Stuttgart, but at the last minute, the Alabamans switched to the Marriott Hotel in Frankfurt, just across the street from the giant convention center where the Frankfurt Motor Show was under way. The Daimler board members had some questions to ask the Alabama team (such as "What is Klan activity like in Alabama?"). When the board meeting ended, the team was told they were no longer needed, but they did not have an answer. Governor Folsom needed to get back to the United States to attend the Southern Governors' Conference in Richmond, but he asked to be alerted as soon as word came about Daimler-Benz's decision. He was taking part in a televised panel discussion when a call came from Camp. "Get me the governor—now!" Camp said. No one had cell phones then, meaning Folsom had to physically come to a telephone, and the panel organizers refused to let him step down from the podium on live TV. The minute the discussion ended, however, Folsom rushed off the platform and went to the receiver, every eye in the room on him. Alabama had won the plant.

The decision triggered a celebration the likes of which few in Alabama had ever seen. The Birmingham Metropolitan Development Board spent $75,000 to erect a huge three-pointed star above a scoreboard at the city's football stadium as a way of thanking Mercedes for selecting the state. "This, my friends, is a new day for Alabama, a day when we move to the forefront of economic development," a gleeful Folsom, sporting a tiny Mercedes star in his lapel, declared at the ceremony to mark the state's selection. More than 4,000 people stood in line to shake hands with the newly arrived Mercedes officials, including Renschler and Bill Taylor, an executive from Toyota's plant in Cambridge, Ontario, who would be the plant's top North American manager. But the fireworks that greeted the plant's announcement were nothing compared to the uproar that erupted when the development package was disclosed. In return for Mercedes's $300 million investment, which would bring 1,500 jobs at the outset, Alabama had pledged $253 million in tax breaks and subsidies. They included the purchase of 2,500 vehicles for state agencies and a sleek black $82,000 S-Class sedan for Folsom to drive as the governor's official car. The money included funds to clear the site, fix roads and install utilities, as well as create a job training center—in fact, every job that Mercedes had promised was going to cost the state more than $60,000. (By contrast, the original package that Ohio gave Honda for its factory in Marysville was a mere $5 million.)

The package put the state on the spot and triggered a flood of negative publicity; even Mercedes had to defend its choice and reiterate that it was happy to have selected Alabama. This aftermath stripped the situation of much of the earlier joy, as state officials were forced to address charges that they had gone out and bought the factory. The drama didn't end immediately: As the plant was under construction, the state struggled to come up with the funding it had promised. Bronner, in order to save the project from collapsing, stepped forward with a loan of $100 million in pension money so that the state could make good on the package. Even today, the incentives are a touchy subject among Alabama business leaders, who point out that the deal was no more generous than what North Carolina and other states were offering. The main difference was that everybody knew what was in the Alabama plan, and that it seemed so lavish in comparison with what other states had paid in the past. But at the time, there was nothing to show for the project except a promise.

Today, there is the Mercedes M-Class, ready for an overhaul after seven years on the market, but a critically important vehicle for the German auto company. The $36,000 vehicle vaulted Mercedes into the luxury sport utility market, helping it keep pace with Lexus and beat BMW. The M-Class was a linchpin of Mercedes's sales expansion during the late 1990s, helping it grab first place for several years among luxury vehicle makers in the United States. More important than just a car, M-Class was a statement by Mercedes that it believed American workers could produce vehicles that were the same quality as those produced by workers in Germany.

Mercedes did hedge its bets, in a way. The Alabama plant is not completely the equivalent of one of Mercedes's production facilities in Europe. It does not produce engines, which come from Germany, and it relies heavily on modular production, like the Nissan plant in Jackson, taking out some of the complexity of building automobiles. But for the state of Alabama, and for the people who work here, this factory is an economic landmark. Mercedes has been Alabama's drawing card for billions of dollars in new investments, not least of which have been Honda's plant in Lincoln and the Hyundai factory outside Montgomery. The factory is a draw for tourists, as well, who stroll through the plant, wide-eyed, watching the gleaming SUVs saunter down the assembly line. The people who work in this plant have been given a level of pay, responsibility and standing in the community that they might never have achieved otherwise.

Among them is Lisa Evans, an assistant manager in the audit quality department. As an engineering student at the University of Alabama, Evans spent a semester working at the same Delphi Thermal Systems plant that Portera had managed to convince GM to spare years before. But Evans had no hopes of landing a job there after graduation, and she had few other prospects in Alabama. While she could have been hired by a company elsewhere, she wanted to stay in the region. However, she realized that with the lack of opportunities, "I might have just ended up managing a fast-food restaurant," she said. Her mother urged her to apply at Mercedes, saying that even if she started on the assembly line, the job might lead to other things. On the last day the company would accept applications, she filled one out. Evans was hired, and was sent to Mercedes's Sindelfingen factory for six months of training, the first time she had ever been on an airplane, let alone to Europe. Though she had experience at Delphi, and an engineering degree, Evans found that neither had prepared her for the demands of a luxury car factory or for Mercedes's expectations of quality. "Mercedes definitely had to develop me," she said. "I'm the last person in the world to say if a product is good or not."

But at least Evans had worked in a factory. Frida Drymon was a housewife with two sons, looking for work after staying home with them through junior high school. "Miraculously, there was Mercedes," Drymon said. And incredibly, her husband also landed a job at the plant, though the two work different shifts so someone will be available for their children. Drymon, who is of Native American descent, said her position in the plant's paint shop has been the equivalent of a university degree. "You go to college out there on the plant floor," she said. Mercedes, and indeed all the new factories in Alabama, Mississippi and elsewhere, have placed a critical emphasis on employee training. All of these plants have elaborate training facilities built, in the case of Mercedes and Honda, by the state of Alabama on the factory grounds or close by, where they put candidates through a rigorous assessment process as they determine who is best suited. The incentive to make it through is valuable, because take-home pay for one of these jobs can be close to $80,000 a year.

The Talladega County Industry Training Center, for example, is set just across the road from the Honda plant in Lincoln, Alabama, part of the $198 million incentive package that included $20 million for training. Nestled back in a stand of trees, the two-story building at first glance looks like a small company headquarters. Inside the entrance is a banner reading: "Honda: The Power of Dreams." All around, there is a flurry of activity. In the auditorium, a collection of Honda managers is hearing a lecture on production techniques. In classrooms, Honda employees brainstorm answers to problems that occurred on the assembly line. The pièce de résistance lies below, on the first floor, a wide-open space resembling a plant floor that is divided into two areas.

To the right is a series of 16 workstations where job candidates practice the kinds of tasks they might be expected to perform on the job. There are bins of parts, labeled according to their use, all manner of tools, including screwdrivers and air guns, and instructions in how to perform the simulated work. It is here that the job candidates have to pass muster, during a 48-hour pre-employment process, before they can be certified as graduates of the state's training program, in turn making them eligible for a job at Honda or one of the state's other manufacturing employers. It is now typical to see requests for state-certified employees in the classified ads run by employers in the *Birmingham News*. Some take themselves out of the running right away, said Steve Sheridan, the project manager in charge of this facility. Sheridan, who keeps a black leather Bible on his desk, said applicants quickly recognize whether they are suited for the repetitive work. The rules are strict. Candidates are allowed one chance to be late; any further tardiness and they are dropped from the training program. The applicants, who come on their own time, are allowed to select whether to come on Monday and Wednesday nights, or Tuesday and Thursday, and they also must devote a full Saturday.

Those who make it all the way through have to be truly committed. Honda, which originally planned to hire 2,000 people at its

Lincoln plant, received 29,000 requests for job applications. About 16,000 people returned them, and out of that number, 5,000 were invited to come for the training program. Some 3,000 completed the program, yielding the 2,000 people who eventually were hired by the factory. Honda used the same system to hire more workers for the second phase of the plant. "You want the ones with drive and determination and stick-to-it-tiveness," Sheridan said. The rigorous process "does allow you to hire the best people," he added.

But getting hired is only the first hurdle. The Honda employees do not set foot on an assembly line for the first two months. First, they are sent back here for further instructions on actual assembly equipment sites. Here, they do what are called practice builds, getting a sense of what their workspace will be like, understanding just how much stamina will be needed to stay on their feet eight hours a day. At the same time, Honda managers are learning about their new employees—in ways they didn't anticipate. Though Honda had the experience of having opened plants in Marysville, East Liberty, and Ontario, the plant's human resources managers still had to adapt to Alabama life. "What hasn't changed is the Honda philosophy, starting with Mr. Honda's vision," said Kathy Jones, senior vice president of business operations. "But we have to be sensitive to the Alabama community. It's different in Lincoln versus Marysville."

One of the first lessons the Honda managers learned was the proper way to deal with the enormous hospitality that the state wanted to offer. As the plant site was being acquired, the state assumed that Honda would want to be right next to the freeway, like the Mercedes plant and the Nissan factory that was built over in Canton. They were about to buy up a strip of land next to Interstate 20, where Honda could put up a big sign declaring the plant's presence, when the Japanese company said no thanks. Instead, the Honda plant sits, virtually hidden from passersby, behind careful landscaping. There is still nothing on the highway that denotes the plant's presence. "We spent a lot of time politely declining. Some who came before us had been a little more aggressive," Jones said in an indirect jab at Mercedes's high profile. "We don't want to give the impression that Alabamans have to learn Japanese customs. We'd rather learn how Alabamans do things."

In the same way, the plant has made many efforts to make its employees feel at home. Honda's plants in the United States and Canada are nonsmoking, but in recognition of the fact that the South is a place where many people smoke, there are tables outside the plant's doors where workers can have a cigarette during their breaks. "We could have had a no-smoking policy, but that would have placed a big burden on our employees," said Andy Ritter, a division manager in the administration department. Likewise, the cafeteria features generous portions of southern specialties, from strawberry shortcake smothered in whipped cream to mounds of pork barbecue and Frisbee-sized slabs of chicken fried steak. It isn't institutional food, either. "We found out that food is a little more important here than in the Midwest," said Ritter, noting that a typical meal is "meat and three sides" of vegetables or starches. "We knew we had to have big portions." Other sensitivities have shown up in the work schedule. Honda learned that it should not hold meetings on Wednesday nights, known as "church night" throughout the region, set aside for Bible study and services. The auto company decided that it would observe the Martin Luther King Day holiday, because of its particular significance to Alabamans, even though it does not give workers at its other factories that holiday off. Since Honda had to make up the lost workday, it decided to keep the plant open on Good Friday, which is not as widely observed in Alabama as it is in Ohio.

The same low-key approach applied when Honda selected the plant. Honda was determined not to see a repeat of the circus that had surrounded the selection of Vance for the Mercedes factory. It had no aversion to incentives themselves. Since any number of states were vying for the plant, the company would have been silly not to have taken advantage of offers to acquire a site, clear the land, build roads and provide a training facility and the like. But Honda manufacturing executive Koki Hirashima was sensitive to the plight the state found itself in with Mercedes when the state fell behind on an incentive payment. Hirashima, in fact, was distressed to learn that the state was going to give Honda a tax abatement on the land it had obtained for the plant. He feared that the state's education system might suffer without the tax revenue Honda expected to pay. Instead of accepting the abatement, he asked how much the state was going to give Honda in tax breaks, and sent a check for double the amount. "Honda didn't base its decision on the incentive package, which was a bit of a mystery to them," Jones said of state officials. "They were ready for us to throw our weight around."

Unknown to the state, Honda had all but decided on Alabama from the beginning. Though it looked at expanding its operations in Ohio, it decided that it had pretty much drained the state of available workers. Plus, the UAW was constantly hovering, and there were fears that should Honda's business there grow too large, it would be impossible to keep a personal connection with every worker, opening the door for an organizing drive. Honda gave consideration to a site in Indiana, but its real interest was in Alabama. Very quietly, it began scouting the state in January 1998, in a project it called Bingo. "It was a project to lose rather than win," said Carroll "Lew" L. Watson, the mayor of Lincoln. The mayor, who has been in office for over 30 years, is an old-fashioned public servant who answers his own office phone at 7:40 A.M., personally handles disputes over citizens' water bills, and knows the security guards at the International Motor Sports Hall of Fame at the Talladega Speedway by name. He found out about the search when state officials began coming up dry in their quest to find a package of land that would be suitable for the plant. They looked up near Huntsville, and had nearly settled on a piece of property in a town ironically called Spring Hill. But "every site they found, something came up," said Watson.

He got a call from Theodore Von Cannon, president of the Birmingham Metropolitan Development Office, asking if he could come up with 1,500 acres. Watson is a real estate appraiser as well as the Lincoln mayor. He can tell you the selling price and assessed value of everything in Lincoln, where a sprawling brick house with a four-car garage sells for $350,000, with annual taxes of $1,200. Watson knew exactly where to go for the parcel: his distant cousins, who owned a stand of farmland within a few blocks of Lincoln's main drag. Town residents now talk about life "before Honda and after Honda," he said. Watson personally knows what the plant has meant to the hamlet. One evening, he heard from a young woman for whom he had done an appraisal so that she could refinance her mobile home. The mother of two had been stretching to make ends meet, working a minimum-wage job. This time, she had phoned to ask Watson if he could come back to appraise the value of a tract of property that sat behind her trailer. "I've just gotten a job at Honda," she said. "It's more money than I've ever made in my life. I'm going to be able to buy this land."

The $158 million Honda package was put together without Bronner's involvement, but he did step in at the end when it looked as if the state was going to lose its chance at landing the $1 billion Hyundai plant in 2002. Project Beach, as that plant was called, had come down to the wire, with both Alabama and Kentucky in hot pursuit. Earlier, Hyundai had eliminated Mississippi and Ohio from its consideration list. Kentucky, eager for another auto plant nearly 20 years after it had landed Toyota, had put together a package worth $125 million, while Hyundai's bid was worth $118 million.

But the difference in price wasn't the only deciding factor. Hyundai was anxious to get started right away, and Alabama had a clear advantage, securing options on 1,600 acres of land that Hyundai could access immediately. Kentucky, meanwhile, had found 1,500 usable acres but was stymied in its attempt to secure a final parcel of land owned by the Howlett family. Its 111-acre parcel was appraised at $800,000, but the family was holding out for much more. In what became a nasty, public spat, the state began eminent-domain proceedings and then decided to negotiate. It reached agreement to pay $6 million for the land, but the argument had soured Hyundai on the Kentucky site. Meanwhile, the Alabama bid had a last-minute sweetener: Bronner came through with $10 million in free advertising on the television stations owned by the RSA and in its 300 community newspapers. It was an offer that Hyundai found to its liking, and Alabama had its third assembly plant. At a news conference announcing the deal, Hyundai chief executive Kim Don-Jin praised the Alabamans' effort. "The state government of Alabama has shown a far more enthusiastic attitude toward luring Hyundai's auto plant investments than its Kentucky counterpart," Kim said. The package, which covered 2,000 jobs, drew little complaint in Alabama.

The Texas market could always be summed up in two words: pickup trucks. And for generations, pickup trucks from Detroit. This is where Toyota executives in the United States took their skeptical Japanese bosses back in the 1980s, when they were trying to make a case for Toyota to build a bigger pickup truck, alongside the little Tacoma. Bob McCurry, the executive in charge of Toyota's sales operations, desperately wanted to see Toyota get into the market, tired of watching droves of Toyota sedan buyers defect to Big Three companies. (It was the same trend that would spur Nissan's product development teams years later into pushing for the Titan.)

But the pickup was a hard sell, because the Japanese market, where development and production of the pickup would take place, simply didn't have big trucks. Moreover, Toyota officials were gun-shy over trade issues. Lee Iacocca, the Chrysler chief executive, had been incredibly vocal in his denouncement of Japanese companies' exports to the United States. "They were sensitive about entering another market, even though it was an important market," McCurry said. But

Fujio Cho, in charge at Georgetown, took a group of visiting Japanese officials to a Dallas Cowboys football game and walked them through the parking lot. They found themselves in a sea of pickup trucks, driven to the game by affluent fans who loved their trucks. Even if they had a car in the garage, they enjoyed getting into their pickups on the weekends for their favorite pastimes, none inspiring more passion than a Cowboys game. That scene helped convince the Japanese executives that Toyota needed to get into the truck market.

However, McCurry didn't win his battle completely. The original Toyota pickup, the T-100, introduced in the 1990s, lacked the size and power of the big Detroit iron from Chevrolet and Ford and Dodge. The T-100 was a "political truck" deliberately dulled down in order to keep Toyota from a barrage of criticism. "It was a truck, but it was not a *truck*," McCurry said. But as with the original Lexus ES 250, or the first Odyssey that Honda sold in the United States, the T-100 was a placeholder. McCurry didn't give up on his push for a genuine big truck, and in 1998 Toyota began building its first real full-sized truck, the Tundra, in its sparkling new plant in Princeton, Indiana. Though the Tundra was smaller than the biggest Fords and the brawniest Dodge Rams, it was functional. It also got a great write-up in *Consumer Reports*. That recommendation was enough to win back some Toyota buyers who had previously bought trucks from Detroit companies, giving Toyota additional time to accumulate pickup expertise. In 2003, Toyota introduced an extended-cab version of the Tundra, its biggest yet, as Nissan was preparing to brave the market with the Titan. Even that Tundra was just a warm-up, because Toyota has bigger plans for the pickup truck market later this decade.

In 2002, Toyota announced that it would build a small truck factory in Baja California, its first Mexican plant. Then, in February 2003, it announced yet another plant. This one would be in San Antonio, deep in the heart of not only Texas but truck country. If all goes well, and Toyota hits the mark with the next version of the Tundra, and the two factories come up to speed and expand in the way that Toyota plants are wont to do, Toyota could end up selling 500,000 pickup trucks a year. Where would it like to sell a lot of them? Texas. "The plant down there is driven as much by market considerations as anything," said Dennis Cuneo of Toyota's North American manufacturing operations. "If we're accepted as a Texas truck, we think that will help us across the country and to really be accepted as a full-size pickup truck."

———

This time out, Toyota's American executives aren't going to let the pickup be developed in Japan. The bulk of the work on it will be done in the United States, at the Toyota Technical Center in Ann Arbor, Michigan, directed by a young executive program manager named Mark Schrage. Although the engineers there had a great deal of input in the Camry, as well as the Solara coupe, the pickup will mark the first time that Toyota has ever entrusted such a critical project to its North American operations, said Cuneo. Toyota also will have key advice from Kurt Ritter, the former general manager at Chevrolet, who oversaw its pickups and SUVs. Ritter left in spring 2003 to join Toyota's ad agency. The move angered GM, and Ritter subsequently opened his own consulting firm. His only client is Toyota.

———

Meanwhile, the San Antonio plant, like all things at Toyota, will fulfill more than just one role. With 65 percent of the area's population of Hispanic descent, the plant will serve as an opportunity for Toyota to attract young Spanish-speaking managers that it can train and deploy to its operations in Mexico, Central America and South America. It will also give Toyota direct experience working with Hispanic employees, who it hopes can give it even more understanding of the Hispanic market. With the nation's population shifting dramatically, and with

Hispanics now becoming the single biggest nonwhite ethnic group, Toyota wants to be able to stretch beyond its traditional customers, Cuneo said. It believes that San Antonio, in addition to its sales experiences in California, where the market is 40 percent Hispanic, will be a key force in helping it to understand what these important buyers want.

———

In Alabama, just before the exit for the Mercedes plant, there is a big billboard. Like the three-pointed star atop the visitors' center, the sign is illuminated at night and is impossible to miss. "Sixty-five years of progress. Standing together as one," declares the sign, which carries the seal of the UAW. It is a visible reminder that the union hasn't given up its efforts to organize these factories. And by rights, the Mercedes plant ought to be the one that it is able to unionize the most easily. As part of the merger that created DaimlerChrysler in 1998, the UAW gained a seat on the company's supervisory board. Chrysler workers in the United States and Canada are unionized, and it seemed logical that Mercedes would be next. Moreover, Mercedes's plants in Germany are all unionized, so the company has plenty of experience in that regard.

———

Yet the UAW hasn't succeeded, either here or at any of the independent factories owned by import auto companies in the United States. The UAW has been defeated in elections at both Honda and Nissan— four times at Nissan alone—and has never called a vote at Toyota, though it has had an organizing office there for years. Bob King, the UAW's thoughtful vice president in charge of organizing, said after the latest defeat at Nissan in 2001 that the company had engaged in a campaign of "fear and intimidation." And indeed, Nissan made a concerted effort to defeat the UAW. Even Carlos Ghosn stepped in with an appeal to workers on videotape. But what keeps the UAW out of these plants isn't the tactics by the companies. It is the fact that workers aren't convinced that a union would make things any better for them.

The absence of the UAW is the primary difference between Detroit-owned factories and the new plants built in the United States by foreign companies during the past 20 years. By and large, the aging brick facilities that the Big Three companies made do with as recently as the 1990s have been shut down and replaced with newer facilities. Even the factories built in the 1970s and 1980s, when Detroit companies went on a plant-building spree, have been thoroughly renovated. To a casual visitor, walking the floor of a Detroit factory seems just the same as visiting Honda's plant in Marysville, Ohio, the Nissan factory in Smyrna, or Toyota in Georgetown. The plants all use robots to assemble their car bodies, and they boast highly automated facilities to paint them. On the assembly line, workstations are organized and labeled according to the tasks that are performed there. The ability to stop the line by pulling on an overhead cord, called an andon, which was once exclusive to Japanese companies, has been instituted in the Detroit-owned plants. Just as they do at the Detroit companies, workers go through training classes and meet in groups to discuss ideas to improve their daily tasks. In a sharp contrast to the past, when the path to a powerful job lay through finance or marketing, the Big Three companies all have men in key positions who were trained in manufacturing, such as Gary Cowger and James Padilla, who head North American operations at GM and Ford, respectively.

But the presence of the UAW is what keeps Detroit companies from achieving the efficiency of the transplant factories in "Detroit South" and elsewhere. This obstacle is best defined by a thick book that contains the UAW's master agreement with each company. In it lie definitions of job classifications and staffing requirements across the plants, as well as the holidays, vacation pay, pensions and other benefits that the UAW workers receive. In addition to the master agreement, there are individual contracts for every assembly plant. All these pages add up to additional cost and complexity that the transplants simply don't have. They also cut into the speed with which information gained on the factory floor can be transmitted to people upward in the organization. It's hard to quantify with any certainty just how many additional jobs this means. But Russ Scaffede, the former manager of Toyota's engine plant in Georgetown, estimated that it was a significant number. Scaffede, who worked at GM before joining Toyota, said that because of the GM contract with the UAW, he would have to have three workers on a GM assembly line to every one at Toyota. Along with more jobs, the UAW contract creates another obstacle: a barrier between the workers and managers. Committeemen are still a part of UAW-represented plants, handling concerns and filing grievances with the company. Often, hundreds of such complaints are open at any time between workers and management. There's little motivation to solve the complaints as they arise, because they can be a bargaining chip between the union and the company at contract time. The national UAW agreement does not allow company-wide walkouts except when the contract expires, but workers can stage local, or "guerrilla," strikes over certain local disputes, such as when leaders feel their health and safety is in jeopardy.

And such areas might be logical places where the UAW could center a case for representation at some of the older transplant factories. Georgetown, Marysville and Smyrna are showing their age, and the novelty of working for Japanese companies has evaporated 20 years on. The pace of the assembly line is relentless, and the pressure to always become more efficient adds a factor of stress. Yet, despite an atmosphere that is at least conducive to an organizing drive, the UAW hasn't been able to convince workers in these plants to join its ranks. Given that failure, the UAW stands even less of a chance at the brand-new factories in Detroit, where workers are eager to have these high-paying, prestigious automotive jobs.

Over the years, Mercedes employees have gotten used to being stopped in the grocery store, the bank or in a shopping mall by people who spot the company logo on their clothing, a giveaway of where they work. It's common to spot workers in Detroit-owned plants wearing UAW shirts, pledging their loyalty to their brethren above the company. But throughout the Mercedes plant, managers and hourly workers alike dress in an array of chambray shirts, sweaters, sweats and golf shirts embroidered with the three-point star. The attire, called "team wear," results in a casual, upscale atmosphere that is more like the members' grill at a country club than an auto plant. It also eliminates any visible distinction between boss and employee, since everyone is dressing alike. That is a subtle way to get across the message that Mercedes is one big family and that outsiders needn't intrude.

A more direct way is through the plant's team representatives, who serve as problem solvers for disputes between the workers and management. These employees serve as de facto committeemen, except for the fact that they are attached to Mercedes's human resources department. Arthur Williams, team representative for the plant's body and paint department, said he believed workers and management are "all one team" but that differences sometimes need to be ironed out. "Our team members come to work wanting to be successful," said Williams, who is also an ordained minister. He has been trained in nearly every aspect of building a Mercedes—"I can do everything but paint the car," he says with a smile—and he said the best solutions to Mercedes's problems come from the workers themselves. "There's never any blame laid. If there's a problem, you go back in and try to find a way to fix it. Nobody is looking at someone to point the finger at. If there's a flaw, you want to be part of the solution," Williams said. Bill Taylor, the plant's president and chief executive, said that relying on workers for input, rather than imposing ideas on them, has been a key part of Mercedes's operating principle. "Technology is exactly the same in the industry. You can buy technology. But deployment of the people and giving them the challenge has unleashed this organization," Taylor said.

That philosophy, expressed by executives at many of the transplant auto factories, has been a key to keeping the UAW out, said Gary Chaison, professor of industrial relations at Clark University in Worcester, Massachusetts. "What the plants are emphasizing, very importantly, is first-line communication," he said. "The transplants have said to themselves, 'Employers create unions. Unions can only organize in an atmosphere where we allow it.'" Chaison said the UAW's two major selling points—better economic conditions and a voice for workers—simply are ineffective in the case of the auto plants. Toyota, Honda, Nissan and the others have been very diligent in pegging their wage and benefit plans to those of the Big Three. The transplant companies pay salary rates of about $25 an hour, which is within range of those earned by a typical worker at GM, Ford or Chrysler. (The exception is temporary workers, hired for the summer or for specific projects. At Honda, they earn half the hourly rate.) Generous even by northern standards, the income is enormous for workers in low-wage southern states. "They're comparing themselves with Wal-Mart, and they're comparing themselves with what their fathers earned, and with clerical jobs in those towns," Chaison said. "The workers understand what's going on. Among the southern workers, the realization is 'You can build the car, or you can fix it' and they'd much rather build it."

As for job-security guarantees, the centerpiece of contracts with the Detroit auto companies, workers in the South understand that their best guarantee of a job is to build a vehicle that sells, Chaison said. They've watched for years as Detroit car plants closed and as steel mills and textile factories shut down. By contrast, the vehicles built by import auto companies remain in demand, the best job assurance that any of these workers can expect. Even Ron Gettelfinger, the UAW's president, acknowledges the fierce challenge that the imports pose to jobs at Detroit companies, saying the UAW isn't "living in a cocoon" and ignoring reality. "We're telling you guys to get in there and design some competitive vehicles. That's what it takes," he said in a March 2003 speech to the Economic Club of Detroit, composed of the city's business leaders. "We wish there were more products and we wish you'd turn them around in a quicker fashion. We've got to get those vehicles out there." But unless Detroit can do so, and unless the relationship between workers and management changes dramatically at the import companies' plants, the UAW is dealing with a lost cause. And Detroit South will undeniably grow in influence. Said Chaison, "The American mark on the auto industry is basically gone. The Big Three have to compete instead of making appeals. They are now fully exposed to the international players, and there is nothing that they can do about it."

But in the past, the UAW has helped the Detroit companies resort to political means to battle the imports. And one question being kicked about in offices, in dealerships, at industry affairs and at other venues is whether there is anything Detroit can do, in the legislature or in the courts, to prevent the imports' further expansion in the United States. Would there be support in Congress, the federal agencies, or the White House to keep foreign-based companies from gaining more market share? Can Detroit fire another salvo like the 1982 voluntary restraint agreement that limited sales of imported vehicles in the United States and forced the companies to build plants here? This time the answer seems to be probably not. The longtime fear among import companies that Detroit will block them from growing has abated. If it had not, former Toyota senior vice president James R. Olson, who joined Toyota from Ford in the 1980s, would have been among the first to say that the imports are still in danger. One of the most outspoken executives on the import scene before he retired in 2004, it fell to Olson, as Toyota's Washington lobbyist in the early 1990s, to defend his company from charges that it was dumping minivans on the U.S. market. Later on, Olson helped the import companies defeat an effort in Congress to restrict sales of Japanese vehicles, including those manufactured in the United States. He had matchless political instincts and never stopped looking over his shoulder. But significantly, Olson is resting easier these days in retirement. He senses that overt protectionist moves are a thing of the past. "I don't see how legislatively they could do it and justify it," Olson said. "We've crossed the threshold."

Olson believes the danger has passed for a number of reasons. First, the Big Three are no more, thanks to the merger of Chrysler with Daimler-Benz, which created DaimlerChrysler. The collective clout that GM, Ford and Chrysler wielded as recently as five years ago is dissipated. It would be next to impossible for Chrysler to support any action that would sanction foreign-based companies, because now it is owned by one. Further, Chrysler's siblings under the Daimler-Chrysler umbrella include Mercedes, Mitsubishi and Hyundai. It couldn't back legislation meant to stall European, Korean or Japanese companies without causing a familial squabble. And if Dieter Zetsche and Wolfgang Bernhard are serious about moving Chrysler's image away from that of Detroit, it would look hypocritical for them to band together with their Detroit brethren to take on foreign competitors. Chrysler's credibility would be on the line, and its legal ability to do so would probably be in doubt.

GM and Ford, meanwhile, both have poured billions of dollars into investments outside the United States during the past decade—GM building new factories in Brazil, Hungary, Poland, Argentina, Thailand and China. Each company has import brands that are sold in the United States: GM owns Saab along with a share of Fiat, and it controls Daewoo, while Ford has a whole collection of import brands, beginning with Mazda, of which it has ownership control and a 34.5 percent stake. Ford also has the Premier Automotive Group, including Volvo, Jaguar, Land Rover and Aston Martin. What would be the point of protecting Ford, Lincoln and Mercury to the detriment of a more prestigious brand that Ford eventually hopes will earn big profits? All that is aside from the extensive foreign operations that Ford and GM have in Europe, Latin America and, increasingly, Asia. Both GM and Ford, along with DaimlerChrysler, are urgently expanding their operations in China, which is poised to become the next automotive superpower by 2010. GM, which expects China to become its second-biggest market after North America, is already talking about exporting engines from China to be installed in cars sold in the United States. Many people in the industry expect that Chinese-built vehicles will not be far behind, not only from the Detroit companies but also from Japanese and Korean companies who are looking at China as a production source. If that happens, there is no way any of these companies could support efforts to limit production by American workers—it would look downright unpatriotic.

Economics and trade aside, there is another key reason that import companies are unlikely to come under a substantive attack from Detroit. They have political friends here now. Toyota, Honda, Nissan, BMW, Mercedes, Hyundai and the others have accumulated plenty of supporters who could be expected to look out for their best interests, or who at least would have to remain neutral in any battle with Detroit. When it comes to assembly plants alone, import companies have operations in nine states—Ohio, Indiana, Illinois, Kentucky, Tennessee, Mississippi, South Carolina, Alabama and, soon, Texas. That's a lot of congressional firepower, and a lot of governors whose states have reaped billions of dollars in investments during the past 20 years. That's not including states with parts plants, like West Virginia, which has a Toyota engine plant and myriad suppliers and dealers spread across the country. If "all politics is local," as former

House Speaker Tip O'Neill liked to say, then these elected officials will have to remember who is employing the people in their states, even if they have Big Three plants, too. Another factor here is popular support for those factories among workers, business leaders and the like. Said Olson, "We've become good corporate citizens. They would come to our defense now and say to Detroit, 'You will not do that.'"

Nowhere is that more true than in Alabama, where community representatives vowed to stand in the way of any arsenal Detroit might fire at Mercedes, Honda, Toyota and Hyundai, whose plants have made such a difference in the state. High atop a downtown Birmingham skyscraper sits the elegant Summit Club, one of the favorite spots of the city's business leaders. Below, the lights of the city spread far and wide as a group of the state's movers and shakers gathered in February 2003 to talk about what the automobile industry had meant to Alabama. Amid drinks and dinner and a lively discussion (which included a lot of joshing about whether Auburn was a "real" university like its rival Alabama), they agreed on two things. One was that Detroit's market share was bound to keep shrinking as the imports attracted more customers. The other was that the imports could count on the support of Alabama's congressional delegation, and their counterparts throughout the South, if they ever needed help. The guests ticked off on their fingers the names of the lawmakers who would rise up to defend their newfound friends.

"The American industry has had a chance to adapt," said Theodore Von Cannon, the Birmingham, Alabama, development official who played a critical role in helping Honda come to Lincoln. "They never got the message. They opened the door for this." He continued, "It's sad. I don't like it either. But these cars are made by American labor. And these companies have listened to their communities and they've become good neighbors." Watson, the Lincoln mayor, said the difference Honda has made in his town is "phenomenal." Meanwhile, Portera, the chancellor of the University of Alabama system, recalling his experience dealing with GM in the 1980s, said he had little sympathy for any lament that might emanate from Motown. "You shoot the enemy, you shoot yourself. These are global companies," he said. "Something happened 20 or 25 years ago with the American consumer. It is second nature for many consumers now to buy what they want." Neal Wade, the director of the Alabama Development Office, said he wouldn't think twice in coming to the import companies' defense should Detroit try to attack them. "Our responsibility is to provide jobs to the citizens of this state," Wade said.

And in doing so, they are creating Detroit South.

CHAPTER NINE

THE END OF DETROIT

IN THE HEARTS AND MINDS of many American consumers, Detroit's traditional Big Three auto companies have lost their grip on the car market. And barring a miraculous rebound during the next few years, they will cede statistical control as well. If things get no worse between now and 2010, and the companies simply lose ground to imports at the same rate they have been doing for the past few years, the Big Three will see their share of the American market slip to roughly 50 percent. Moreover, unless a phenomenal renaissance takes place, it is likely that at least one of them will not continue in the same form that it is in now. Neither size, in the case of GM, nor the presence of the Ford family at Ford, nor the protection of Daimler-

Chrysler for Chrysler, can shield them from further deterioration.

The consensus among many Wall Street analysts, industry experts, executives from competing companies and even those inside Detroit is that GM, Ford and Chrysler face three potential scenarios. The first—and most likely—is that one or all of the companies will shrink further, forced by financial crisis to restructure, even beyond the cutbacks they are already making. And in the most extreme situation, one of them could seek Chapter 11 bankruptcy protection. Under the second scenario, the two remaining U.S.-based players, GM and Ford, seeing their market share depleted, might combine to form a dominant American player (assuming that federal regulators would allow it). And in a third scenario, one of them might seek a foreign partner, as Chrysler was bought by Daimler-Benz, placing the fate of yet another Detroit company in foreign hands. These possibilities were out of the question five years ago, when Detroit seemed to be strong. And there are people who still react in shock at the thought. Surely, GM is too big and powerful to fade away. Certainly, the Ford family would act en masse to protect the family's company. And Daimler-Benz, having bought Chrysler, would certainly do everything to make it stronger, they say. But as the steel industry discovered, as the airline industry found out, as retailers learned, as dozens of famous names in American business know from painful experience over the past few years, no company is immune from demise, no matter how storied its history.

There are two primary reasons for this pessimism. First is that the composition of the American automobile industry has fundamentally changed as it begins its second century, compared with its first 100 years. Rather than be dominated by companies taking big chunks of the market, as GM and Ford did for much of the twentieth century, the industry is fragmenting into smaller pieces, following the same model as has the European auto industry. Indeed, there may be room for a dominant player, taking perhaps one-fifth to one-quarter of industry sales. But the market simply does not have room for two mass market companies without clear identities, not when there are so many competitors who know exactly who they are, building vehicles that precisely pinpoint their customers' needs, and most important, who have spent years building their reputations for quality, durability and reliability. Because Detroit companies are ruled by the cult of personality, letting the latest whims of a CEO steer them in one direction or another, they have to stop every few years to reinvent themselves. The best import companies, by contrast, keep building on their foundation, pausing for breath sometimes, regrouping occasionally, but continually moving forward.

A second reason for pessimism is the danger that the companies will not earn enough money to support their vast and tangled operations, from the executive suite to the factory floor. The infrastructure has become so heavy, and the burden of health care and pension costs for retirees so great, that there is not enough profit being generated to support this mass for the long term. Scott Sprinzen, the automobile analyst at Standard & Poor's, the Wall Street ratings agency, said GM faces a $50 billion health care liability going forward, on top of a pension fund with a $23 to $26 billion shortfall. (In June 2003, GM sold more than $17 billion in bonds meant to address the pension underfunding. But the liability remains.) Ford's health care liability, meanwhile, is an estimated $27.4 billion, and its pension fund in 2003 stood $15.6 billion underfunded. George Borst, the chief executive of Toyota Financial Services, likens GM and Ford's plight to that of the U.S.S.R., which seemed indestructible for the first seven decades of its existence, only to disintegrate in its final two years. "They're all set up on world domination, and the world has changed," Borst said. Gregory L. Kagay, an industry analyst with Auto Market Scope, said Detroit has only itself to blame. "The Americans are guilty of myopia, stubbornness, and bureaucratic malaise, among other maladies," he said. "Detroit came to the starting line to win the wrong race. It faced not only a nimble competitor, but a wily one as well."

However, GM, Ford and Chrysler will not go down without a fight. Nobody, certainly not executives at the Japanese, Korean or European companies, underestimates these companies' ability to push vehicles out the door. As fast as the companies run into crisis, they can rebound. Repeatedly, competing executives insist it would take only a handful of strong-selling cars and truck models to vault the Detroit companies back to leadership. The companies have a valuable weapon in their big networks of dealers, who are capable of moving vast amounts of sheet metal. "No matter what you think of Ford, they still sell 10,000 cars a day," said Denny Clements, general manager at Lexus, who began his career at Ford. And, as the Detroit companies have proved during the past two years, they can deluge the market not only with rebates available to anyone, but also with discounted sales to rental car companies, to their employees, retirees, dealers, dealers' families, suppliers and everyone else with even the most tenuous connection to them. Another resource is the rental car market, which accounts for about 30 percent of Detroit's vehicles. The Big Three have enough power to sell a lot of cars and trucks to somebody, no doubt about it. But when it comes to the most desirable consumers, those who have a choice, who willingly give Detroit their business, Detroit has lost valuable ground—first the car market, and now, increasingly, its leadership in the market for trucks. If it's to get back on top, Detroit faces a Herculean task. Said Jim Press, Toyota's executive vice president: "They have to do to us what we did to them."

That is going to be difficult. Detroit is simply not luring import customers back to its showrooms; it is just selling to the same people, over and over again. Auto companies aim to attract a healthy mix of return customers, as well as those trading in competing vehicles, which are called "conquests." All auto companies value loyal customers, but they simply have to keep new blood coming into their showrooms so they don't eventually run out of business as their existing customers age and purchase fewer vehicles. But in 2002, 88 percent of Detroit's customers previously owned Detroit vehicles, according to the AutoPacific Group, based in Thousand Oaks, California. Only 10 percent of Detroit customers traded Asian nameplates for Detroit automobiles, and just 2 percent traded in European vehicles, giving Detroit a dismal conquest rate of only 12 percent. At the same time, both Asian and European companies were attracting Detroit buyers with alacrity. About 43 percent of sales by Asian companies came from people who previously owned Detroit vehicles, the AutoPacific numbers showed, while 5 percent came from people owning European cars, giving the Asian companies a conquest rate of 48 percent. The performance was even better for the Europeans. About 32 percent of European car buyers traded in Detroit vehicles, and 33 percent traded in Asian vehicles, giving them a conquest rate of 65 percent.

If Detroit could have held its own, and hadn't lost buyers to the imports, GM, Ford and Chrysler could have sold 1.5 million more cars than they did in 2002, said George Petersen, an AutoPacific analyst. "Domestic buyers are defecting in very large numbers. These are very sobering statistics," Petersen said. "With the huge numbers of competitive products coming from the Europeans, from the Japanese, each one is taking a little bite. It's like a kitten getting thrown in a pool of piranhas."

The defection rate is having a significant impact on Detroit's profitability. The automobile industry has always been a cyclical business, with Detroit used to peaks and valleys of demand, just like other traditional sectors of the economy. Over time, Detroit companies raked in billions of profits during good years, hoping they would offset the deep losses during the bad years. But in Detroit's case, the peaks are not as high as they once were, and the valleys are getting deeper. In 1963, when the Big Three had nine-tenths of all sales in the country, they earned a profit margin of 17 percent on sales of cars and trucks, according to Merrill Lynch, the Wall Street brokerage firm. From then on, margins began their slow deterioration. In 1973, just before the Arab oil embargo slammed into the industry, profit margins were an average 11.4 percent. In 1983, when Japanese companies were making serious inroads, profit margins were 7.3 percent—the best they would be for the rest of the twentieth century. Even with the industry's shift to supposedly high-profit pickups, minivans and SUVs during the 1990s, the high cost of incentives had devastated Big Three profits by the start of the new millennium. In 2002, the companies' collective profit margin was a mere 1.4 percent—a bare fraction of the profits that they were earning 40 years earlier.

By contrast, Toyota, Honda, Nissan and BMW all earned operating profit margins of 10 percent or greater in 2002. To be sure, some of that performance was due to currency fluctuations. But a greater part of it was simply due to the fact that while import companies certainly offer incentives, they have not had to discount their vehicles in the same way the Detroit auto companies do. And they are constantly cutting the cost of developing new cars and trucks so that they can keep investing in their expanding businesses. Toyota has ordered its engineers in Japan to cut the cost of vehicles by 50 percent going forward, because it is concerned about the danger posed not by Detroit but by Chinese companies, whose labor costs are minute compared with the expense of employing workers in mature markets such as Japan, the United States and Europe.

What are the implications? Simple. Without adequate profits, Detroit cannot invest in the future, let alone pay the enormous pension and health care liabilities that the companies face. In 2002, analysts estimated that the Detroit auto companies faced a $1,200-per-car burden, called the "legacy cost," because of the benefits earned by its retired workers. Without adequate profits, Detroit will have trouble simply treading water against the imports, let alone finding the resources to develop lineups of vehicles that could defeat them. It is a reason why, all across the industry, executives are questioning how any of the Detroit companies can hope to get through the next few

THE END OF DETROIT ■ 237

years as they exist today. The companies are becoming like an upside-down pyramid, with a smaller and smaller tip trying to balance the vast expense of vehicle development against employee and retiree expenses.

Yet the corporate culture of bigness that is so inherent in Detroit and, indeed, in the American business world in general, does not lend itself to the belief that these companies will shrink. Voluntarily slimming down to a realistic and manageable size just isn't part of the way Detroit does things. Gary Cowger, president of GM's North American operations, said GM has no intention of letting Toyota push by it to become the world's biggest carmaker, nor does GM plan to let its market share shrink any further. "We want to be the best American player. Not only the biggest, but the best," Cowger said. But others see the handwriting on the wall. "If there is one thing that has done the most harm to the Big Three, it is the word 'big,'" declared Jim Schroer, who was Chrysler's executive vice president of sales and marketing until he was forced out in May 2003, after Chrysler stumbled in its attempts to keep pace with its domestic and foreign competition. Said Schroer, "We are beset by trying to achieve quantities of scale that require enormous volumes. And then you look around the industry and you see that the advantage is where companies are not big."

GM vice chairman Bob Lutz is among the most vocal proponents of the idea that the auto industry has seen the end of Detroit—at least, the old definition of Detroit as a monolithic industry whose players were merely big and its vehicles interchangeable. At 72, Lutz, a former marine fighter pilot, is on the last and most critical mission of his career. He is striving to craft a new identity for GM as an aggressive company with exciting products, defeating the imports' charge with vehicles that outpace them in flair and are their equal in quality. He is about the only man in Detroit who would be capable of handling the job, for he is hands down the most famous automobile executive in America. Ramrod straight, with gleaming white hair and an eaglelike gaze, he unabashedly wears the mantle of celebrity that was once shouldered by Lee Iacocca, his former boss at Chrysler, who refused to name Lutz as his successor and instead brought in Bob Eaton from GM. To this day, Lutz insists that it wasn't his performance but his brash persona that lost him the job—specifically, a quip at a University of Michigan conference that Chrysler had been a woman on her deathbed, which Iacocca took as an insult. He left Chrysler before its merger with Daimler-Benz, to sit in relative obscurity for a few years as chief executive at Exide, a battery company, before GM's CEO, Rick Wagoner, appealed to him to come to GM's rescue.

The challenge that Lutz faces will have far more of an impact on his legacy than everything he did at Chrysler. The actions he is taking will determine whether GM can remain the world's biggest auto company and hang on to leadership of the American market in the face of the imports' drive. Under Wagoner's predecessor, Jack Smith, GM spent the 1990s on its restructuring efforts, coming out as a leaner company financially but with continually eroding market share owing to a bloated lineup of vehicles that with few exceptions seemed out of sync with what consumers wanted. In the nearly three years since Lutz arrived as vice chairman of GM, with all of its product development operations under his wing, he has charged through GM's engineering and design laboratories like hell on wheels. He has attacked the protocol and lethargy that kept GM's product developers from getting their best ideas to the car market, handing out stickers reading, "Says Who?" each time someone suggests that GM's tradition is to do things a certain way. He has insisted on a new identity for Cadillac, which he wants to see become the leading luxury brand in the country. Every utterance, every move results in a hail of publicity, which only serves to fuel the Lutz mystique. "He is an icon that everyone can rally around," said Jeremy Anwyl, chief executive of Edmunds.com.

Even as Lutz tries to yank GM away from the past and forward into a new reality, the vestiges of old Detroit cling to him like the scent of the expensive cigars that he loves to smoke in a charming if thoroughly alpha male fashion. Asked over lunch in GM's Detroit headquarters which car he felt represented everything he wanted buyers to think about GM, Lutz unhesitatingly chose the Chevrolet Corvette. Certainly its legions of enthusiastic fans would agree, but to an import audience the 'Vette seems distinctly rough-edged, more *The Sopranos* and less *Sex and the City*. Moreover, executives at Toyota would undoubtedly choose the Camry, Honda executives would select the Accord and BMW's leaders the 3-series as their standard bearers, all of which are within reach of many consumers. But Lutz contends that the Corvette is the market's premium sports car and as fine a vehicle as GM is able to build. He's proud to have it speak for the company.

Likewise, when asked which primary advantages GM has over import companies, Lutz answered that GM is able to build an endless number of V-8 engines, and that American customers always show a weakness for as many cylinders as GM can offer them. And, when the conversation turns to hybrid-electric vehicles, which GM had yet to introduce by mid-2003, Lutz dismisses the ecology-minded vehicles from Toyota and Honda as PR moves (to the consternation of Tom Kowaleski, the GM public relations executive on hand for the interview). But lest it be thought that Lutz is a relic of Detroit's past, completely out of touch with the American car market, he parries with a series of thrusts that show exactly how clearly he understands the threat that GM's import competition poses.

Throughout the 1980s and 1990s, Ford was widely considered to be the strongest of the Big Three auto companies, reigning as the company producing the best-quality vehicles, as the industry's lowest-cost manufacturer and as the one with the highest profits. Now all those titles go to GM, which spent the past few years completely overhauling its factories, unloading the Delphi parts division, and streamlining its product development operations. But, says Lutz, GM knows full well that it can't just be better than Ford to maintain its hold on the American market. Such theories are like the folk tale of two hunters in the woods, racing to escape a threatening grizzly bear. "I don't have to outrun the bear, I only have to outrun you," he said with a sly smile as others in the dining room laughed at the punch line. "We don't see it that way. It would be dangerous to see it that way." Nor can GM discount any of its competitors. Two years ago, Lutz said, he was ready to write off Nissan, only to be impressed by its swift comeback. The "fear factor" is a powerful motivator, he said, ticking off Toyota, Honda and BMW as companies that he particularly watches.

But Lutz rejects the notion that GM must be like a batter in a cage, whirling 360 degrees to bat at balls from all directions. He doesn't want the company to develop vehicles just because its competitors have them. In fact, he'd like GM to step out of the batting cage and get into an adjoining cage, scoring hits with vehicles that are a surprise to the car market. "*We* are going to be the home-run machine," Lutz declares.

In 2003, the best example was the Hummer H2 sport utility, a modern street version of the Humvee military vehicles that were so prevalent in the two Gulf Wars. GM can't take credit for developing the H2 itself—it bought marketing rights to the Hummer brand in 1999—but it has scored an unmistakable success with the SUV, a favorite with well-heeled baby boomers, and which was consistently the only GM vehicle during 2002 and 2003 on which it did not have to offer zero percent financing and huge rebates. Excitement over the H2 was only heightened when the second Gulf War began in March 2003. "When I turn on the TV, I see wall-to-wall Humvees and I'm proud," said Sam Bernstein, an antiques dealer in Marin County, California, and owner of an H2. "They're not out there in Audi A4s. I'm proud of my country and I'm proud to be driving a product that is making a significant contribution." (The H2's pre-

mier status was sullied a bit when it was ranked dead last in a quality survey by J.D. Power & Associates. Owners were disappointed
when it achieved poor gas mileage, estimated at around 12 mpg.
But then, no one ever claimed that it would be economical.) As
with all hot cars, the H2 eventually had cooled by 2004, despite the
continued conflict in Iraq, and GM was forced to offer incentives
on it.

The H2 was a notable exception to the situation GM faced elsewhere in the market. Despite all the streamlining efforts during the
past decade, GM by far has more car and truck brands than any other
company. And though Oldsmobile is gone, GM still must feed product to Chevrolet, Saturn, Pontiac, Buick, Cadillac, GMC and Saab,
along with Hummer. All that complexity just makes the job so much
harder for GM, which is facing competitors with finely honed identities and whose lineups are clear from top to bottom. Yet it is loath to
give those brands up. To GM, which began life in 1908 as a collection
of brands joined together by William Crapo Durant, brands are a sign
of strength, not weakness, no matter how confusing they might be to
customers or the burden they pose as GM tries to compete. Its experience with Oldsmobile, whose dealers filed suit to stop GM from elim-
inating the division, demonstrates the difficulties it faces in getting rid
of any of these nameplates.

Even so, GM might be able to justify keeping all those brands if
each one had a specifically designed image and mission, with models
designed from the ground up to fulfill a specific purpose. However,
GM somehow lacks the will and the confidence to put its power
behind a single vehicle as proof of its expertise. There is never just one
mid-sized sedan, like Camry, or one pickup, like Nissan's upcoming
Titan. A case in point is minivans, which had been offered by Chevrolet, Pontiac and Oldsmobile. In 2003, GM said it would give minivans
to Buick and Saturn, too. Doubtless Lutz believes that they will fill a
need for customers at each brand, but with so many available, there is

just no way that GM can hope to replicate Honda's success with the Odyssey, or to fight it head-on, as Toyota can with Sienna.

Moreover, a minivan won't begin to address the problems at Saturn. Saturn reached the market amid incredible fanfare in 1990. Its small cars attracted owners of Hondas and Toyotas, and its no-hassle approach charmed customers. But Saturns earned only minimal profits, a cardinal sin in the eyes of GM's bean counters. GM starved it of new products in the mid to late 1990s, stymieing its potential before it had a chance to grow. By the time Lutz got to GM, Saturn was being folded into the rest of GM's operations, no longer a stand-alone company. Though its lineup eventually was filled in with a tepid mid-sized car and a small SUV, and Lutz has vowed to revive it with high-performance vehicles that GM has dubbed "Red Line editions," much of the goodwill that GM had generated with Saturn has evaporated. In 2003, it was just another GM brand, joining the rest in GM's zero percent financing drive, expressly against its original vow not to resort to incentives. GM's focus on incentives, in fact, has stolen attention away from the renaissance that Lutz is trying to achieve. Zero percent financing wasn't anything new to the auto market when GM embraced it in September 2001: Months prior to that, Mitsubishi had offered zero percent financing, zero down and zero payments for the first year on its cars and SUVs. But it was a big deal when GM turned to the concept as a way to jump-start sales following the September 11 attacks. Its Keep America Rolling campaign was a direct response to an appeal by members of President Bush's cabinet who traveled to Detroit days after the attacks to plead for GM's help.

Had it been a short-term offer, GM might have basked in congratulations for doing its part to stimulate the economy. Instead, it made zero percent financing available in one form or fashion throughout the next two years, resulting in a barrage of criticism from its competitors and industry analysts, who contended that GM had made customers expect such deals. Chrysler's chief executive, Dieter

Zetsche, was among the most critical, likening the constant flood of offers to automotive heroin. Indeed, the incentives seemed to exemplify a constant complaint that the Detroit automakers, and GM in particular, were guilty of short-term thinking, sacrificing their future sales to expand market share now. In fact, zero percent financing and the rebate deals stopped GM's market share slide and helped it pick up 0.2 points of share during 2001 and 2002, returning it to 28.2 percent of the market, albeit at a tremendous cost. In one sense, GM's decision could be justified. Job-security provisions in UAW contracts required the company to pay workers virtually their entire pay and benefits even when they were laid off, meaning that GM didn't have the flexibility to save money on labor costs by cutting production. Every additional sale helped GM spread its legacy costs over a little broader base.

Also, GM booked its sales when vehicles were shipped from the factory to dealers; since it had reduced its manufacturing costs, the sales generated by the incentives allowed GM to eke out a few dollars more in profits. That aside, the strategy still seemed risky, given that the company has a large number of attractive new vehicles planned for the 2004 model year and beyond. Since his arrival, Lutz has been laying ground for a variety of cars that he thinks will make GM the industry's hottest company. GM executives initially missed the shift by consumers from cars into trucks, and it was not until the late 1990s that GM finally caught up with Chrysler and Ford in SUVs and pickups. Starting in 1999, GM introduced a well-received wave of vehicles, such as the Chevrolet Silverado pickup and Tahoe SUV, the GMC Envoy SUV and the Cadillac Escalade, which brought the company a raft of new customers for luxury sport utilities, some of whom traded in imports. The SUVs helped Chevy push past the Ford division for leadership in the truck market, although the F-series remained on top as the best-selling pickup, as it had been for more than three decades.

But in shifting so much attention to trucks, GM fell far behind in the car market, to imports' advantage. Lutz knew that to remain the leading industry company, GM had to refocus its attention. The car market is where he has put most of his thrust. Among the most important vehicles that GM plans to introduce are incarnations of the Chevrolet Malibu family car and the Pontiac Grand Am compact. It will be tough enough for GM to convince customers that these are vehicles worth owning instead of Accords and Camrys. And it faces an additional hurdle: These two cars have been known as rental cars, much as the Taurus has become. (Lutz, who got to GM after development had started, said it was too late for him to order a name change for Malibu. But GM changed the names of the other cars, such as the Cavalier, which became the Cobalt.)

The GM product plan also includes more vehicles for Cadillac, which has been undergoing yet another widely publicized revival effort for the past few years. As part of the effort, GM was giving every Cadillac an aggressive angular appearance, meant to make the cars stand out from their more-rounded import competition. The look was not to everyone's taste, including that of Lutz, who recoiled from it when he first stepped into a Cadillac styling studio upon arriving in 2000. But Lutz had since become an enthusiastic supporter of what Cadillac was trying to do, and he was confident that future vehicles in the Cadillac lineup, including the XLR coupe and the SRX luxury sedan, would be hits. Yet, despite Lutz's vow to make Cadillac the world's best luxury brand, GM put incentives on its lineup in 2002, because its marketing department decided that the company's message came across better if every vehicle in every division was included, no matter what kind of exclusive image the company was trying to create. GM contended that the deals haven't hurt Cadillac's image and points to a good first-year performance by the small CTS sedan, which replaced the dreadful Catera.

But analysts saw still another problem with the incentive offers: They were pulling potential customers for GM's new vehicles into the market before the vehicles went on sale, endangering the launch of those critical vehicles later on. Moreover, by enticing so many buyers into showrooms, GM had triggered a flood of trade-ins, whose presence on used-car lots was destroying the resale value of cars and trucks still in owners' hands. Those lower values, in turn, angered customers, who would be upset at seeing so much of their investment dwindle away though they had demonstrated their loyalty to GM by purchasing its cars and trucks. Further, and perhaps most important, the situation was exacerbating the division in perception between domestic and import vehicles, making the former less attractive to customers for the latter, whom GM had to capture in order to be successful. Lutz, not surprisingly, disagrees that the torrent of incentives will make it harder for GM to sell its future vehicles. He said consumers have short memories, have proved time and again that they want to be the first to own the industry's hottest vehicles and will be happy to pay dealer markups to do so (although auto companies officially frown on the practice of charging more than the sticker price). "If the new stuff is good enough, it will sell without incentives," Lutz said. "They will go from rebates to [markups] quicker than the blink of an eye."

Besides, he contends, import companies have always offered incentives; they just disguised them, offering cash to dealers to help sell vehicles—"money in the trunk," he said—instead of publicizing the size of their rebates. Lutz noted with delight during the spring of 2003 that Toyota was offering zero percent financing on some of its vehicles, while Honda was again offering low-payment leases on the Accord. "We've pressured them out," he declared. "They're no longer the little start-up companies that can nibble away with impunity" at Detroit's market share. "They're no longer the lovable little underdogs." Going forward, Lutz said, there would be no such division between domestic and import companies. The winners would be the manufacturers who were able to execute their vehicles the best, to offer the best quality and the more desirable products.

As in Europe, where companies compete across the Continent and in Britain by product, not by stressing their national origins, the American market eventually would put aside such distinctions and compete as one big marketplace, Lutz said. GM's secret weapon, he said, would be vehicles that are pleasurable and satisfying versus the bland and boring. Added Cowger, "At the end of the day, we can style better" than import companies. But GM knew that its task was monumental, and one that could not be achieved unless its lineups were filled with exciting vehicles. Said Cowger, echoing DeLorenzo, "Each and every one of them has got to be a hit."

But the initial report card has been mixed. GM got off to such a slow start in 2003 that it lost the market share it had gained in the two years before. And while its executives were confident they could recover their lost ground in 2004, the first quarter of the year was marred by a huge spate of recalls, involving more than 7.5 million vehicles, nearly as many as GM had recalled during all of 2003. Also GM saw its market share fall further in the first half of 2004. It faced having to offer what one analyst called "nuclear" incentives to clear out huge stocks of unsold cars—among them some of its freshest models.

Peter DeLorenzo, whose father, Tony, was GM's legendary vice president for public relations during its glory years, is enthusiastic about Cowger and Lutz's efforts. Regardless, he thinks GM faces an enormous task. "GM's squawking that there is a perception lag for American consumers is absolutely true. But when you have almost a 20-year legacy of consistently bad or mediocre products, that perception gap will take time to reverse," he said. Indeed, GM made the perception gap the center of a highly controversial series of ads that it began running midway through 2003. Officially called "The Road to Redemption," and known around Detroit as "the apology ads," the print campaign admitted that GM's quality was terrible in the 1970s and 1980s, but assured buyers that they could now trust GM and that its vehicles, going forward, would be superb. The ad campaign sparked outrage from Bob Garfield, the astute columnist for *Advertising Age*.

"This is a company that consistently fails to divine the desires of the marketplace and translate them into the right product for the right time," Garfield wrote. "It is a company that, having spent decades and billions achieving quality parity, is unable in its ordinary divisional promotion to communicate that achievement to the world. And it is a company with priceless brands containing unimaginable reserves of equity—equity inaccessible to the owners who can't seem to find the combination to the vault. So now they're telling us this isn't your father's General Motors . . . and we're supposed to believe them? We don't believe them." In the end, said DeLorenzo, GM stood a chance to stage a comeback only if it could follow through on its promises. Nothing short of that would suffice. If GM creates hits, as Cowger vows, and builds them with high quality, "all the doomsday scenarios are put on hold," DeLorenzo said. But he added, "That's admittedly a big 'if.'"

———

While GM plans to face down imports head-on, Chrysler would like to be considered as one of them—in every way but location. Like GM, it is striving to separate itself from old Detroit and to forge a path that moves away from its roots. But it is facing an enormously difficult time in doing so, given its past reputation for substandard quality. Further, there are real doubts in the industry about whether Chrysler has the resources to stave off GM and the imports long enough so that it can create vehicles that can shift consumers' mind-sets away from its past quality mistakes. By mid-2003, the damage from GM's incentives had become painfully clear. Chrysler, which had seemed on a clear path to recovery, stunned Wall Street and the industry in early June with an unexpected warning that it would not make the $2 billion profit it had predicted for the year, and would be lucky to break even. The turnaround, it appeared, would need a turnaround of its own. Meanwhile, DaimlerChrysler was roiled with management tumult that nearly cost CEO Juergen Schrempp his job, and in April 2004 resulted in the shocking ouster of Wolfgang Bernhard, universally thought to be the industry's brightest young executives, whose promotion to lead Mercedes was scrapped. Once again, Chrysler, always trailing well behind GM and Ford, was in trouble. "They have turmoil in their DNA," said Art Spinella, an auto industry analyst with CNW Marketing Research of Bandon, Oregon.

Five years after the DaimlerChrysler merger, it was hard to find anyone who believed in its wisdom. It can be argued that Robert Eaton was right to link up with Daimler-Benz at the point in time when he did so. An independent Chrysler could be a fast-moving, innovative and highly profitable company, thanks to its lineup of light trucks, but it was in no way capable of surviving the onslaught from the import companies on its own. Simply for that reason, Chrysler, in theory, seemed much better off under the umbrella of DaimlerChrysler than it would have been as an independent company. It was able to draw from the resources of brands like Germany's Mercedes, Japan's Mitsubishi and Korea's Hyundai, of which DaimlerChrysler owns a 10 percent stake. But Eaton's reasoning for the merger, denounced by distraught employees for years as a betrayal, seemed less compelling with each misstep that the German-controlled Chrysler made. Indeed, the mistake that both he and Schrempp made was in trying to sugarcoat the truth: calling it a "merger of equals" when in fact it was a takeover by the German company. The angst of the merger might have been over much more quickly if Schrempp had simply deployed the German executives he eventually sent in 2000 to rescue Chrysler from two years of postmerger bungling and crafted a strategy much sooner.

In Zetsche, the chief executive, and Bernhard, the intensely focused chief operating officer, Chrysler seemed to have two of the smartest executives in the global auto industry. They attacked Chrysler's operations with vigor and determination, with new, streamlined processes for developing vehicles, a concentrated effort aimed at improving quality and theoretically well-defined plans for all of its brands, Chrysler, Dodge and Jeep. The energy that each of them exudes permeated the eighth floor of the executive tower at Chrysler's technology center in Auburn Hills, 30 miles north of Detroit. When it's time for his next appointment, Zetsche doesn't wait for a secretary to usher in his visitors. He appears at the door of his office, hands in his pockets, eyebrows lifted in expectation. The conversation begins right away, Zetsche slinging his leg over the side of an armchair as he talks, completely relaxed, his eyes bright above his trademark walrus mustache. "We want to get out of this box of being one of the Big Three. That's not us," he said. "I don't believe success in the marketplace is defined by location of headquarters, the shape of your eyes, or anything like that. It's defined by your strategy." Added Bernhard, who has a chiseled face, laserlike eyes and jet-black hair, "We have completely—in our business strategies, in our product strategy—turned away from what GM and Ford are doing. This is not the issue anymore. We do not even look at them anymore." When it came to vehicle quality and product features, Bernhard said, Chrysler's role models were the Japanese companies. On the cost side, it was the Korean companies, and on innovation, design and prestige, the Europeans. "No Ford. No GM. The cars that we are comparing are the Europeans and the Japanese. No Americans," Bernhard declared.

It is a blunt assessment, one that Zetsche and Bernhard began honing from the day they got to Chrysler in October 2000. Their arrival could not have been more inauspicious. Their first few months in Detroit were marked by financial and directional uncertainty, manifesting itself in anti-German sentiments spewed on Internet message boards and local talk radio. In breathtakingly quick fashion, Chrysler had lost not only billions of dollars but its reputation for efficiency. For the third time in a decade, it needed another rescue plan. The two executives wasted no time in rolling one out. By January 2001, less than 90 days after they began, they had delineated a strategy. First up came suppliers, who were asked to cut prices by 5 percent for 2001 and by another 10 percent over the next few years. Product spending was sliced from $48 billion to $36 billion. Finally, Chrysler said it would close or cut back six factories, forcing the loss of 26,000 jobs. At the same time, Chrysler made plans to grow. Zetsche lured Schroer, the marketing executive, from Ford, and they immediately began working on new identities for each of Chrysler's brands, which are beginning to become apparent as the auto company introduces new vehicles. It wasn't as difficult as it might have been were Chrysler laden with the nameplates of a few years earlier. Even before Zetsche and Bernhard got there, Chrysler had announced it would discontinue Plymouth, so the repair job was made simpler.

And on paper, it all seemed logical. Schroer was satisfied with Jeep's image as a symbol of outdoor ruggedness. He did little to tinker with Dodge, simply emphasizing its boldness, making the appearance of its cars and trucks as gritty and gutsy as possible. The real centerpiece of the strategy was to transform the Chrysler nameplate into something with style, class and elegance, instead of a collection of vehicles with little in common. The *New York Times* called it "upscaling" the Chrysler division. That would take an entirely new series of vehicles. But the first—and most important—of them stumbled from the starting gate.

The Chrysler Pacifica, introduced in spring 2003, was the company's first entry in the crossover category, where Toyota had competed for the past five years with the Lexus RX and the Toyota Highlander, and Honda with the Pilot and the Acura MDX. Pacifica's design seemed like a combination of a Chrysler minivan and the PT Cruiser, as big as the first and with the retro influences of the second. What people primarily noticed, however, was its price: $32,000, more than many vehicles in the Chrysler lineup, and in the same strata as some luxury vehicles. While Pacifica initially received favorable reviews, some journalists who drove it felt it was underpowered and noted that it lacked the sophisticated, five-speed transmission that buyers of cars in that price range had come to expect. By summer, Chrysler was offering lease deals on the Pacifica and talking about how it could save the bungled launch. By 2004, the Pacifica had become a poster child for miscalculating the car market, a lesson that Zetsche said he would never forget.

At the same time as it was pondering how to revive Pacifica, Chrysler began selling the Crossfire, a two-seater built in Germany that almost would seem more at home in the Mercedes lineup than in Chrysler showrooms. That wasn't by accident, since the Crossfire draws heavily from Mercedes's expertise and was a key part of a controversial strategy, unveiled by Schroer before his departure, to link Mercedes and Chrysler. And that is at direct odds with how the merger started out: Both Chrysler and Mercedes insisted their brands would remain separate, with no overlap in products or identity.

But it is no surprise that Chrysler ultimately decided to travel that path, since both Zetsche and Bernhard each knew Mercedes intimately. Zetsche had been chief engineer at Mercedes just prior to the merger, while Bernhard, born in Boehen, Germany, a town in Bavaria, had run AMG, the brand's performance vehicle division. They both knew the resources that they could draw on at Mercedes, where engineering was not just a function but a craft. It took months of negotiations, delays and discussions to sort out, but it was finally decided that Chryslers would be part German under their skins, the first being the Crossfire. Yet despite its jazzy looks, the Crossfire turned into another missed opportunity for Chrysler. It never generated the buzz that is so vital for a limited-edition image car. Rather than create a stir, the Crossfire simply seemed to keep pace. That meant even bigger stakes for the vehicles Chrysler began introducing in spring 2004: the Chrysler 300C and the Dodge Magnum. They are being built in Ontario, on a chassis whose centerpiece is a transmission borrowed directly from Mercedes. With them, Chrysler is taking a huge risk. It is moving away from the front-wheel-drive platform that has been the underpinning of its cars and minivans for the past 20 years. Instead, they are rear-wheel drive, a feature that has not been on mainstream Detroit vehicles in years.

Chrysler isn't alone in offering rear-wheel-drive vehicles: GM and Ford both plan a return to the configuration over the next few years, although none of Toyota's or Honda's cars feature rear-wheel drive, with the exception of a couple of Lexus models. There's no evidence that Americans are anxious for it to return, especially those who live where weather is a challenge (including California, where traffic can be slowed to a snail's pace by heavy rains). Indeed, a whole generation of buyers has grown up driving nothing but front-wheel-drive cars, although rear-wheel drive is prevalent on SUVs. The thinking among car executives, however, is that rear-wheel drive results in a more enjoyable driving experience. Trevor Creed, Chrysler's executive vice president of design, is clearly energized by the opportunity. Creed, 52, is a sandy-haired Englishman who has been on Chrysler's design staff for years. During the 1990s, he participated in the development of some of Chrysler's most notable cars, like the Dodge Viper, the Plymouth Prowler and Chrysler's family of LH sedans, which introduced the idea of cab-forward design, in which the wheels are moved out to the sides and the passenger cabin slung forward, to maximize interior room. Yet Creed was overshadowed at Chrysler by Lutz, its swaggering vice chairman, and Tom Gale, his well-respected predecessor as Chrysler's chief designer. It always seemed as if Creed was in the wings, waiting for his chance. He has it now, in the designs that will make or break Chrysler going forward.

Sitting in his conference room at the Chrysler Technology Center, with big color drawings of Chrysler's concept vehicles on the walls, Creed shows off photographs of what Chrysler has coming up, pointing out the long hoods and roomy passenger compartments that a rear-wheel-drive chassis makes possible. The Dodge versions have strong, almost growling front ends, while the Chryslers have a sleeker, more rounded appearance. In his stack of photographs, too, are a collection of future Jeeps that keep Jeep's traditional prison-cell grille but look much more spunky and modern than the squared-off vehicles that have been in the brand's lineup in prior years. "The challenge to me has been how can we grow and distinguish ourselves?" says Creed. "We've got to deliver now. We all know that."

But Chrysler has a huge hurdle to overcome in the perception of its quality. There are too many disappointed owners of Jeep Grand Chero-kees and Chrysler minivans who will never give the company another chance. Dave Long, who lives in Dallas, is one of them. Long, 32, a soft-ware engineer and the father of four children, set out in 1998 to buy a minivan for his wife to chauffeur their family around. Price was an object: Long likes to pay cash for his vehicles and didn't want to spend more than $25,000, which ruled out the higher-priced Honda Odyssey. He settled on a Plymouth Voyager, for which he paid $19,000, knowing going in that the vehicle wasn't likely to be as durable as the Honda he'd passed up. However, Long got more headaches than he'd bargained for. "It's garbage," Long said of his minivan. First, his transmission went out at 18,000 miles. Then the electrical components stopped working. To protect himself from future repair bills, he bought an extended warranty in 2001, but he grumbled over it. "The car shouldn't bleed money," Long said. In spring 2003, Long went car shopping again, and this time he was ready to spend the money on an Odyssey or a Toyota Sienna. "It would take a long time to convince me" that a Chrysler minivan could match up to either vehicle, he said. "I will never look at another Chrysler again, and I can't think of what they could do [for me] to look at another Detroit product. They've got to do something seriously to revamp their products. At the end of the day, this car is junk."

Chrysler executives are quick to insist that such experiences are rare and that the company's rankings on surveys from J.D. Power and Associates and even *Consumer Reports*, which rated it the best among the Big Three for 2003, show it is doing much better. "A vehicle is a very complicated system. The possibility of having a glitch is very high. The likelihood that you will be perfect is very low," said Bern-hard. But he adds, "Without quality, there is no future." One strategy that Bernhard has implemented is to demand better-quality parts from Chrysler's suppliers. He was distressed upon coming to Detroit to see the shoddiness of the components the company was buying from some of the same suppliers that Mercedes dealt with in Europe. Digging for answers, Bernhard found that Chrysler, in many cases, simply wasn't expecting enough. Without a knowledge of what suppliers were doing in other parts of the world, it simply accepted the parts that it was sold, not realizing it could ask for better materials and get them for the same price. "We are telling them that it matters," Bernhard said. "I don't want to be a second-class citizen anymore. I'm not going to accept wrinkled seams on seats. No more butts of elephants." He continues, "It makes me freaking mad. It's that attitude of 'good enough.' It's over. 'Good enough' is not good enough. If we decide we're fine, that our new car is so much better than our old car, and we just make incremental improvements, we'll always be behind."

The Chrysler executives acknowledge that to catch up with the Japanese companies will take years. But they have a long-term horizon. Zetsche's timetable stretches out to 2007, when he wants Chrysler to have returned to the 16 percent of the American car market that it held in 1998, before the merger. At the same time, he wants Chrysler's vehicles to sell with minimal incentives, as against the thousands of dollars per vehicle in rebates and zero-interest financing plans that it has been forced to offer to keep pace with GM. That will be difficult. Chrysler tried in fall 2002 to cut off incentives cold turkey, alarmed at the damage they were doing to resale values of used cars and to the company's brand image. "We've all become like Persian rug merchants around here, with our going-out-of-business sales," said Schroer. But customers walked out of showrooms when they found that Chrysler was not matching GM's offers, and its market share plunged from about 14 percent to 11 percent in one month. Until its lineup is remade, it will have to keep offering rebates, lease deals and zero-percent plans, said Schroer. He said Chrysler would be back on the programs as it introduces new vehicles, sharing Lutz's assumption that the freshest cars won't need them. A cold-turkey approach would be too abrupt. "We've got to get out of this slowly," he said.

But Schroer is not there to see that happen. Early on a Friday in June 2003, Creed was driving into the executive garage at Auburn Hills to attend a marketing meeting, only to see Schroer pulling out. The executives rolled down their windows, and Creed asked Schroer where he was going. "That meeting's about me," Schroer said. With Chrysler losing ground as GM piled on incentives, Schroer had been pushed out and replaced with Joe Eberhardt, a German executive who had been in charge of Mercedes's sales in England. Eberhardt's appointment meant that the top three jobs at Chrysler—chief executive, chief operating officer and head of sales and marketing—now were in German hands. And only two years after the crisis that brought Zetsche and Bernhard to Auburn Hills, these German executives faced another financial emergency. Zetsche, like Ghosn at Nissan, had been able to bring Chrysler back to profitability in quick fashion, only to see the company falter in 2003. He vowed that Chrysler would be back on track in 2004, but in the meantime, it had fallen behind.

There are many similarities between Chrysler and Nissan, leading to comparisons between the turnaround efforts. Both companies have strong leaders, both are leveraging the assets of their various partners—Nissan by sharing platforms with Renault, Chrysler by drawing from the expertise of Mercedes, and by sharing development of cars with Mitsubishi and engines with both Mitsubishi and Hyundai in a $1 billion project. Both, too, are using design as a key in their comeback efforts. And there's another similarity: Just as Ghosn has promised that a Japanese executive eventually will be in charge again at Nissan, Zetsche and Bernhard have pledged to put Chrysler back in American managers' hands, even though in 2003 it looked as if just the opposite was happening.

Until the unexpected reversal of fortune, it seemed that Zetsche would eventually go back to Germany to succeed Schrempp and that Bernhard would run the company when he left. But that scenario was stood on its ear in 2004. Winter brought the surprise announcement that Bernhard would go back to Germany that August to replace Juergen Hubbert as head of Mercedes. It was an impressive promotion for Bernhard and a seeming endorsement of the skill with which he had reorganized Chrysler's operations. What's more, he seemed just the rejuvenating force that Mercedes, beset by quality problems, and hampered by an old-boy network of relationships with German parts makers, would need to regain its luster. Bernhard's job was slated to go to Tom LaSorda, the Canadian executive schooled at GM who had joined Chrysler to run its manufacturing operations. But before that could happen, something went horribly wrong, namely, DaimlerChrysler's global strategy.

Despite constant rumors that Schrempp was on shaky ground, and despite the difficult legal battles that he had encountered with Chrysler's largest shareholder, Kirk Kerkorian, the DaimlerChrysler board extended Schrempp's contract in March 2004. That did not come with carte blanche, however. Schrempp argued that Daimler-Chrysler should invest close to $6 billion in Mitsubishi, the Asian corner of his framework, so that it could fix its quality problems and expand its lineup. The board refused, saying Mitsubishi would have to go elsewhere for capital. DaimlerChrysler's money would be better spent at Mercedes and Chrysler.

In the course of a few days, Mitsubishi's German chief, Rolf Eckrodt, had stepped down, and Schrempp offered to quit. The board voted to let him stay: but as a safeguard against giving Schrempp too much unchecked authority, it decided that Hubbert should stay on as well. That meant Bernhard would not be promoted. That put the company in an awkward spot, given that his old job was filled, and he had no other assignment.

The news shocked Detroit and Stuttgart and led experts to question why one of the brightest talents in the industry had been set adrift. DaimlerChrysler's spin doctors went quickly to work. They whispered that Bernhard was difficult to manage, and that he had gotten into arguments with Hubbert over the deep cuts he insisted Mercedes would need in order to become competitive. As he had done at Chrysler, Bernhard had wanted to tear up Mercedes' parts network in order to drive down prices, a move seemed too drastic at the tradition-laden company.

Bernhard's handling was more evidence of the personality clashes inside the company, and it overshadowed the improvements that Bernhard, with Zetsche, had made at Chrysler. Few doubted that Bernhard eventually would land on his feet. But once more, Chrysler had become an automotive soap opera. Perhaps sensing that the task would never be easy, Bernhard had talked presciently in 2003 about the difficulties the company faced. Sounding very much like Carlos Ghosn, Bernhard said, "We don't look for short-term successes. We have to get things right, or we will get things terribly wrong. Failing is not an option. We can't, we will not, fail."

———

At precisely 10 A.M. on June 16, 2003, the one hundredth birthday of Ford Motor Co., a door opened inside the Ford Conference Center across the street from the Henry Ford Museum and Greenfield Village in Dearborn. Into an auditorium came the five living generations of the Ford family, nearly 80 in total. Almost like a scene from *The King and I*, the parade began with a stream of handsome youngsters, the boys in blue blazers and khaki pants, the girls in neat summer dresses and skirts, followed by their smartly attired parents, uncles, aunts and eventually the elder generation of Fords, led by William Clay Ford, Sr., grandson of the company's founder. His son, Bill Ford, Jr., watched the process, beaming, from a stage at the front of the room, where he presided as chairman at Ford's annual shareholders' meeting. "Your support means more to me than I could ever express," Bill Ford said.

It was a day awash in nostalgia for Ford and everything that the Ford name represented, capping a five-day celebration of the company's centennial.

The festivities had been in the planning stages for more than six years—and on the surface, they were a success. Indeed, the weekend saw the Ford family bask in admiration from thousands of Ford owners, employees, dealers and retirees who had descended on Dearborn. They cheered at concerts by Toby Keith and Beyoncé Knowles, sighed in delight at dozens of classic Ford cars and gazed in fascination at the machinery in the new Rouge manufacturing plant. They lined up for autographs from Anne Ford and Charlotte Ford, Henry Ford II's daughters, and Bill Ford Junior's cousins, snapping pictures of the normally private women as if they were Hollywood stars. "They're our royalty. They're our Kennedys," effused Guy Gordon, then a news anchor at Detroit's Channel 7, which broadcast special reports from the centennial festivities every night.

But as it staged the celebration, the auto company was trying to surmount its latest crisis. Since 1998, when Ford had smashed profit marks, it had gone from being Detroit's strongest auto company to the one whose future seemed most unclear. Whereas once there was talk of Ford surpassing GM as the largest player in the U.S. car market, Ford's market share by 2003 had plummeted; it lost $6.4 billion in 2001 and 2002, almost as much as it earned in 1998. Ford earned $495 million in 2003, and would have achieved its target of a $1 billion profit had it not been for restructuring costs. This is a pittance compared with its performance in better years; not so long ago Ford would have earned more than that in a single quarter. Compared with the swift results achieved at Nissan by Carlos Ghosn, Ford's pace seemed merely plodding.

Bill Ford's leadership of Ford was seen as a valuable link to Detroit's glorious history, a unique asset that no other auto company could boast. But Ford did not seem to be attacking his task with vigor, more a sense of pained responsibility. And no matter how valuable the distinction of being born a Ford—he frequently said that he "bleeds Ford blue"—he did not have the hands-on training, the background or the business acumen that other CEOs typically receive. In contrast to GM's chief executive, Rick Wagoner, who has been a senior executive at GM since 1992, when he was named chief financial officer, Bill Ford had never held a corporate position that important before becoming Ford's chairman in 1998 and its chief executive in 2001. Aside from his board seat, his most significant job had been as head of its climate control division. And, stymied in his efforts to gain more authority within the company, he quit Ford in the mid-1990s, concentrating on the family's Detroit Lions football team and coming up with a strategy to return to the company as its chairman, with Nasser as CEO. He had never envisioned that he would eventually hold both positions, or that he would have to assume responsibility so fast. It was on-the-job training under the toughest pressure imaginable.

Slight in stature, with a genial, low-key personality, Ford is known to show up after a morning run for a double espresso at a coffee bar in Ann Arbor, Michigan, where he moved his family several years ago, without anyone paying a moment's notice. (That wasn't the case in Dearborn, where he had to stop going to the Starbucks near his office because he'd be asked to pose for pictures or listen to a complaint about a Ford car.) Despite his famous name, and despite the commercials in which he appeared on behalf of his company, Ford lacked the buzz of a Ghosn or the snappy determination of GM's Wagoner. (But he retained his casual style. "Now we'll move on to the more mundane stuff," he said at one point as the annual meeting progressed.)

The most difficult situation that Ford ever faced was the crisis that befell the auto company in 2001. Only three years before, Ford had reveled in record profits, earning nearly $7 billion in 1998, out of a collective $16.7 billion in net income earned by all three Detroit companies. Ford's performance stood as an industry record until 2002, when it was broken by Toyota. Bill Ford was not yet a household name when 1998 began, but behind the scenes, he was maneuvering for power. With Nasser, an Australian by birth, Lebanese by descent, Ford had concocted a plan that would elevate Nasser, head of Ford's automotive operations, to CEO, replacing Alexander Trotman, with Ford as chairman. It was a combination that dazzled the industry: the 41-year-old chairman, bursting with enthusiasm about the future of the company, and the 49-year-old CEO, vowing to vault Ford to a position of industry leadership. The pair seemed destined to run the company for a generation, and when they were through, it seemed possible that Ford could eclipse GM. No small ambition, but the only thing small about Nasser was his size.

Nasser was an executive in a hurry. He departed from the industry's long-held practice of rising with an entourage. True to the saying, Nasser moved swiftly by traveling alone. Beginning in Australia, he climbed Ford's ladder primarily through its operations outside the United States, and it was as head of Ford of Europe in the early 1990s that most people became aware of him. Nasser bustled with nervous energy, setting a frantic dawn-till-evening pace that wore out the people who worked for him. He had his sights set well beyond the auto industry. His pacesetter was Jack Welch, the chief executive of General Electric. And like GE, known best for being a standout company first and a maker of lightbulbs, aircraft engines and other products second, Ford, in Nasser's vision, had a future beyond the auto industry. He wanted it to join the pantheon of the best consumer products companies and retailers, like Disney, Nordstrom and Nike, known first for their reputations. He thought Ford could expand far beyond its Dearborn roots. So he took the company on a buying spree, first snapping up Volvo Cars for $6.45 billion (a price immediately criticized as too high), then purchasing a collection of ventures, from junkyards to Internet sites. All that was great when Ford was enjoying prosperity.

But when the Firestone crisis hit, Ford stumbled in a devastating way.

To his credit, Nasser reacted quickly once reports of the exploding Firestone tires escalated. He took to the airwaves in a series of ads to defend the safety of the Ford Explorer, assuring viewers that his family rode in an Explorer. He defended the company in numerous appearances and interviews. But Nasser—or Ford's public relations department—slipped up when Congress came knocking. Ford turned down an invitation by Rep. Billy Tauzin's subcommittee to testify on the situation, even though the CEO of Bridgestone, the Japanese parent of Firestone, agreed to appear. The criticism of Ford was brutal, and the company was forced to backtrack. Nasser got his comeuppance when he was forced to sit behind the speakers' table for hours into the evening before getting a chance to speak. He could not fidget, talk on a cell phone, or leave the room—agony for someone like him. Furthermore, the Firestone crisis sparked a division within Bill Ford's own family. His mother, Martha, is a Firestone, and the Ford and Firestone companies had been linked for more than 90 years. Harvey Firestone was one of Ford's first tire suppliers, and he often joined Henry Ford, Thomas Alva Edison and whoever the president of the United States was at the time on camping trips. (A photograph depicting one outing hangs on the wall behind Bill Ford's desk.) However, Firestone angrily severed its ties with Ford amid the furor. And the situation prompted Bill Ford to skip a speech he had promised to give at the 2000 Firestone family reunion. He sent his mother, wife and children instead.

The Firestone situation eventually died down, and Nasser might have outlasted it, but his internal conflicts and Ford's slipping performance conspired to force his ouster. Nasser felt Ford was laden with too much deadwood—too many lifetime employees who were collecting generous benefits and a hefty paycheck with too little productivity. He vowed to shake them out of the company, and he instituted an evaluation system that assigned grades for performance. In the past, Ford's evaluations had been relatively benign and hardly anyone was fired or demoted, though many were invited to take early retirement or were shifted elsewhere in the company. Under Nasser's grading system, however, job levels were no longer guaranteed to those who did not achieve. Employees who repeatedly were rated as underachievers were in serious danger of losing their jobs. At the same time, Nasser instituted leadership development programs, personally mentoring the candidates he felt were the most promising. And he brought in a completely new management team, with 40 percent of his vice presidents coming from the outside, including companies like GE, Whirlpool and RJR Nabisco.

The moves put Ford into an uproar, and on top of it, the Firestone crisis had cost the company dearly. After dozens of profitable quarters during the 1990s, Ford began to slip. Out of eight quarters in which Nasser was chief executive, Ford was profitable in only five. By 2001, the company was on track to billions of dollars in losses: It would lose $6.4 billion over 2001 and 2002, almost as much as it had earned during its record year in 1998. By October 2001, it had become clear that Nasser had to go. Though there had been rumors of nasty exchanges between Nasser and Bill Ford throughout his brief tenure—one story, which Ford denied, had them coming to blows on the twelfth floor, where the executive offices were located—the final parting of the ways was actually handled in a gentlemanly fashion. According to Ford, Nasser came to his office at 5 P.M. on October 29 and said he had decided to leave for the good of the automaker. The next morning, a work crew arrived at his office, bearing big rolls of bubble wrap. Shortly afterward, Ford strode to the front of an auditorium in Ford's world headquarters, to the applause of gathered employees. "We need to get our focus back on the basics of our business, back to building great cars and trucks," he said.

But Ford didn't seem to know where to look for help. He didn't have his own troops to replace Nasser's management team, a number of whom had left with Nasser or were now planning to depart. He had no go-to guy or experienced surrogate who could carry out his orders with full authority. Years before, Henry Ford II relied on a British aristocrat, Walter Hayes, for blunt direction and P.R. advice. But Hayes, sadly, died just as Bill Ford became chairman, and no one that savvy emerged to replace him. "The one thing Ford needs is individual leadership that moves the organization. It's a huge company. As long as there is fuzzy thinking and lack of clarity, it is delaying what needs to happen," said Jeremy Anwyl, the president of Edmunds.com. "I'm sure he's committed to the company, but we're talking about a superhuman effort. I'm not sure he's interested in that, and if he's not up to it, he should delegate it." Stephen Girsky, the veteran auto industry analyst for Morgan Stanley and a longtime friend of Ford, shared Anwyl's concern. He worried that Ford didn't have lieutenants he could trust to get the organization in line and the company up to speed with GM and Chrysler, let alone face the challenge from its import competitors. Ultimately, Bill Ford would pick his team in 2004. But as with Chrysler, the process would turn out to be ugly.

Those factors are a large reason why Ford has been enveloped in continued speculation that it must ultimately embark on a significant restructuring. At the annual meeting in June 2003, Bill Ford took pains to dismiss the speculation and members of the Ford family vowed they would hang on to their shares in order to prevent the restructuring from happening. In an interview with the *New York Times*, Anne Ford noted that the car business was "so cyclical. Ford was on top for so long and General Motors was not. We've gone through this before, so we're all prepared. But you can't be too prepared." She added, "We back Billy and everything he's tried to do." While the Ford family's faith is an immeasurable asset, there is never any guarantee in the tumultuous auto business that a family will always stand strong. The Ford family's vow to keep their shares is one thing; whether they would contribute their own money to fund the company's future is another.

Witness the Agnelli family at the Italian automaker Fiat; when their company hit upon rocky times in the late 1990s, they sold a 5 percent stake to General Motors in a bid to raise much-needed cash.

As another defense, Ford officials point to the company's hefty cash balance, which stands around $26 billion, and its ability to tap capital markets. But Ford needs every penny of that cash as a hedge against a swift and sudden industry downfall, because it no longer enjoys the sterling credit rating it held during its glory years in the 1980s and 1990s. In 2000, Chrysler proved just how fast an auto company could burn cash when it was caught off guard by an industry slowdown. It ran into trouble again in 2003 when it failed to offer incentives fast enough to keep pace with GM. As Ford learned with the Firestone tire situation, a crisis can knock the wind out of an unsuspecting company very swiftly, and Ford, to analysts, seems particularly vulnerable.

And there is another reality at play. The American marketplace has never been kind to No. 2 companies in any industry. They face problems from above them and beneath them. They must deal, first, with the difficulty of competing with their industry's largest player, which by nature has more resources, and second, with the constant nipping at their heels by smaller and sometimes wilier players. In the airline business, United Airlines was forced into bankruptcy in late 2002; it was not as broad or efficient as the biggest carrier, American Airlines, and significantly, it had high costs that made it impossible to fend off attacks from nimble, low-fare airlines like Southwest and JetBlue. The retailing industry's second-biggest company, Kmart, also had to file for Chapter 11 protection in 2002, unable to battle the strength of Wal-Mart and fend off the rivalry it faced from well-defined smaller players such as Target and Kohl's. In the movie business, the huge studios can occasionally console themselves with monster hits, but the vast majority of Academy Awards go each year to Miramax, the leading independent studio, which is able to put together beautifully written scripts that appeal to today's most talented stars. In all those industries—airlines, retailing and entertainment—there are lots of choices, and simply being a big player is no protection.

At its heart, Ford's revitalization campaign is based on the slogan "Back to Basics," and its executives talk of 50 new models that it plans to introduce in the United States over the next five years, from cars to crossovers to more luxury cars. Yet consumers will have to be convinced that these models are right for them, because plenty of auto companies, from Toyota and Honda to Hyundai, offer good, basic vehicles. The market is not crying out for more choices. "From an economic standpoint, Ford could go away, and the marketplace wouldn't miss them," Anwyl said. That would have been hard to imagine in the 1980s, when cars like the Taurus were admired for their styling and quality, and in the 1990s, when Ford's SUVs and other truck models were flying out of showrooms, many at sticker price or more. For many years, Ford was considered on a par with Toyota, in part because of its corporate slogan, which pledged, "Quality Is Job One." But it would be hard to make that same assertion today. The company lost endless amounts of goodwill over the past few years with substandard quality, the Ford Explorer situation aside. The old jokes about what the letters in the name Ford stand for—"Found On Road, Dead"— aren't funny to owners of the small Ford Focus, a European-rooted car that has been recalled more than a dozen times in the past four years, or to buyers of the first Ford Escape sport utilities, which suffered five recalls in its first month on the market. By 2003, Ford, once the industry's best-built brand, had been eclipsed by a flood of competitors on quality surveys, including Korea's Hyundai. And as the Ford Thunderbird proved, the company had trouble getting the quality right on one of its showpieces.

The excitement that surrounded the T-bird when it debuted as a concept car in 1999 seemed exactly in line with the new era that had begun at Ford, where just months before Ford and Nasser had taken charge. The industry vibrated with speculation that the pair was intent on making Ford the biggest American company within a few years. Its rising market share had surpassed that of GM, whose share was sinking. The T-bird was just the kind of vehicle that would set Ford apart, with its heritage as a sports car, its instantly recognizable name and especially the pretty styling that the concept car displayed.

But the T-bird didn't fly the way Ford expected. Two more auto shows and three agonizing years would pass before Ford got the vehicle to dealers. By then, the excitement that Ford had fanned so successfully with the original concept car had died out. Ford dealers had waiting lists for the T-bird but had a terrible time filling orders. Production was delayed several times, and when Ford's Wixom, Michigan, plant finally began building the car, it had to shut down the assembly line when it discovered that an engine fan could catch fire. The experience was particularly upsetting to customers who had bought their cars through the Neiman-Marcus Christmas catalogue, which made it the featured vehicle in its 2000 Christmas Book. Though they had not been given a firm delivery date for their cars, many were under the impression that the Neiman-Marcus T-birds would be the first that Ford built. Some were still waiting for their automobiles in fall 2001, after dealers had received their regular allotment of T-birds, and several dozen didn't have the cars when the next Christmas catalogue was published. (Neiman-Marcus made sure that it had the complete supply of its next Christmas car, the Lexus SC 430, on hand before they went on sale.)

Once it went on sale, the T-bird received mixed reviews. Though raters liked the car's appearance, they were disappointed by its lack of power and its soft handling. Ford had been trying to capture the boulevard ride that the early T-birds had boasted. But by 2002, T-bird had lots of competition from other two-seaters, such as the SC 430 and BMW's Z-3 sports car. Because it was competing with those fast cars, customers had certain expectations. People getting behind the wheel of a T-bird wanted to punch the accelerator and go. Instead, the car floated down the road, certainly in keeping with the easy ride that Ford intended but not what consumers wanted. Ford insisted that a more powerful engine was coming. But the T-bird never recovered from the bungled launch. By the winter of 2003, a row of brightly colored T-birds sat, covered in snow, out in front of Varsity Ford, the big Michigan dealership that was among the largest in the country. By that spring, only a year after the T-bird's debut, Ford had bowed to the inevitable and offered rebates on a car that had once been its prize and subsequently said it would be discontinued, although it said it planned to revive the T-bird name again in the future.

As the T-bird roiled, so did Ford's management ranks. Far more than GM, so prescribed in behavior as to rival the Pentagon, Ford has always been a company where individuality pays off. When other auto executives seemed drab bean-counters, Ford always had somebody fun to watch within its senior ranks. And, perhaps because of the cult of personality that surrounded its executives, Ford also always seemed to be the most susceptible to management gurus and the flavors of the month that they touted as the way to prosperity. In the 1950s, the Whiz Kids took charge under Henry Ford II, himself an industry legend for his flamboyant lifestyle. In the 1960s and 1970s, Lee Iacocca provided the catalyst for both Ford's success, with cars like the Mustang, and high drama, when he was fired in 1978 by Henry Ford II, who famously said, "Sometimes you just don't like somebody." In the 1980s, Ford brought in W. Edwards Deming, the aging quality expert who had studied Japanese plants after World War II and came up with a set of 14 points that a company's management should follow to get the most out of its employees. Simultaneously, Ford's chief executive, Donald Petersen, received vast attention for returning Ford to industry prominence with the Taurus and its other top-quality cars. But Petersen, and then Trotman, and later Nasser all left because of unsettled circumstances and clashes with the Ford family.

In previous times, Ford simply picked up and went on under whoever the new chief executive was. But the brain drain that occurred when Nasser left meant Bill Ford had to rely on a team of elder statesmen whom he nicknamed his "grumpy old men." They included Carl Reichardt, the retired chief executive of Wells Fargo, who agreed to serve as vice chairman in charge of Ford Financial Services, and Allan Gilmour, who had retired as Ford's chief financial officer in 1994 but returned at Bill Ford's request to once again serve as CFO. Another such senior executive was the chief operating officer, Nicholas V. Scheele, who had run Jaguar, and to whom fell the day-to-day responsibility of leading the turnaround effort.

Scheele, an ebullient British executive who had been knighted by Queen Elizabeth, loved to expound about the wonders of Ford's vehicles, and he could spin marvelous yarns about the car business. But throughout 2002 and 2003, he was rumored to clash with David Thursfield, the taciturn, no-nonsense head of Ford's international and purchasing operations, over the pace and form of the revitalization plan. Thursfield could be as chilly in demeanor as Scheele was warm. (When he cut his finger to the bone over Christmas 2002, Thursfield darkly joked that in the view of some of his colleagues, he was "too mean to bleed.") Thursfield, who had directed a restructuring at Ford of Europe in the late 1990s, reportedly wanted to push Ford faster to achieve its cost-cutting targets; Scheele argued for a more measured approach. While waiting for direction, Ford's market share continued to slip, plateauing at about 18% by 2004. There were times when it seemed as if GM, sensing weakness at its rival in Dearborn, was deliberately bombarding the market with incentives in a bid to push Ford over the brink. GM executives denied that that was their aim.

In April 2004, the outcome of the battle was clear. Ford, whose performance had been slowly improving from the dire days when Bill

Ford took charge, surprised Wall Street by posting first quarter profits that were double those it had earned the year before. Its automotive earnings eclipsed those of its financing operations for the first time since the downward spiral had begun in 2000, due in large part to the cost-cutting drive that Thursfield had directed. Finally, the Ford revitalization plan was taking root, if not as dramatically as everything that Carlos Ghosn had pulled off, at least in a solid way. Thursfield's reward? He lost his job. Ford named James Padilla, who had worked with Scheele at Jaguar and had since run Ford's North American operations, as its new chief operating officer. Thursfield, the company said, had elected to "retire." Despite the results, his prickly style had simply proved too much.

By then, Ford thankfully knew that the latest version of its F-150 pickup truck had become a hit. There were more new Fords on the scene, including the Freestar minivan, and its pipeline was full with new models, including a wealth of cars, from the Mustang to the Ford 500, a family sedan that would eventually supplant the Taurus. The real excitement lay in the Ford GT, a super-charged sports car, which drew its inspiration from Ford's race cars of the 1960s and that would command a six-figure price tag.

But it isn't clear whether they will be enough to fend off GM, Chrysler and the numerous imports, and help the company boost its share. The deluge of coverage leading up to the Ford centennial questioned whether they would. "A Century at Ford, But Will It Be a Happy Birthday?" asked the *Financial Times*. Meanwhile, *Newsweek* depicted Bill Ford as a conflicted CEO who had turned to sleeping pills and tranquilizers to ease his worries about the company. The denouement came from *The Economist*, which in the week of the Ford centennial displayed a rusted Ford pickup on its cover. Indeed, as with GM, Ford faced huge inventories of unsold cars in summer, 2004. Despite the F-150's success, little else in Ford's lineup was catching hold, hardly the best launching pad for its many new vehicles.

Undoubtedly, Ford would have far preferred to bask in an atmosphere that Edsel Ford did in the months leading up to the centennial celebration. The son of Henry Ford II, Edsel Ford had spent years at the auto company, working in a series of marketing and sales jobs, and had once been thought to be a contender for the job his cousin ultimately landed. But he had wound up as president of Ford Credit, spending most of his time smoothing relations with Ford's dealers. Ultimately, Trotman told him that he would receive no more promotions. Thus, he left Ford in 1999 (although he kept his board seat) in order to pursue his own business interests, including corporate aviation, and to play a leading role in national and local charitable causes.

Unfailingly jovial, with a down-to-earth manner and infinite patience, he showed off classic Fords on a New York City street to the hosts of *Fox & Friends,* and sat chatting one evening about company history with public television's Charlie Rose, making no mention of unpleasant issues like the Explorer or the financial crisis that faced his family's company. It was as if, by dint of the family's historical significance, Ford could make all the questions about its future fall away and be supplanted by images of its marvelous past. But the approach seemed much like the commercials that Detroit companies love to run, filled with footage meant to trigger memories of the era when they sold Americans their dream cars. All the fond memories of the past do not change Ford's present. And unless it can address the competitive challenge that it faces from GM, Chrysler and the imports, its next 100 years may be bumpy indeed.

CHAPTER TEN

WHAT DO CUSTOMERS
REALLY WANT?

MARK SANDLIN, a 29-year-old graphic designer who lives in
Everett, Washington, is just the kind of buyer that auto companies
long to attract. He grew up loving cars and still treasures his case of
Hot Wheels that he collected when he was a kid. His enthusiasm was
fueled by his father, who owned more than 30 different models when
Sandlin was young—domestics, imports, sedans, pickups, you name
it. He's an avid Web surfer, constantly checking out various automotive sites and dropping into car discussions. On weekends, Sandlin
will stop in at car dealerships to see what the latest models look like,
fending off salespeople who descend on him like locusts, eager for
his business. "I say, 'Quit it, I know more about cars than you do,'"

Sandlin said. Through his knowledge of design, he can analyze every concept car that GM and Ford have put on display at auto shows over the past few years, such as the Ford 49 and the Chevrolet Nomad.

Sandlin is excited that Bob Lutz has taken charge of GM's product development, and he's glad that Lincoln is trying to make its interiors more luxurious. But Sandlin has no interest in owning a Detroit automobile. He drives a Volkswagen Jetta, his second import, bought after trading in a Honda Accord coupe. His wife still drives a 1995 Accord, and his friends own Subarus and Toyota Corollas. "There isn't any American car that evokes any kind of passionate response from me at all. So many of them have been so bean-counterized that they just make you yawn," Sandlin said. What does it symbolize that he and so many other American consumers are buying cars with import nameplates? Sandlin shrugs. "I think it says we're tired of Detroit making crap," he said. "I think the domestic companies are learning that they can't just support their business by waving a flag anymore. People want something to be proud of while they're waving their flag."

Lou Nunez, who lives in the New Jersey suburbs outside New York City, isn't a car expert like Sandlin, but he has always believed in Detroit, having come from a family of Ford owners. He set out specifically to buy another Ford in 1999, aiming to use up more than $1,000 in credits on a Ford Visa card. Nunez, 43, took home a Ford Contour SE Sport Edition, which joined his brother's 1998 Contour in the family's stable of Fords. But a week after Nunez bought his Contour, the compact would not start and had to be towed back to the dealer. Then, when the car was three years old, the speedometer stopped working, requiring a $350 repair. That happened a few months after the air-conditioning died in the middle of a hot New Jersey summer, requiring a new shot of coolant. In addition, his Contour is afflicted with excessive wind noise on the highway, as well as "mysterious creaks, groans and rattles" from the dashboard, he said.

Nunez decided to get rid of his Contour "before it really caused me headaches" and took the car to a used-car lot for an appraisal, only to find out that a car for which he had paid $18,820 four years earlier was worth less than $3,500. A key reason was that Ford had sold countless Contours over the years at deep discount prices to rental car companies. They, in turn, unloaded them onto the used-car market. Some dealers even refused to look his car over. "One guy said to me, 'Look, I'm not buying this. I've had a Contour sitting on my lot for more than six months,'" Nunez recalled. In spring 2003, Nunez broke with family tradition and set out to shop for a Subaru Outback. He figures the car will be reliable, since one of his neighbors has owned one for a dozen years with no major problems. Nunez, who runs the information help desk at a local college, said the experience with his Contour has erased his loyalty to Ford. "Ford, as far as I'm concerned, just has not been loyal to their customers," he said.

Sandlin, in Washington State, and Nunez, in New Jersey, each live in a state where customers are buying imports at a faster rate than the national average, a trend that is accelerating with each passing month. The growth is greatest on both the East and West Coasts, and increasingly in western and southern states. It is as if the imports took a map of the country, colored in two sides of it and then began coloring in the adjoining states. The pattern is just like the import companies' strategy for eating into Detroit's market share: The imports are nibbling at the edges as the traditional American companies cling to their core strength, the industrial heartland. To be sure, Detroit companies have not lost their grip on the states where they've always been strong.

In Michigan, the nation's automobile capital, where more than 1 million people are directly or indirectly employed by the auto companies, domestic brands have an 87.2 percent share. It is possible to sit at a stoplight at the intersection of Telegraph and 12 Mile Roads, two main thoroughfares 20 minutes from the headquarters of each of the Detroit companies, and not see a single import vehicle among two dozen waiting for the light to turn green. Other midwestern states are overwhelmingly loyal to Detroit, too. Domestic vehicles still have two-thirds to three-quarters of the market in Indiana, Minnesota, Wisconsin and even Ohio, despite Honda's presence there. But that's to be expected. What is more alarming is that Detroit is losing ground in some of the wealthiest states of the country, with some of the country's most sought-after buyers.

Californians have always bought import cars and trucks in droves, attracted by their fuel economy and cleanliness in a state where environmental issues have long been in the forefront. Japanese auto companies made their first inroads there, followed by the Koreans, while European cars with their posh reputations have attracted status-seeking Californians for decades. In almost a reverse picture of what it is like to drive in Detroit, a motorist can sit in a sea of traffic on Interstate 405 in Los Angeles at rush hour and see but one Detroit vehicle—an SUV. But California is no longer the only state where imports have more than 50 percent of the market.

In California, Connecticut, the District of Columbia and Massachusetts, import nameplates took more than half of all automobile sales in 2001, according to statistics from R. L. Polk & Co., which tracks vehicle registrations. In another 13 states—Arizona, Colorado, Florida, Hawaii, Maryland, New Hampshire, New Jersey, New York, Oregon, Rhode Island, Virginia, Vermont and Washington State—import sales constituted more than 40 percent of the market, above the national average of 38.7 percent. On the flip side, there are only three states where imports made up less than 20 percent of all sales. They are Michigan, of course, plus the two Dakotas, hardly a groundswell of support for the Detroit auto companies.

Consumers' switch to imports coincides with the greatest availability of car-buying information that the industry has ever seen. Thanks to the Internet, buyers can tap into more statistics about vehicles than many engineers at the auto companies used to be able to access. This wealth of data is revolutionizing the way people think

about vehicles and the way they approach their car and truck purchases. Anwyl, of Edmunds.com, feels the situation has created a
whole new dynamic among consumers, car companies and their
dealers. "People aren't as afraid as they used to be" about the car-buying process, Anwyl said. "They feel empowered. Even though car-buying is still a battle, it is a battle that consumers feel they can win." As
recently as five years ago, auto companies did not know what to make
of the Web. Some companies saw it only as a marketing tool, a place
to stash brochures and dealers' addresses. Others panicked. For a time
in the late 1990s, the industry was awash with predictions that the
traditional automobile showroom was headed for the dustbin and
customers would be buying cars with a click of their computer mouse.
"This Guy Is Outta Here!" a cover story in *Business Week* declared in
1999.

That did not exactly turn out to be the case. Internet purchases are
rare, comprising less than 5 percent of all auto sales each year. But Internet research has become the norm. Consumers from all walks of life,
from senior citizens to the industry's youngest buyers, are arriving at
showrooms armed with information, already experts on the vehicles
they want to buy without being handed a brochure. Some 60 percent of
customers research their vehicles on the Internet, whether on the auto
companies' sites or independent sources. Even so, a number of dealers
and their parent car companies have been slow to realize the transformation that has occurred, still convinced that their primary job is to sell
the sizzle, not the steak.

For decades, consumers got the bulk of their quality data from
magazines like *Consumer Reports*, which served as a bible for customers who demanded high quality. Dealers got used to shoppers
walking in the door with dog-eared copies of the magazine under
their arms. Although the magazine barred companies from citing its
reviews, and still does, a favorable rating in the publication could lead
to the "*Consumer Reports* effect," triggering a sales increase of as much

as 25 percent in the year after the review appeared. The magazine's repeated endorsement of Toyota and Honda vehicles throughout the 1970s and 1980s helped launch those brands in the United States. Likewise, its declaration of the Suzuki Samurai as unsafe led to the small SUV's demise and triggered an angry lawsuit from the Japanese company. But *Consumer Reports* was far from the only source of information: For generations, car enthusiasts have turned to magazines like *Motor Trend, Car & Driver, Road & Track, Popular Mechanics* and, more recently, *Automobile* for their opinions and for their wildly entertaining articles.

In the 1980s, another place to look for advice popped up: the marketing firm J.D. Power & Associates, which issues a series of ratings every year on vehicle quality, reliability and the service provided by dealers. Unlike *Consumer Reports*, J.D. Power allowed the auto companies to use its ratings in their ads. And by the 1990s, its endorsement had become a very visible imprimatur on the automotive scene. But these automobile raters proved to be only a run-up for the explosion of information about automobiles that is now available on the World Wide Web.

One of the most widely accessed sources is Edmunds.com, which is based in Santa Monica, California, and which draws 2.7 million visitors a month to its omnibus site. The Edmunds company has been around since 1966, and it became known for its annual series of buyers' guides for both new and used cars, domestics and imports, that were then the size of *Reader's Digest.* Along with other publications, Edmunds helped buyers figure out the mysterious process of car shopping, cautioning them about the ways dealers calculated prices, alerting them when vehicles were likely to be poor values. In 1994, the company took the leap to the Internet with a site that now rivals *Consumer Reports* in its reach and impact on the car market.

Unlike the magazine, however, Edmunds.com is a freewheeling site, focused as much on data as it is on opinions and reviews. Its phenomenally popular "Town Hall Forum" invites car owners, shoppers and enthusiasts to post their views on everything from financing to future vehicles and to volunteer to be interviewed by the media.

What Edmunds.com and some of its rival sites have done is bring the concept of data transparency right into the faces of the auto companies. Just about any statistic about any vehicle sold in the United States can be found on the Web, whether it is new or used. The data on Edmunds alone seems endless.

Manufacturers' list prices are just a beginning. There are list prices and invoice prices for vehicles and features like CD players and antilock brakes. There are pages that compare everything about a vehicle across a grid that stacks it up next to its competition. Buyers can find out what vehicles are selling for within their zip code and elsewhere, allowing them to get an idea of the price they can expect to pay, a feature that Edmunds calls the True Market Value. It's a way to figure out how deep discounts are running, and also to tell how hot a vehicle is, by determining how close to sticker price deals are ranging in their area. "In any car purchase, the biggest fear that people have is the fear of making a mistake," said Robert Kurilko, vice president of marketing at Edmunds. "One of the things they want to do is buy a good car at a good price," he said. To that end, customers can check out the kinds of incentives that the auto companies are offering and how they compare to what's available on other cars. They can look up financing information, print out pictures of future vehicles, and arrange for insurance. They can also find out the kind of damage that discount lease deals, incentives, zero percent financing and other special offers are doing to the resale value of their vehicles, and figure out whether vehicles are reliable. In March 2003, Edmunds introduced a feature called the True Cost of Incentives, which showed an alarming discrepancy between import and Detroit vehicles. At that time, the site found that for every $1 that was being spent on incentives by Japanese companies, Korean companies were spending $1.15,

European automakers were paying $1.67 and Detroit companies were paying $3.39.

Executives view Edmunds and other sites as a sea change. "The better informed a customer is, the worse it is for Detroit," said Denny Clements, the Lexus general manager. "No matter what they try to say, the quality gap hasn't narrowed. Just look at the data that you can find out there on the Web." While disagreeing with Clements, GM's Bob Lutz said he likes the sites for another reason: The more information a consumer has, the more GM can combat mystiques about other companies, he said. But the flood of information is taking a key element out of the car-buying process: raw emotion. Detroit has long operated on one basic premise, which was that in the end, people bought cars that stirred them inside. That perception still lingers today, and it helps to explain why Detroit companies still place so much emphasis on niche vehicles, like sports cars, as proof of their expertise. In the world of Detroit, which is so relentlessly male in focus, people buy cars because they are sexy and exciting. It is a *Maxim* magazine approach whose validity is fast being eroded by imports.

All across the country, buyers of all types—male, female, white, black, Asian, Hispanic and so forth—increasingly don't use sex appeal as the key determinant in their car purchases. First of all, what gets lost in the great quest to attract male consumers is that half of all vehicles are purchased by women, and women have a say in 80 percent of all automotive purchases. Of course, women love good design, but they put many other considerations ahead of styling, including durability, reliability, safety and comfort. The flood of working women into the car market in the 1980s was a key factor in launching imports' upward climb, and it's a factor that the smartest import companies have never forgotten.

Second, a car or truck these days costs a lot of money. The average vehicle costs $29,000 new, and there are dozens of vehicles, particularly sport utilities, that cost well above that. A car is a major purchase for many households, and it is one that requires days, weeks or months of research. While emotion definitely gets people interested in a vehicle, and a portion of the car-buying population actually will go out and buy one based on their reaction to its appearance, the grand majority of buyers are making their decisions based on practicalities. "Emotion is what I feel when I look at a new car," said Joe Hammell, the Atlanta BMW 5-series owner. "I would buy a car that doesn't look good to me, but I would never buy a car because it simply looks good."

Buyers' behavior is changing in another way: No matter how much fun they have behind the wheel, consumers these days have far less tolerance for cars that don't live up to their expectations for quality and value. Two German brands, Volkswagen and Mercedes-Benz, are discovering that the hard way. Only five years ago, Volkswagen was the industry's hot car company, enjoying an enormous renaissance from a dismal performance in the mid-1990s when its American sales dropped to only 49,000 a year. Throughout the decade, there was no more hotly anticipated product than the Volkswagen New Beetle, the rejuvenated version of the mass-market car that was VW's trademark during the 1950s, 1960s and 1970s. In 1994, when VW showed a concept version of the Beetle called the Concept One, its display at the Detroit Auto Show was mobbed. Within a week, dealers across the country were deluged with deposits for a car that VW had not yet decided to build. The strong response signaled that people were ready for the Beetle to return, and eventually, VW went ahead with plans to build the Beetle in Puebla, Mexico. It arrived in the United States in the summer of 1998, with the auto industry enjoying a banner year.

There were waiting lists for Beetles at almost every VW showroom. There were circles worn in the grass outside showrooms from the footprints of people who surrounded the car to peer inside. Beetle owners got used to being waved at, their cars admired by passersby and borrowed by neighbors for test drives. The joy over the Beetle seemed endless, and it was the linchpin of a marketing campaign that turned VW into a truly hot company. Both the Beetle and the Passat mid-sized car were blowing out of showrooms, the latter helped by a rave review in *Consumer Reports* that said it was better than an Accord or a Camry. The endorsement brought people into showrooms who had never bought VWs before, and VW added to the excitement over its vehicles with memorably quirky ads that were the talk of the industry. As the Beetle had done for VW in the 1960s, it seemed destined to do for VW in the late 1990s: make it a cult car with young consumers. Volkswagens of all kinds seemed to be what the kids wanted, and the company basked in its long-awaited glory.

It seemed too good to last, and it was. When things got particularly tough for VW in the mid-1990s, it rolled out a two-year free-maintenance plan, covering most repairs and defects that a buyer might encounter, taking a page from Hyundai in an effort to convince consumers to come back. The plan remained in place as VW sales began to swell, but what seemed on the surface to be a great selling point ultimately backfired. VW dealers, who had grown accustomed to slower business, found themselves with more customers than they could handle. Their repair bays filled up with cars from the free-maintenance plan, requiring owners to make appointments three weeks and more in advance. Moreover, owners were discovering that their vehicles weren't as trouble-free as they expected, particularly the people who had traded Japanese vehicles for them. There would be irritating issues, like turbocharged engines that misfired because of bugs in their computer chips. There would be long waits for parts that had to come from either Mexico or Germany. And there were some major problems, too, like a widespread ignition glitch that afflicted hundreds of thousands of cars.

VW also reacted far too slowly in building on the excitement over the Beetle. It took five years for the Beetle convertible, promised when the original car was introduced, to arrive in American showrooms.

(Then, in a fluke of timing, it went on sale in winter 2003 just when much of the country was paralyzed by snow.) In Germany, VW's parent company was running into financial trouble, forced to acknowledge that it had to address the quality issues, even as it expanded its lineup into much more expensive vehicles, such as a sport utility called the Touareg and a luxury car called Phaeton. VW sales fell in 2002 and dropped again in 2003, proof that its moment of heat had cooled.

At the same time that VW was enjoying its rush of excitement, Mercedes had an unquestioned hold on luxury buyers. What the 1980s had been to BMW, the 1990s were to Mercedes. The company didn't seem to take one wrong step. It launched a series of well-received vehicles, like the E-Class sedan, the M-Class sport utility, and a series of smaller cars such as the SLK coupe and CLK convertible. No longer was Mercedes a brand that appealed to the most conservative, stodgy luxury car buyers. It was hip and happening, thanks in part to a magical advertising campaign that featured an Elvis impersonator and a chorus line of autoworkers singing "Falling in Love Again." As it came time to introduce the next version of its flagship S-Class sedan, it seemed that Mercedes was bulletproof. But it was not. The S-Class, which debuted in 1999, immediately was beset by complaints that its quality trailed behind that of competing vehicles from Lexus and BMW. Its starting price of $72,000 was well above the $55,000 cost of the Lexus LS 430, which had reached the market to rave reviews.

Mercedes's sales didn't plummet, but the buzz that it had enjoyed in the 1990s began to diminish, and by 2002 it had been passed by both Lexus and BMW. Quality issues began to surface. In 2003, it actually fell behind Chrysler on a J.D. Power survey of long-term reliability, stunning the industry. Then Mercedes took a step that further afflicted its brand image. It introduced the cheapest car in its lineup, the $24,950 C-Class coupe, based on the C-Class sedan. Mercedes had always had an entry-level vehicle, but the C-Class coupe was cheaper than anything that either BMW or Lexus offered. Among buyers of more expensive Mercedes models, the coupe caused grumbling that the German company was cheapening its reputation, something that neither it nor its sister company, Chrysler, could afford to see happen, since Chrysler was pinning its future on the idea of being connected with such a heralded brand. Even worse, the cars didn't sell and Mercedes found itself with a growing supply that it attempted to clear out with discounted leases.

It was an indication of what could happen if a company strayed too far from what its customers expected. But Mercedes couldn't be blamed for trying to reach beyond its traditional buyers in an effort to attract younger customers into its showrooms. That's exactly what BMW will be hoping to do, too, as it brings in the 1-series later this decade. In fact, every single player in the auto industry is trying to figure out what the next big generation of consumers will want.

———————

The Honda Element looks like a sport utility that married a Brinks truck, with as much headroom as a Greyhound bus. Honda calls it a dorm room on wheels, with seats that can be turned around, pulled out, folded flat, hosed off and stacked with gear. It is so unlike the rest of Honda's lineup that it stands out like a Frank Gehry building in an industrial park. And it isn't the only such oddity. The Toyota Scion xB seems like homage to a Chrysler minivan, but shrunken and brought down to curb level. It has the dramatic edges of a Japanese *anime* cartoon, all exclamations and drama. There aren't any controls in front of the steering wheel to distract the driver. They're off to the center above an ear-blasting Pioneer stereo, prewired for satellite radio. The sound system's controls dwarf the fan and air-conditioning dials.

Ye Chen, a 26-year-old graphic designer from Brooklyn, is enamored of both, especially the Honda. "The Element is different. It's not pretentious. It's not trying to look good. It's a box. I like it," said Chen. Alisha Broberg of San Antonio isn't interested in either of them. "I think the Scion is awful," she said. "When did designers start thinking that boxy equals cool for the under-30 set?" Given an unlimited budget, Broberg, 25, said she'd replace her 1990 Jeep Cherokee with a Nissan 350Z, a Honda Accord or a Toyota RAV-4 SUV. Such polar-opposite reactions are just one illustration of how perplexing it can be for car companies to figure out what will appeal to buyers under age 25. Known to marketers as Generation Y, these customers have little buying power now, purchasing only 5 percent of the 17.2 million cars and trucks sold in the United States in 2003.

But just wait. By 2010, buyers born after 1977 will constitute 25 percent of the car market. And by 2020, they'll be 40 percent, which, if sales stay at roughly the 2002 rate, means they'll be purchasing 8 million vehicles a year. In an industry fraught with competition, and beset with marketing experts who dissect buyers' behavior to the specificity of a DNA molecule, it isn't too soon for the auto companies to start worrying. Honda and Toyota, otherwise known for their general conservatism, are employing the most radical approaches. One of the biggest champions of Honda's approach is its recently retired chief executive, Hiroyuki Yoshino, who believes Honda needs to keep a fresh supply of customers coming into its showrooms. "If you're young, you have a young future," said Yoshino. Consumers in his generation "have only so many years left. For example, cars like Cadillac capture a certain generation and they age with the car. You've got to get them young."

Honda has a secret weapon, he said, in its robot, Asimo, who is an icon with Japanese children and is becoming widely known in the United States as well. "Small kids are so attracted to that robot," said Yoshino. "If small kids come to like Honda because of him, it will be a help to us later." It's no accident that Asimo, who walks and talks, moves his arms and legs, and nods in recognition, is four feet tall and proportioned like a child. That's so children will find him approachable, Yoshino said. "We're not just miniaturizing a large robot," he said.

Toyota's approach is different but just as unique. In 2003, it created an entirely new nameplate, Scion, which will eventually house a collection of vehicles meant to appeal to the trendiest slice of the Generation Y market. Scion went on sale in June 2003 in California, and then rolled out nationally. Its initial lineup includes the xB and the xA, a subcompact car that seems to be a marriage of a Toyota with a VW Golf. Both Scions are based on cars sold by Toyota in Japan, where the xB is sold as the BB and the xA is called the Ist (pronounced "east"). Toyota hasn't introduced a new brand since Lexus in 1989, and there was plenty of debate over whether it needed to add another brand, or whether the original Toyota nameplate would suffice.

Opponents of the separate approach noted that in the 1970s and 1980s, Toyota did great with baby boomers, so there was no need to branch out. But the company's research, and surveys by industry analysts, showed that Toyota had a fairly stodgy image with the children of those buyers. Even though Toyota's buyers, at an average 41.1 years of age, are younger than their counterparts at GM, Ford or Chrysler, the company decided that it had to do something different to appeal to Gen-Y. And one of the biggest advocates of the idea was Fujio Cho, Toyota's chief executive. He admitted that he had no feel for the market himself. "I'm not the kind of person who can tell [what young customers want]," he said at the 2003 Detroit Auto Show. But he added, "This will have a tremendous strategic influence 10 or 20 years in the future. If we can capture them at 15 to 24 [years of age], we can enjoy their business for years to come."

Toyota, in its typical way, has studied these consumers inside and out—literally. It knows that they've gone to the movies more than seven times in the previous six months, spend up to 30 hours a week listening to music, another 7 to 10 hours a week playing sports, eat out three times a week and visit a museum maybe once every six months. They may don hot-colored jackets for outdoor activities, but they don't like bright colors in cars, so the Scions will be offered in the same muted tones that are on Lexus automobiles. To start, Toyota has relatively low expectations for Scion. It hopes to sell about 100,000 a year eventually, once it fills out the lineup with a third model, a subcompact coupe. It priced the first two cars daringly low, given that the average vehicle in the country costs $30,000. The Scions each cost less than $14,000. And there's a twist. Scion buyers will be able to pick out all kinds of features for their cars, kind of like outfitting a condominium. They can choose between a manual or automatic transmission; select the style they want for the wheel covers; choose the colors of the lights behind the dashboard gauges (you can have an amethyst radio display), and choose among different reflector lights and seat covers, which are available in a leopard print. Toyota dealers, who are spending $125,000 each to set up separate Scion displays in their showrooms, will relay the choices to Toyota and then the car will be outfitted at one of the company's shipping centers and sent to the dealer within seven days. This customizing process, known as "tuning," is a widespread trend in California, where Honda has been one of its biggest beneficiaries. (The phrase is borrowed from the process of tweaking the valves of an engine so that it features a distinctive roar.)

Tuners use their cars to display their sense of personal style, and their favorite vehicle, hands down, is the Honda Civic. Drive through the streets of West Hollywood at night or down Interstate 405 from Los Angeles and you'll see Civics and other cars streaking by, with magnesium wheel covers that can cost hundreds of dollars, colored sidelights, booming radios and loud engines. Tuners were featured in the movie *The Fast and the Furious*, which made Vin Diesel into a Gen-Y icon, and the tuning movement, with its "have it however you want it" attitude, surprised Honda and the rest of the industry. They're all trying to capitalize on it without looking "really uncool," according to Chen, the Brooklyn graphic designer. "The youth market is a lot more savvy than the car companies give them credit for," said Todd Turner, president of

CarConcepts, Inc., a California firm that studies automotive trends. "If they think it's specifically made for them, they're not interested. If they discover it and adopt it, they like it."

That's the strategy that other companies are following in various ways. Hyundai has done almost nothing special to attract young customers, but pulls them in anyway with its low-priced lineup and its 10-year, 100,000-mile warranty. The average age of a Hyundai buyer is just 35.8, according to CNW Marketing Research of Bandon, Oregon. Finbarr O'Neill, the former Hyundai chief executive, was skeptical about trying to attract any single age group. "You don't break people down by ages. I just don't think that it works out," said O'Neill, banging his hand on a conference table for emphasis. "You can slice and dice the market too thin. You have to look at broader categories, because you otherwise lose the definition of who you are."

Mitsubishi came up with its own formula: aggressive styling, pulsing music and free cars. At least, free for the first year, under the program it has offered for the past couple of years. Its television ads, with head-bobbing drivers and contortionist passengers, plus some of the industry's most flexible financing terms, helped make Mitsubishi the fastest-growing automaker in the United States the past four years, with its sales up 81 percent since 1999. What's more, 40 percent of its customers were under the age of 35. "We've become a very cool and hip company in the eyes of our customers," boasted Pierre Gagnon, president of Mitsubishi Motors North America. But that hipness, like Gagnon's tenure, was short-lived. Mitsubishi had thought vehicles like the entry-level Lancer and the sporty Eclipse would help shake the company free of a fuzzy image as a second-tier Japanese player to Toyota and Honda. Gagnon, in fact, insisted Mitsubishi could sell as many as 600,000 cars a year by mid-decade, up from just 190,000 in 1999. But the flame of popularity that engulfed the brand was quickly extinguished. Mitsubishi's overly generous credit terms to its young customers resulted in a repossession rate much higher than the industry average. Simultaneously, its parent company ran into financial problems in Japan. Ultimately, Gagnon was let go in 2003, and Finbarr O'Neill, who had revived Hyundai, was lured to run the brand. He gave few hints of where he planned to take the company, and his task seemed unenviable, no matter how hot the company and its young customers had been just a while back.

All the maneuvering to attract young customers amuses Helmut Panke at BMW, who has his own youth car, the $20,000 Mini Cooper. There are no special deals on the Mini, still in demand after 18 months on the market. Like O'Neill, he's willing to sell one of his cars to anybody, no matter their age, as long as their state of mind matches that of the retro British automobile. "People who are 96 years old are buying the Mini, as well as 20-year-olds, and I'm happy about it," Panke said. "It's good to have a customer. What's wrong with that?"

After an afternoon spent in Los Angeles rush-hour traffic, the Honda FCV is as serene as a monastery. There is no noise when it starts, and just a quiet whir as its transmission engages and the car moves forward. The front-wheel-drive compact glides up to 35 mph in no time. The car's speedometer and other gauges are displayed on a screen above the center console. Its ride is as comfortable and safe as that of any other Honda. The FCV has undergone crash tests and been certified by the Environmental Protection Agency. But the FCV isn't for sale, unless you are the city of Los Angeles, which took delivery this year on the first of a fleet of five FCV cars.

The FCV is powered by hydrogen, which is captured in a fuel cell and used in place of gasoline. Its only emissions are water vapor, and it can be refueled in five minutes. The FCV, which costs $300,000, can travel for 170 miles on a full fuel cell, and there's another benefit: The same home generation unit that would be used to produce hydrogen for a customer's car can also make natural gas to heat a home. That won't happen soon. Hydrogen fuel cell cars are far from ready for the conventional car market and may not be sold to the public before 2010 or well after.

But hybrid-electric vehicles are already being sold across the country, and they are demonstrating that there is a group of consumers, though limited at the moment, that is interested in exploring automobiles powered by something other than an internal combustion engine. These cars, powered by battery-driven electric motors and gasoline engines, came into vogue in 2002, when spiking gas prices and the backlash against SUVs made them seem not only sensible to many ordinary consumers, but hip to Hollywood stars like Cameron Diaz and Leonardo DiCaprio. Detroit has resisted offering alternative-fuel vehicles for years, saying that there was no sign that customers would be interested in them, and no possibility of making a profit on such expensive research. But Ford and GM are finally being dragged into the alternative-fuel-vehicle market because Honda and Toyota are already there, selling 50,000 hybrid-electric vehicles a year. "They're about building hype. We're about building products that people want," said Jim Press of Toyota, which has sold the hybrid-electric Prius (pronounced "PREE-us") in Japan since 1997, and in the United States since 2000. As for Detroit's conversion to the wisdom of hybrids, Press says, "I'm glad they see this giant walking down the hallway, but they saw it too late."

For, as Detroit companies introduce their first hybrid-electric vehicles over the next few years, with Ford bringing out the hybrid Escape SUV and GM promising pickups and a hybrid Saturn VUE sport utility, Honda and Toyota are on their second-generation hybrids and Toyota also plans to introduce a hybrid Lexus RX 330 in 2005. While Bob Lutz talks about giving American customers more cylinders and Chrysler brings back rear-wheel-drive cars, executives at the Japanese companies firmly believe that hybrid vehicles are set to move beyond experiments. In 2002, Honda added the hybrid Civic to a lineup that was launched with the Insight in 1999. Now the hybrid Civic accounts for 10 percent of all Civic sales and a hybrid Accord is coming. "Honda likes technology, but engineers feel they're successful only if they can put it into the market," said Ben Knight, vice president of Honda's Research & Development Center in Torrance, California.

The automobile industry has examined ways to power cars with something other than gasoline since its earliest days. The Stanley Steamer, powered by steam power, was the first car bought by the American government while Theodore Roosevelt was president. Electric cars were curiosities through the 1920s, when gasoline engines firmly took charge, and Chrysler had a brief fling with jet-engine-powered cars in the 1950s, ordering up a fleet of them. There have been diesel-powered automobiles for generations, enjoying a spike in popularity in the 1970s, due to the rise in gasoline prices in the wake of a pair of oil embargoes. But the idea of a vehicle powered by anything but gasoline died out until the 1990s, when California passed a regulation requiring that 5 percent of all vehicles sold in the state be nonpolluting by 2000. The auto companies vigorously fought the idea. But in the meantime, GM decided to give electric vehicles a try.

It spent $1 billion to develop a small electric car, the EV1, which was available through Saturn dealers in California and Arizona. GM leased rather than sold the EV1, and its owners had to install charging stations in their garages and be interviewed by the company in order to be sure they understood all the requirements of an electric vehicle. The biggest problem with the EV1 was its short range, especially in California's stop-and-go traffic. The air-conditioning system could sap the car of power, and more than one owner had to cancel meetings that were more than 100 miles round-trip, fearing that they couldn't get back home. Put on the market in 1995, GM discontinued EV1 in 1999 after developing just two versions of the car, concluding that there wasn't sufficient demand. "We couldn't give them away," said Gary Cowger, president of GM's North American operations.

In retrospect, EV1 was a good starting point for GM and earned it a lot of loyalty among its small group of owners, some of whom filed suit in 2002 to keep their cars instead of turning them back in to GM when their leases expired. But instead of using EV1 as a launching pad into hybrid vehicles, the auto company saw it as wasted time and money and simply decided that customers weren't interested. "EV1 was frankly what held us back on hybrids," Cowger said. "When the hybrid thing started, people said, 'Show me the business case.'" Added Lutz, "A product that loses money is not a legitimate product." But Lutz is quick to congratulate Japanese companies for sensing the inklings of public interest in hybrid vehicles. "Was it smart PR? Of course it was. Do we wish we had them? Of course we do."

Nobody is more unhappy that GM doesn't have hybrids yet than former GM chief executive Robert Stempel. Since resigning form GM in 1992 in the midst of the company's financial turmoil, he has become a tireless advocate for alternative-fuel technologies, devoting the bulk of his time to the development of hydrogen fuel cells and lean-engine concepts. "I'm furious," Stempel said in March 2003. "GM had the technology. The lead [over Japanese companies] was there. I know it." But the Japanese companies got a leg up on their Detroit competition for a couple of reasons. First was the deeply held belief by executives at both Toyota and Honda that the environment mattered.

Throughout his life, Soichiro Honda had constantly dogged his engineers to keep the environment at the forefront as they developed engines. He actually approached GM decades ago with some of his environmentally friendly technology, Stempel said, but the auto company turned him away. Likewise, in 1996 Toyota said that internal combustion engines most likely would someday have to disappear, in order to protect the world's shrinking energy resources. Overall environmental consciousness seems much higher, on a daily basis, in Japan than it is in the United States, some green communities aside. For one thing, Japan is an island. The sea is never far away from any point in the country, and Japan has taken enormous efforts to preserve its parks and shrines, despite the intense crowding that occurs in its cities and on its subways and on its highways. Gasoline, as in Europe, costs $5 a gallon and up. Long before fears over severe acute respiratory syndrome, or SARS, circulated in Asia during spring 2003, Japanese pedestrians could be seen walking through major cities wearing face masks to protect themselves against the air pollution that permeates urban areas.

Both Toyota and Honda developed electric cars and then segued into hybrid vehicles as a way to maximize fuel economy of gasoline engines. A hybrid vehicle's battery is recharged by the gasoline engine and by collecting energy when the car brakes. The battery powers an electric motor that boosts and occasionally replaces the power of the gasoline engine. Honda and Toyota use the power a little differently. On Hondas, the electric motor helps out the gasoline engine when the car is climbing hills or accelerating sharply. On Toyota models, the electric motor takes over completely at slow speeds. In both, the gasoline engine shuts off when the car comes to a stop at a traffic light or stop sign. (Jay Leno quipped that he'd once had a car that did the same thing. It was called a Yugo, he said.)

The first hybrid car that was introduced in the United States was the Honda Insight, an aluminum car shaped like an upside-down bathtub that definitely was a stretch to get used to. The two-seater was originally available only with a stick shift, and it was uncomfortable, appealing only to the most serious devotees. Honda has solved that quirkiness question with the hybrid Civic, virtually the same as the conventional compact save for a $2,000 premium. But Knight says that Insight, since updated and made available with an automatic transmission, has been important for Honda. "I don't consider it an experiment. The Insight really helped prepare the market [for hybrids]," Knight said. He brushes aside criticism of the Insight's space-age looks, saying, "The public recognized they were real cars."

Appearance wasn't an issue with the Prius, which is about the same size as a Toyota Corolla and has significantly more headroom. It required no compromises space-wise, and its conventional appearance was a strong selling point for dealers. "When you look at what's happening with the world and the availability of oil reserves going forward, they really hit the nail on the head with the Prius," said Greg Penske, owner of Longo Toyota, the country's largest Toyota dealer. In 2002, Toyota passed a milestone, selling its one hundred thousandth Prius worldwide since the car went on sale in 1997. Toyota is aiming to sell 400,000 hybrids a year by 2005, and by 2010, the company would like to sell 1 million hybrid vehicles a year, according to its chief executive, Fujio Cho.

Toyota's approach differs from Honda's in that it sees two ways to apply hybrid technology. One is the conventional hybrid system; the other is called a mild hybrid, in which fuel economy is boosted about 10 percent on the company's biggest vehicles, like its minivans and larger cars, by use of the electric motor when the car is idling in traffic. That might not seem like much, but on a vehicle that gets 25 mpg, even an extra 2.5 mpg can reduce gasoline prices in places like Tokyo. Stempel, for one, says this fuel-economy-boosting hybrid is an important development. "The biggest payback on a hybrid is not on a smaller car. It's on the bigger stuff," said Stempel, chairman of a company that is developing hydrogen fuel cells. "The bigger it is, the better it is." Honda, by contrast, has just one kind of hybrid and doesn't think a mild hybrid has much use, since it can get a 10 percent increase in fuel economy out of its conventional engines. "Words are meaningless," said Knight of Honda R&D. "Ours is a high-efficiency hybrid. There are many ways to package it. What counts is performance."

Actually, what counts more is whether customers across the United States are ready to embrace something other than the big engines that Lutz thinks they will always want. The shift to hybrids has been fairly slow in the United States, where about 50,000 were sold in the first few years they've been available. But thanks to high gas prices in recent years, the little interest in them has skyrocketed, and those who've purchased them are enthusiastic about their potential. "It's always great to go 500 miles on less than $20 in gas," said Jim Alden, a Hollywood computer network engineer. He is on his second Prius, having bought his first in 2001 and his second in 2003. In California, Alden was paying $2 a gallon and up for gasoline for his frequent business trips. But he wasn't just interested in saving money. "I was motivated by the technology, and it's so good for the environment," Alden said. The hybrid market is set to shift into a new phase in 2005, when hybrid versions of the Lexus RX 330 and Toyota Highlander will both be on sale. Officials at Toyota are excited about it, as is Stempel, who thinks that it will trigger interest in hybrids in an entirely new group of buyers. "What's important about the Lexus is that it's so damn quiet," Stempel said.

That's just what some people in the industry think is a drawback about hybrid vehicles. They lack the zoom-zoom quality of internal combustion engines. And that's disconcerting to people who grew up with the sound of roaring V-8s and turbochargers. The silence can take the joy out of driving. But Stempel said hybrids can be tuned to have the performance of traditional engines, just as Lexus is promising it will do with the 400 H. "Do I like the boy-racer feel? Sure," Stempel said. "But this will set a new standard for comfort." Whether hybrids will exist on their own as the country's favorite form of alternative power, or lead to hydrogen fuel cell vehicles, isn't certain. Hybrids' biggest advantage is that they don't require anything special. They needn't be plugged in like electric cars, and they can run on gasoline.

But there are vast uncertainties. It's not clear yet how hybrids will hold up under rugged driving conditions, whether repairs will be expensive, how they'll do on the used-car market and whether interest in them will stay strong should gasoline prices plummet back toward $1 a gallon. One of the biggest skeptics about them is Chrysler, which had a hybrid Dodge Durango under development and ready to be introduced in 2002, only to pull it back because its parent company,

DaimlerChrysler, insisted that diesel-fueled vehicles were a better way to go. Diesels are common in Europe, where 25 percent of all vehicles are sold with diesel engines, and it is logical that DaimlerChrysler wanted to focus its efforts in an area where it could yield more sales. However, the fight to convince consumers to try diesels will be a difficult one in the United States, where consumers remember diesels as dirty, chugging and noisy, with engines that knocked and performed poorly, except in the case of turbocharged engines.

Hybrids are another story, gliding softly along American roads like swans on a still pond. They are more than just cars—they are a statement about society, said James Lentz, Toyota's vice president for marketing. "Toyota feels they are a way to give back," he said, a statement that some in Detroit feel is hypocritical, in view of the fact that Toyota has expanded so deeply into the market for pickups, SUVs and minivans. But Lentz isn't completely starry-eyed. He said Toyota believes that as with other vehicles, future buyers of hybrids will gravitate to companies with experience in the technology when they decide it's time to buy their first gasoline-electric car. "We'll have a huge competitive advantage when we get to generation four and five," Lentz said.

All of which makes Stempel even sadder that his old company missed out on its chance to lead in yet another market that import companies captured first. "In the face of fluctuating gasoline prices, the situation in Iraq and an uncertain economy, consumers are saying, 'Isn't there a better way?'" Stempel said. Whoever hears those voices first, throughout the car market, will have the upper hand. And when it comes to the youth market and the potential for alternative-fuel vehicles, imports' sense of hearing seems to have been more acute than that of Detroit.

THE WORLD IN 2010

TOKYO, JAN. 1, 2011—Confirming what the global auto industry had come to consider as inevitable, Japan's Toyota Motor Co. said today that industry statistics for 2010 would show it had become the world's largest automobile company, breaking an 88-year hold on the title by the General Motors Corporation.

The historic acknowledgment came in a New Year's address to Toyota employees by Akio Toyoda, who became the company's chief executive last year. Mr. Toyoda, a descendant of the company's founder, Kiichiro Toyoda, spoke with employees around the world via a satellite hookup. Even while noting that company's achievement, Mr. Toyoda, 53, cautioned company employees not to become complacent. "We take this position with humility and with the knowledge that our customers can change their minds at any moment," said Mr. Toyoda, who last year became the first member of the Toyoda family to run the company in nearly 20 years.

Mr. Toyoda made special mention of the auto company's operations in the United States, by far its largest market, which now include 10 assembly plants and a series of engine and parts plants that employ more than 100,000 hourly workers. Mr. Toyoda noted that Toyota's sales of pickup trucks in 2010 had topped 500,000 for the first time, and that it sold a total of nearly 2.5 million vehicles in the United States in 2010, solidifying its hold on third place there.

He also mentioned that Toyota's sales of hybrid-electric and other alternative-fuel vehicles had exceeded 1 million worldwide in 2010, including over 600,000 sold in the United States last year.

Toyota's sales in 2010 are expected to give foreign auto companies nearly 50% of the American car market, their greatest proportion in industry history, according to an estimate from Nextrend Inc., the Los Angeles automotive consulting firm. In Detroit, GM was closed for the New Year's holiday, and officials could not be reached for comment.

Whether Toyota actually passes GM by 2010 to become the world's largest company, or simply remains the same size it is now, seems to be moot. There is already a grudging consensus in Detroit that it is the world's leading automobile company, not merely the world's best when it comes to manufacturing. Bob Lutz may turn up his nose at Camry's looks, and others may declare Lexus cars to be anonymous. But a simple fact remains: Many Americans consider Toyota's vehicles to be superior to the Detroit automobiles that they once admired and that will live on as icons of American design. Even more, Americans have come to embrace vehicles built by foreign manufacturers as substitutes for those made by GM, Ford and Chrysler. And the longer they own them, the more difficult Detroit's task becomes. Customers, as *Advertising Age* columnist Bob Garfield said, simply aren't listening when Detroit argues that its quality has improved, promises that what's coming next will be even better or tries to guilt customers back into the fold by evoking patriotism and nostalgia.

That isn't to say that America is losing its automobile industry. Far from it. With every gain made by the imports, Americans are enjoying the fruits of a new automobile industry in which American workers build fine cars and trucks in American factories. No, the owners of those plants aren't based in Detroit. But the outlook for the automobile industry is bright. There will be more new plants opened in the United States by 2010, more new choices and more jobs introduced into the car market. Those vehicles won't be sold by Detroit companies, most of those new plants won't be built by Detroit companies and those factories won't employ United Auto Workers members. The emergence of this parallel American automobile industry is an astounding prospect, considering how deep Detroit's roots are sunk into the American culture. But the Detroit companies have had plenty of time to get used to the idea—since the 1980s, in fact. Stopping imports' growth between now and 2010 may be impossible, primarily because American consumers simply won't allow it.

"I just find that cars built by American-run factories have slumped over the past 15-plus years," said Mike Iace of New York City, who owns a Subaru WRX and an Isuzu Trooper. "They have nice designs, but they cut corners so much that the reliability factor makes them difficult to purchase. It is fairly typical of the American mentality of 'do as little work to get the job done as possible,'" he said. A. J. Teixeiria of Washington, D.C., turned to Subarus and Mazdas after owning several Detroit models. He is of Brazilian descent and wanted to keep supporting the U.S. companies, but he gave up when he was repeatedly disappointed by the vehicles' poor quality. "Americans are smart consumers and will buy the best product for their hard-earned money. Buying U.S. products out of pity helps no one," Teixeiria said.

Ed Gjertsen II, of suburban Chicago, who owns both a Chevrolet Tahoe SUV and a Volvo S80 sedan, offers a glimmer of hope for Detroit. Gjertsen said he'd buy his Tahoe again. But he wouldn't buy a traditional Detroit car brand. He'd either stick with Volvo (good news for Ford, which owns it) or buy a Toyota next time out. "Detroit has been behind the curve for over 30 years. There have been some great years, but sprinters do not win marathons," Gjertsen said. He'd tell Detroit executives to work hardest on developing vehicles with consistent quality, high safety standards and, most important, good value. "This is what Detroit needs to focus on. I believe if it was not for competition, Detroit would be still sitting on its laurels," Gjertsen said.

Detroit has rallied in the past when its back was against the wall, and there are people who think that's just what will happen during this decade. Far from conceding defeat, GM, Ford and Chrysler all say they are better than they've ever been. They all have new vehicles in the works over the coming years, and they vehemently argue that this next wave will finally turn the tide in their favor. They will prove, once and for all, that they can defend themselves from the imports' relentless attack. Yet that assumes that these vehicles will be introduced into a vacuum and that the imports will simply stand still and let Detroit catch up. That isn't going to happen. Even if the upcoming Detroit vehicles are exciting, and their quality the equal of their counterparts from outside the United States, Detroit will have to convince import owners to convert. And it will be very difficult. "Once people have driven a Toyota or a Honda for 15 years and liked it, why would they switch?" said Greg Penske, the veteran Toyota dealer. That is the only way the Detroit companies can prove that their efforts have worked. And it is the fundamental hurdle that Detroit simply fails to understand.

What owners of foreign cars have come to value most is consistency. Whether it's Hyundai at the bottom of the market, Toyota and Honda in the middle, or BMW at the top, the companies deliver what they promise and rarely disappoint. Whether it's a $10,000 sedan or a $60,000 SUV, these companies' reputations for quality, durability and reliability are like an oak tree that stands straight and tall and whose roots are sunk deep into the earth. The tree may be blown by a storm, but it does not topple. Detroit companies have improved, and they are the first to congratulate themselves for doing so, but in these critical areas, they are not the equivalent of the imports. In gardening terms, they are like weeds or annual plants, grabbing at the soil with root systems that are shallow. Every time there is a recall, and every time another customer is disappointed, those roots get yanked up. Over and over again, Detroit executives say that the situation can be changed only with new products. But new products, in and of themselves, are not the solution.

In the long term, the Detroit companies have to display the same heritage for vehicle integrity that the imports have gained over two decades. That is a process that will take patience, consistency and clear direction. If the Ford Taurus and the Saturn division are any evidence, this is not a game that Detroit has yet learned to play. And in the coming years the auto industry will be affected by a series of forces that will greatly determine whether it will be able to do so.

THE MARKET

Market trends show that the future holds more growth by the import companies. Christopher Cedergren, the veteran industry analyst at

Nextrend, sees a steady erosion of Detroit's market share this decade, despite the efforts by GM, Ford and Chrysler to introduce new vehicles and gain ground. Detroit's share fell to just above 60 percent in 2003. By 2010, Detroit's share will have dropped to 52 percent, he says, and it will decline to 50 percent by 2012. Cedergren said consumers simply consider import nameplates to be the ones they want to own.

Bob Lutz counters that imports' appeal stems from the stigma the media has placed on domestic vehicles. He believes Detroit's problems are primarily perceptual. And Lutz takes issue with the whole concept of dividing the market up between Detroit-based companies and foreign manufacturers. He said differences are vanishing. By 2010, he says, consumers will be weighing Detroit vehicles and the import nameplates equally, and choosing those that make sense for them. But by then Lutz will be retired from GM (presuming he doesn't stay around until he is 78) and the vehicles that he brought to market will long since have been introduced. By then the market will know whether he has managed to instill some excitement at GM—and whether the company will increase its market share—or whether GM's market image was irreparably sullied by its relentless emphasis on incentives.

By 2010, the automotive market will have changed dramatically from the playing field in which the companies are competing now. And there is not much time to get ready, since it takes the auto industry between four and five years to develop a new vehicle. The end of the decade is only one and a half product cycles away. That causes trepidation not only in Detroit but elsewhere.

Yoshi Inaba, who was, until summer, 2003, the president of Toyota Motor Sales, the automaker's top executive in the United States, is so concerned about what lies ahead that he has asked Toyota's strategists to look at the market differently. Inaba has no interest in seeing whether Toyota can expand its sales by selling more rental cars or moving into segments where it doesn't now compete, like full-sized vans. He also knows that Toyota simply can't capture the most hard-core Detroit loyalists. All that aside, Inaba, who is returning to Japan to take charge of Toyota's North American operations, is looking for a definition of the "relevant market"—where Toyota will see its biggest challenges in attracting buyers and its greatest opportunities to attract new business going forward. Inaba is careful about predictions that Toyota will easily smash through 2 million sales a year in the United States, on its way to 2.5 million a year by 2010. "That's a good place to go," Inaba says with a smile, but he adds, "It will not be as easy as the last five years or so. This phase is a little different."

By 2010, the oldest baby boomers, on which Toyota has relied most heavily for its growth, will be 64 years old. They'll be the youngest-thinking and youngest-acting senior citizens in the history of the country, but nearing retirement age nonetheless. Hard on their heels will be Generation X, and coming behind them, the initial crop of Generation Y buyers. Many of them will have grown up in a world where their parents and even their grandparents owned import nameplates, where the nation's favorite car was a Toyota Camry, and where they don't have to choose among a car, a pickup, an SUV and a minivan. They're going to have a flood of new choices in the crossover market, the next big category on the verge of developing in the car market. Crossovers, or sport wagons, based on car platforms, will be to the market in 2010 what SUVs are to the market now. Imports got the initial advantage in this market, with vehicles like the Toyota Highlander, Lexus RX 300, Acura MDX, Honda Pilot, Nissan Murano and Infiniti FX 35, and there's no reason to think they can't hang on to it as they broaden their lineups. After all, if they've already beaten Detroit in cars; why wouldn't they beat them in car-based SUVs as well? Simply because Detroit enters a category doesn't mean that it has to be the dominating force, as some in the Motor City still fervently believe. But a telling factor here will be manufacturing flexibility. The companies that build multiple kinds of vehicles in their factories will have a leg up on those companies that build only one or two types of vehicles. Toyota, Honda and Nissan already have the equipment in the body shops of their American factories to allow them to build as many as eight different types of automobiles. That will let them change production on the fly, according to consumer demands. Detroit will have to prove that it can react as swiftly. GM, Ford and Chrysler already are beginning to convert their plants to this manufacturing capability; whether they can shift their mind-sets to be ready for a world where tastes change even faster remains to be seen.

An unknown for every manufacturer is the role that alternative-fuel vehicles will play. For its part, Toyota is determined to turn hybrids from curiosities into mass market vehicles. It wants to sell 600,000 hybrids a year in the United States by then, which would be the equivalent of the combined sales of the Camry, the Avalon and the Sienna in 2003. GM, not to be outdone, says it's going to sell a million hybrids a year by then, but it is only now introducing its first ones and must prove that its customers are interested in them. Before it decided that it, too, had to get into the hybrid market, GM had spent most of its time talking about hydrogen fuel cell vehicles, showing the Autonomy at the 2002 Detroit show, which is a platform onto which its fuel cell vehicles would be built.

Fancy stuff, but hydrogen fuel cell vehicles are much farther out than 2010, at least where the average customer is concerned. And, in a tactic that most likely will lead to further delays, Detroit companies want the government to foot a good part of the research bill, requiring $1 billion or more in subsidies. In the same vein, they've argued that there should be tax breaks, as well, for customers who purchase hybrid vehicles. Even while he talked excitedly at Ford's shareholders' meeting about the upcoming Ford Escape hybrid, Bill Ford, an avowed environmentalist, argued for a $3,000-per-vehicle credit to convince customers to buy it. The jockeying for government help comes despite the fact that

Honda, Toyota and Nissan have already sold their first fuel cell vehicles to government fleets, and Honda and Toyota have already established a foothold in hybrids.

POLITICS

In the past, Detroit companies have never hesitated to turn to the political arena when they needed help to compete. Here they have a weapon that the imports cannot wield. What role could the United Auto Workers play, either in a protectionist political debate or in helping the Big Three companies return to prosperity? No matter how powerful the UAW has always been in Democratic politics, it has little say these days in the nation's capital, dominated as it is by the Republicans. "Obviously, we do not have a lot of friends in Washington to help us," said Ron Gettelfinger, the UAW's president. Some would say that the UAW hasn't been much of a friend to the Big Three, either. But to blame the union alone for what's happened to the Detroit companies is just plain wrong. Detroit's problems haven't been caused only by the fact that its workers are unionized and those at the transplants are not. There are two signatures on every union contract—one from the UAW, the other from the auto companies.

The work rules, wages and benefits at the Detroit companies weren't imposed on them—they were agreed to. Nobody twisted Detroit's arm—although the UAW has never hesitated to get its point across through strikes and work slowdowns. The UAW has stood up for its members over the years, and it has won some generous benefits that white-collar workers in many professions can only dream about: fully paid health care, legal advice, child care, pensions, vacation time, education benefits and job security. Clearly, it has been a positive force in their eyes, no matter how the Detroit executives complain about legacy costs. They have only themselves to blame, for in every instance an auto company agreed to go along.

What will it take to change that? It will require vision and courage, not just from one side of the table but from both. Until that happens, nothing will change in the master contracts or in the way of thinking that permeates Detroit. Even though the union granted modest concessions to the auto companies in negotiations in 2003, progress will not be made unless there's a collective acknowledgment at the companies and in the UAW that the landscape has changed and that things need to be done differently. There are numerous examples—in Ohio, Kentucky, Tennessee, Alabama and elsewhere—that unions aren't necessary for American workers to build some of the finest cars and trucks in the world. That wasn't a reality 20 years ago, but it is now. The newest auto plants in this country prove that Americans can produce quality vehicles. They just aren't unionized. That's something both the Detroit companies and the UAW have to concede, as much as it hurts to.

It doesn't do any good for Gettelfinger to get up in front of the Economic Club of Detroit, as he did in March 2003, and try to make a case for why America needs more unions. That's not the issue in the auto industry, where union jobs are still disappearing and nonunion jobs are proliferating. The UAW needs to help the Big Three (beyond the minimal contract changes that it has grudgingly accepted) be as competitive as the import companies are without the UAW. And likewise, the Detroit companies have to help the UAW tell its members that the contracts they've worked under during the past 20 years are not saving their jobs. It's an incredibly difficult cultural, political and financial task, and it can't be done with old ways of thinking. It may take a revolution like the one that created the UAW in the first place in the 1930s, and it may take the same kind of revolution in thinking that convinced the Big Three to accept the union back then.

There is a precedent for all of this. From 1979 to 1982, the UAW agreed to a series of concessions, including wage cuts, pay freezes, the elimination of cost-of-living allowances and other steps meant to save Chrysler and help GM and Ford get back on their feet. There are two reasons why this happened: One is that the UAW had to give in or Chrysler would die. It was a pragmatic situation that Lee Iacocca played to his advantage. The other reason is the work by a number of creative executives and union leaders who arrived on the scene just when they were most needed. At the UAW, it was the president, Douglas Fraser, the vice president in charge of Ford, Donald Ephlin, and the Canadian union leader, Bob White, all of whom knew that the futures of their workers were in doubt unless things changed.

At Ford, the revolution was brought about by Peter Pestillo, the labor relations vice president who had come to Detroit with a strategic plan to change the atmosphere and find new ways for labor and management to work together. Fraser and White are long retired, Ephlin is dead and Pestillo is winding up his career as chief executive of Visteon, the auto parts supplier that was once part of Ford. But the 1982 agreement between Ford and the UAW, which GM later accepted, was a landmark in that it traded concessions in return for the union getting a look at the company's books and, ultimately, a say in certain affairs in its manufacturing plants. The agreement proved that the UAW and the Big Three could face reality and move forward. Eventually, the union won back all their pay, and relations between the union and the companies turned rocky again, culminating in the devastating strike at GM in 1998 that shut down the company for seven weeks and cost it billions of dollars in lost sales.

For such a revolution to take place in the auto industry again would require the companies and the UAW to sit down together and find new ways of doing business. People who are familiar with his style say that Gettelfinger realizes the threat that the imports pose. But he can't step forward alone—and especially not without the support of his union members. That would be political suicide, because those workers have a say in whether Gettelfinger will get reelected. He's got to get help from CEOs and other leaders at the auto companies, who would also have to pledge to overhaul the way they do business.

That might be too much to expect from Detroit companies, permeated as they are with the culture of bigness. But as Chrysler is trying to change its focus from domestic to import, as GM is trying to become the strongest American player, on a par with the best imports, as Ford searches for an identity, there is hope that eventually some kind of change can come about. In the meantime, there will be hundreds more automotive jobs created in this country by 2010. They just won't be at Detroit's Big Three.

Jim Olson of Toyota doesn't completely discount the possibility of minor actions, on the part of the union or the Detroit companies, to stymie the imports' growth. One such showdown has been over fuel-economy regulations. In 2002, the UAW tried to convince members of Congress to impose standards that would have required auto companies to improve their fuel economy according to a set percentage. That would have hurt import companies more, because the fuel economy of their vehicles is generally higher than that of Big Three automobiles. The effort was defeated, however. Said Olson, "We're always wary. They can get us in little ways, with sharp elbows and heels to disadvantage us, but they aren't able to drop a big thing on us."

Besides, he noted, every major automotive company building vehicles in the United States except Honda is a member of the Alliance of Automobile Manufacturers. Representatives of the group meet twice a month to talk about issues in Washington and elsewhere, which has removed some of the Detroit companies' incentive for attacking their foreign counterparts. "It's difficult to do that with someone that you meet with every two weeks. You can't hide it anymore," Olson said.

THE PEOPLE

One of the places where Detroit has come to expect change is at the top. In times of crisis, the Detroit auto companies replace CEOs almost as frequently as sports teams do coaches (which, in the case of the Detroit Lions, owned by the Ford family, has become an annual occurrence). It's become a favorite pastime among company insiders, the media and the Wall Street community to lay odds on whose star is rising and whose is falling. And almost no attention is paid to the import companies' own leadership developments. But a very important one is taking place at Toyota.

Yoshi Inaba, the president of Toyota's U.S. sales operation, is considered a candidate to become the next chief executive, succeeding Fujio Cho, who was 66 in 2004. Inaba is a relaxed, smiling executive who speaks perfect English and is a keen student of the auto industry. He has directed Toyota's operations in the United States during its most aggressive and successful period, seeing its sales top 1.75 million a year, owing in part to its expansion into the truck market and its ever-growing collection of factories in the United States, Canada and Mexico. Were he to replace Cho, it would mark the second time in recent years that a Toyota executive had taken the top job after holding a key position in the United States—and it would be only fitting, now that the United States is Toyota's leading market.

Understandably, Inaba doesn't think it's appropriate to discuss succession issues where his own future is concerned. But he's one of the few people at the company who will discuss the future of another Toyota executive—Akio Toyoda, 47, the latest member of the company's founding family to play a role at the automaker, and a man who many feel will become its eventual CEO. "Whoever is next [as chief executive] is bridging to Akio Toyoda," Inaba said. Roughly the same age as Bill Ford, Jr., Toyoda could be as important to his family's company as Ford has been to his. And indeed, the pair of automotive scions could be in place at the same time, since Ford plans to be at his family's company the rest of his career.

It has been nearly 10 years since a Toyoda family member ran the company, and in that time both Cho and Okuda raised Toyota's profile on a global level, bringing it beyond its Japanese roots. In view of his background, Toyoda is most likely to stay with that path. Named to the company's board in June 2000 as its youngest member, Toyoda's journey has been unusual compared with that of other family members, but in a sense completely appropriate for a future CEO given the direction Toyota is taking. He attended prestigious Keio University, outside Tokyo, but earned an MBA degree at Babson College in Boston (the alma mater of Edsel Ford II). Toyoda joined Toyota in 1984 as a regular trainee, and then served as vice president at NUMMI. In 1998, Toyoda founded Gazoo.com, a cybermall that became one of Japan's trendiest Web sites; it sold CDs, DVDs, used books and PCs and included a link to Toyota's financing Web site. Toyoda's latest assignment has been with the automaker's Chinese operations, which will be critically important both to feed the developing Chinese market and as a potential source of production. Toyoda, who sports glasses and close-cropped hair, has said that he doesn't feel qualified to talk about his future. "I try not to think about my heritage. But I'd be lying if I said nobody around me is conscious of it," he told *Business Week* in 2001. Sounding impossibly modest, he went on, "I'm just happy doing whatever I can for the company as sort of a jack-of-all-trades."

If he ascends to the CEO's job, Toyoda would take charge of a company that has gone well beyond its Japanese roots. Inaba has said he feels that Toyoda would embrace Toyota's emerging global philosophy. "Toyota is now a giant company striving for change," Inaba points out. "Whoever comes next should go along those lines." In the same way that he expects Toyoda to take charge, Inaba also would like to see an American in the job he holds. That would be a step forward for a Japanese company in the United States: Neither Toyota, Honda nor Nissan has Americans completely in charge here. But Inaba thinks the time is coming, if Toyota is truly to be considered an American player. "I wish I could tell you that we were much more Americanized.

There are still a lot of hurdles to face to truly call us an Americanized company. But this culture within Toyota can be perfectly carried forward through an American CEO," he said.

Toyota has no shortage of candidates for that job among its American managers and, significantly, no shortage of talented Americans throughout its operations, much to Detroit's chagrin. It's a sign of imports' enduring success that these companies continue to lure the best and the brightest from Detroit to join their operations. Among those hired by Toyota in 2002 was a manufacturing executive named Jamie Bonini, who had been with Chrysler for 15 years. Bonini, 40, was by all accounts a rising star in the American automobile industry. A graduate of Princeton University with a master's in mechanical engineering from the University of California at Berkeley, he was profiled on the front page of the *Wall Street Journal* in 1997 for his work helping to streamline the auto company's Windsor, Ontario, minivan plant. He played a key role in developing the Chrysler Operating System, based on the Toyota Production System. As a reward, Chrysler sent him to Brazil, where he was the codirector of a prestigious engine production venture the company launched with BMW.

Bonini loved Chrysler and had no intention of leaving, especially as the company pushed forward under Dieter Zetsche. But in 2002, he joined Toyota, taking an assistant manager's job inside the engine and transmission factory in the Georgetown, Kentucky, complex. The position would be seen as a demotion in the hotly competitive world of Detroit, where executives spend as much time managing their careers as they do managing their operations. But for Bonini, it was a start in a company that he hopes will be "a good long-term fit," he said. "I came to Toyota knowing it was going to take several years in my early time in the company to really understand the philosophy and lead with that philosophy," Bonini said.

He made his decision to leave Chrysler after months of discussions with Sam Heltman, the executive in charge of human resources at Toyota Manufacturing North America. As interested as Toyota was in Bonini's skills, Heltman said he wanted to make sure that Bonini would embrace Toyota's culture and that he'd be happy inside the company, starting out in a job beneath his abilities but that would give him a chance to learn how Toyota worked. Bonini, for his part, said he was impressed by the thorough interview process, which involved his family, too. "I really love manufacturing. I love working on the shop floor. I thought I was a really good fit with what Toyota was trying to do."

Within days of joining the company, Bonini was on a plane for Japan, where he finally visited Toyota's factories not as an outsider looking for tips on how to improve Chrysler's operations, but as a Toyota employee. After his 15-year career in manufacturing, the trip was a seminal experience. "The difference is that Toyota has been at this for such a long time. The skill level is so high, they are able to practice it at a higher level of detail and precision," Bonini said. Returning home, one of his first tasks was to participate in a continuous-improvement session on the assembly line in Toyota's West Virginia engine plant. There, managers and workers had studied the employees' wrist motions as they put engine parts together and had measured their movements down to a fluctuation of 10 centimeters. Bonini had taken part in plenty of such *kaizen* exercises, but "not to that level of improvement," he said, his voice showing that he was impressed.

In their own way, American consumers can sense that difference, too. They are not buying imports reluctantly, or for a single reason such as fuel economy, as they might have done 20 years ago. That was a reason Detroit could understand and make allowances for. But two decades or more after the energy crises that caused Americans to sample Japanese cars, they now are willingly and enthusiastically buying import cars and trucks, because the vehicles meet their needs and satisfy their expectations. The fundamental damage to Detroit has already been done.

To be sure, the end of Detroit's influence on the American automobile industry is a tremendous loss for Detroit. A quick drive around Detroit and its suburbs gives a sense of just how important the auto industry is to the region. In every corner of Wayne, Oakland and Macomb Counties are office parks and low-rise buildings that are home to suppliers, engineering firms, advertising companies and public relations agencies who owe their existence in some way to GM, Ford or Chrysler. Every time a budget is cut, every time a new car project is canceled, each time incentives have to be raised in order to move metal from dealers' lots, thousands of people feel the pain.

But there is a victory in all of this for American consumers. The imports' success is being enjoyed by the people who have bought Hondas and Toyotas, Hyundais and BMWs, and who love their vehicles. Yes, the demise of Detroit is a tragedy for Michigan and other states that depend on the Big Three companies. But investments by foreign companies are a boon to Alabama, Tennessee, Kentucky, Texas, California and other areas. As for the argument that the profits earned by foreign companies go back to their home countries, consider this: In the 1990s, as it shut two dozen plants in the United States and eliminated 75,000 jobs, GM invested more than $1 billion in new plants all around the world. During the same period, Toyota invested more than $1 billion to expand its Georgetown, Kentucky, plant, build a truck plant in Princeton, Indiana, and start up an engine plant outside Charlestown, West Virginia, creating more than 20,000 jobs. Which decision was better for the U.S. economy? Which did more to raise the standard of living for people in the United States? By any measure, most people would say the money was better spent here. In June 2003, *Detroit News* columnist Daniel Howes argued that because of its growing market clout, Toyota had a responsibility to fund the charities, schools and cultural institutions in the Detroit area in the way that Big Three auto companies had done for years. If it was to be considered the industry's leading company, Howes said, Toyota had to assume a leadership role in Detroit, the epicenter of the American automobile universe.

That misses the point. Toyota has no such responsibility to Detroit, nor do any of the other foreign manufacturers. Their responsibility lies wherever their customers live, their dealers sell cars and their workers manufacture vehicles. The American automobile industry no longer rests in one place; its influence is being felt all across the United States. And what's more, import companies' popularity has resulted in a much better American automobile industry. It may no longer be in Detroit's sole control, but that is what happens in a country like the United States, where consumers are free to buy whatever they like. And they have those choices because of the efforts of countless Americans who have played a role in creating vehicles to suit American buyers' tastes.

No one has enjoyed his role more than Robert McCurry, the Toyota executive, now retired, who set the company on its expansion path during the 1980s and 1990s. "Once I was there for about a year and got to know the people in Japan, I knew it was a great company. I knew they were going to be very successful. I was happy to be a part of that," he said. Having worked in Detroit, he found that Toyota's "system, their honesty and doing what you wanted done, was phenomenal. I knew they could accomplish what they wanted to accomplish. They're loyal to quality, both at Toyota and at Lexus. They've accomplished that reputation, and that's why they continue to grow, grow and grow." Detroit, he said simply, "lost that."

If the Detroit companies are to win back customers, they can't simply flood the market with new vehicles and hope that will somehow generate more sales. Nor can they simply dump cars onto rental car lots, because the rental companies are only a last resort. Detroit's survival cannot be based on leveraging history and making promises about a grander "next year" that somehow never comes to pass. To get it right, GM, Ford and Chrysler have to do what their foreign counterparts do: They must make every vehicle they develop uniquely special and targeted precisely at the consumers who will own it. They must make a concerted effort every time out. Every pickup, every car model, every minivan has to be the best of its kind ever built, and every generation after that must be the same. Detroit companies have to put in the kind of effort that Honda did with the Odyssey minivan; take the risk that Nissan is taking with the Titan pickup; stretch the imagination as Toyota has with its Camry and all its derivatives.

There can be no more compromises, no excuses about the need to save money, no halfhearted moves with a vow that "this will hold the place until next time." Customers have moved far, far beyond that. And they know the difference as soon as they get behind the wheel. They don't have to make choices based on patriotism or guilt. There is no need to make allowances or wait around until Detroit is ready with its entries. Customers can walk into any import showroom and drive home in whatever they desire, confident that they've chosen wisely and, just as important, as excited about their new car or truck, minivan, SUV or crossover as their parents and grandparents once were about cars from Detroit. Unlike past generations, Americans now stand an excellent chance that however long they choose to keep their vehicles, they will be rewarded with reliability. Whether the company that makes their vehicle is based in Japan, Germany or Korea, American consumers know they can find something that fully meets their needs. And that knowledge has ultimately spelled the end of Detroit.

THE PUBLICATION OF *The End of Detroit* in September 2003 kicked off a debate in the auto industry that was long overdue. Why, people asked, had things gotten to this point? And what, they asked, could be done about it? In fact, the question I was asked most frequently, in all my interviews and public appearances, was "How would you fix Detroit's problems?" Readers and interviewers seemed disappointed that *The End of Detroit* offered a diagnosis but not a cure. Many not only wanted to know what was wrong, they wanted to know how it could be fixed.

But there is no easy solution to the dilemma Detroit finds itself in. The Big Three's decline stems from mistakes that were first made at least a generation ago and that have now had time to eat away at their dominance. For Detroit to regain its old grip will be next to impossible. Yet there are some ways the Big Three can strengthen themselves, prevent the loss of any more jobs and provide strong competition for their rivals from abroad.

1. GIVE CONSUMERS
WHAT THEY WANT

Given that Detroit companies have lost roughly 10 market-share points to import rivals since the end of the 1990s, and given that in

2003, they lost yet another 1.5 points, you'd think that the Big Three would have faced up to the fact that their dominance was eroding. Yet, in the year since *The End of Detroit* was published, Detroit's defenders have repeatedly insisted that, as in the 1980s and as in the 1990s, the decline is simply temporary. Once all the new products that Detroit has in its pipeline are introduced, the imports' market-share gains will vanish, these people insisted. Sure, buyers might have defected over the past few years because the Big Three ignored the car market, didn't have competitive minivans and didn't offer hybrid-electric vehicles. But now we have them coming, they claim, "and we'll stage a comeback that will knock their socks off." According to their thinking, anyone who dares to predict Detroit's demise—me, for example—will simply be proved wrong.

Put simply, these true believers are in a state of denial. "The basic problem is that the American people are not buying American cars," said Douglas Fraser, the former UAW president. Toyota and Honda, in particular, and other foreign brands in general, have now had decades to cultivate their customers and integrate themselves into their lives. Their early converts from the 1970s and 1980s have now bought multiple numbers of import vehicles. Now their children buy them. At the same time, foreign companies have invested billions of dollars in American and Canadian factories. Collectively, they employ tens of thousands of workers, whose well-paying jobs have spurred economic development in the states and towns where these plants have been built. Further, the import companies' lineups have been broadened to cover virtually every corner of the market for cars and trucks.

The quality of these vehicles, the foreign companies' decision to build plants in North America, and the number of choices that they offer, have significantly negated the need among consumers to feel loyalty solely to Detroit. Among these owners, it does not matter whether the Detroit companies claim their vehicles have improved.

These buyers don't care about apologies for shoddy quality in the past, like the one General Motors offered in its "Road to Redemption" ad campaign. These buyers haven't been waiting around for Ford to introduce a crossover vehicle, like the Freestyle, which will reach the market this year, long after Honda brought out the Pilot, Toyota the Highlander (and even Chrysler the Pacifica). These owners have no interest in 24-hour test drives of cars and trucks that they simply do not intend to buy, except out of curiosity or to reinforce their confidence in the vehicles that they own.

These people have been lost for good. And what's more, as the data from AutoPacific shows, they continue to take more people with them, every year. During the past year, I have had numerous e-mails from readers and encounters in bookstores with customers who were loyal to Detroit for generations only to have ultimately abandoned its cars, in some cases with great reluctance. Other times, I talked to people who still owned Detroit products but were eager to give them up, such as the wife of an executive with a major parts supplier who came up to me after a luncheon speech. "I can't wait for him to retire so that we can get a Camry," she confided. On the floor of the Detroit auto show, I ran into a former GM executive who had retired and left Michigan to join a well-known California consulting firm. His first purchase after he got there, he said with a smile, was a BMW.

Far more important than making converts, Detroit's most important task at this point is to stop losing its core buyers. If Detroit can simply stabilize its market share at its current level, around 60 percent, that would be an extraordinary accomplishment. Fraser calculates that if Detroit carmakers had kept the portion of the market they held at the beginning of the 1990s, the industry could have saved ten assembly plants and roughly 50,000 jobs. As it was, the UAW's membership in 2003 dropped to the lowest level since 1942. Even more stark, two-thirds of the assembly-plant jobs that Detroit had at its peak were gone. Fraser noted Detroit's market share losses have come during the strongest sales years in American automobile history. "There's nothing wrong with the market," he said. "Everybody in Detroit ought to be rich."

Rather than try to convince owners of Toyotas, Hondas and Hyundais to switch, Detroit's better bet would be to focus on keeping its customers in the fold, make sure they are happy and hope that they become ambassadors for its products. Aim for the trees, not the forest, in other words. Once that happens, Detroit can use those satisfied customers to reach out to others who have slipped out of its grasp. Yet marketing experts say the job of regaining a customer is ten times harder than retaining one. It takes determination and time. And patience is not a Big Three virtue.

The second and probably more difficult task for the Detroit carmakers is to become more contemporary in the way they reach out to consumers. No matter how broad and deep the lineup of the Detroit companies is, their advertising campaigns often seem to fall into two categories: one, selling muscle cars to young males or two, leaning on nostalgia. At times, Detroit's ads seem to have only one theme—squealing tires, dramatic statements and flashy styling—making it hard to tell the companies' products apart. I'd be the last to suggest that Detroit strip its lineup of sexy cars and only make bland products. Performance cars will always make the covers of car magazines and captivate car reviewers on TV. They're fun for everyone to drive, they are the projects that every engineer and designer wants to work on and they are why many people get into the car business.

But not everybody who buys a car is a car buff, and a dwindling number of people actually remember Detroit's glory days, which is another issue that the Big Three simply can't seem to understand. Cadillac, Chrysler and Ford, to name just a few, lately have all reached back into the 1960s, 1950s and even earlier, in advertising their twenty-first century lineups. That might make executives feel cozy but out at street level, such ads come off as an extension of the History

Channel. By now, half the population of the United States can't remember the original Ford Mustang, and I've been asked more than once during my appearances what a "Hemi" is, proving that no matter how much buzz the engine has, Chrysler better not assume it will automatically mean something to every buyer.

To dwell constantly on this muscle car/nostalgia approach ignores the fact that the market is populated with all types of customers beyond young white males and car buffs—women, for starters, who make up half the market, as well as Asians, Latin Americans and African Americans, to whom such images have little resonance. "One of the problems with Detroit is that it sees itself as the epicenter of the auto industry, but it's so removed from what the rest of the country is thinking about cars," said Ron Pinelli, the auto analyst. Put off by Detroit's approach, or perhaps simply ignoring it, these buyers have helped provide the foundation for import companies' market gains in the United States over the past decade, with women in particular.

Occasionally there is an exception. Cadillac has understandably congratulated itself in recent years for its ability to make the Escalade and other vehicles attractive to the "urban" market (a code word for black consumers). But Cadillac is far from the only brand that African American consumers buy. Lately, the Chrysler 300 C has become the "it" car in the rap community. And even so, as I appeared on radio programs aimed at black listeners and talked to black car and truck owners over the past year, a number raised the same complaints that I heard from consumers of other backgrounds. Namely, they were disappointed in the quality of the vehicles they had bought from Detroit, and like other customers, they could not afford to take any more risks. Some of these people had long ago switched to buying Toyotas, Hondas, BMWs and Hyundais, reflecting trends across the population.

This was true even if their parents and grandparents had come north to work in auto plants, as so many members of the black community did from the 1920s to the 1960s. More than anything else, consumers of all ages, backgrounds and attitudes are concerned about quality, in every definition of the word. And in this regard, Detroit car companies have got to get real, as well.

2. QUALITY MATTERS

No one denies that Detroit's vehicles are far better than they used to be. But almost nobody buys a vehicle because it is an improvement over a lemon they owned in the past. Until Detroit can make cars that are nearly as good after five years as they are when buyers drive them off showroom lots, its problems in competing with the best foreign brands will continue. It does no good for executives to insist that poor quality is simply a perception problem, as Gary Cowger, president of GM's North American Operations suggested in 2003. It is not. In just the first quarter of 2004, GM recalled 7.5 million vehicles, almost as many as it recalled during all of 2003. Included in those recalls were some of its best-selling models, such as the Chevrolet Silverado pickup, and new vehicles, like the Cadillac SRX crossover wagon. The cost of the recalls, GM estimated, would be $200 million.

Such problems give consumers plenty of evidence, and their own experiences are more than enough to back up their view that vehicles from Detroit simply do not hold up as well over the long term, on average, as those from the best foreign brands. Said the UAW's Fraser, "If you plunk down $20,000 and you have a bad experience, you are certainly not going to go back."

Detroit's failing has been to define quality as a measurement of defects—what I would call statistical quality. But a customer's definition of quality today encompasses the entire vehicle, from exterior to interior. It covers the ease of operation: How simple is a car or truck to understand? And few consider a vehicle to have been a good value based solely on the purchase price. One element is what Edmunds calls the "cost of ownership"—not just the amount a vehicle costs up front, but the amount of money an owner spends to insure, maintain and run it over five years. In April 2004, Edmunds published a list of vehicles with the lowest ownership costs, ranking them by price and market segment. The list measured the money that owners laid out beginning in 1999.

Of the 27 cars, trucks, SUVs and minivans on its list, 26 were from foreign nameplates. Only one, the Ford F-150 Heritage pickup (the predecessor to the newest version of the F-series), was from Detroit. Moreover, 15 of the 27 vehicles were from Japanese nameplates, and seven of those were from Toyota. "It's always good to know how deep the pool is before jumping in the water," said Bob Kurilko of Edmunds, arguing that with such information, consumers could protect themselves "long after the new-car smell has worn off."

Only a few weeks before Edmunds's study came out, *Consumer Reports* had published its own quality study, which Detroit companies had greeted as good news. It showed that for the first time in a generation, the quality of their vehicles in the first year of ownership was better than those from European manufacturers. Detroit vehicles, on average, recorded 18 problems per 100 vehicles in the first year, compared with 20 for European models. Even the initial quality of Chrysler's automobiles beat that of its sister luxury brand, Mercedes-Benz. Especially pleasing to Ford was that its Focus, which had gotten off to such a rocky start with 11 recalls in the first year it was on sale in the United States, was ranked by *Consumer Reports* as one of the industry's best cars.

But the good scores for Detroit did not match those of Japanese and Korean brands, whose average was 12 problems per 100 vehicles. In fact, the average for all vehicles in the survey was 17 problems per 100 cars and trucks, so Detroit's score of 18 problems was actually below average, no matter that it had beaten the Europeans. And when the numbers for three-year-old and five-year-old cars were considered, the gap between Detroit and its Asian rivals simply widened further. Another shock came on J.D. Power's 2004 Initial Quality Report, which showed that while Detroit had made improvements, Korea's Hyundai had made a startling leap in quality, surpassing them as well as the Europeans and even the Toyota brand (although not Lexus). Zetsche, at Chrysler, acknowledged that the battle was far from finished. "Ultimately, we cannot settle for any in-between position," he told me over lunch in March 2004. "Our objective has to be to compete with the best."

Incredibly, as its recalls were soaring, GM went on a campaign to convince journalists that such numbers were good news. It maintained that improved lines of communication with consumers and dealers meant that it was getting data on faulty cars and trucks more quickly, and could initiate repairs much faster than in the past. GM, which borrowed from techniques used by the Centers for Disease Control to track outbreaks of viruses, argued its case in a dogged and detailed way, pointing out that 84 percent of its recalls were voluntary (as is true with most such campaigns). But it will take years for consumers to think of the word "recall" in a positive light, if ever. In the meantime, Detroit has to focus on making every single vehicle as good as it can be, not just when it rolls off the showroom lot, but over time. Given Detroit's current situation, every recall campaign is a step backward. And there is little the Big Three can do to change that reality.

With tools like Edmunds, *Consumer Reports* and through their own word of mouth, customers can find out what to expect from the cars and trucks they are considering, well apart from anything that the car companies claim. And until the numbers significantly change in Detroit's favor, a large portion of the buying public is simply going to take their business somewhere else.

3. CREATE GREAT PRODUCTS

There is a mantra in Detroit that has become dangerously close to becoming a cliché: the phrase "It's all about product." Detroit executives, from Robert Lutz at GM to Bill Ford at Ford and Dieter Zetsche at Chrysler, continually tout the number of vehicles in their pipelines, confident that consumers will be impressed by the dozens of automobiles that are on the way. Ford, at the 2004 Detroit auto show, even declared that it would be "the year of the car" at Ford, standing out front as a phalanx of models like the latest Mustang and the Ford 500 sedan drove onto the stage. Yet as with quality, numbers alone do not tell the story. One thing that the ultra-clogged car and truck market has proved is the importance of designing every vehicle so that it stands out from the crowd in some fashion, while meeting customers' needs spot on. Automakers have to hit their target with laserlike precision, so that they create demand, not just buzz. For, even if a vehicle seems eye-catching, it does not always make sense.

Dan Neil, the talented car reviewer for the *Los Angeles Times*, who won a Pulitzer Prize for his work in 2004, made just that case with the Chevrolet SSR, a pickup truck with a stylized front end and a convertible roof that opened and closed at the touch of a button. The flamboyant SSR had been the talk of the Detroit auto show a few years before, and Chevrolet put all its marketing clout into making it visible. But what made a splash as a show car did not necessarily translate to the street, said Neil, after driving it around L.A. "It's kind of like a postmodern hot rod pickup truck. I mean, it's like a pickup truck from Toontown," he said on National Public Radio. "I mean, you feel ridiculous driving it. It's one of those vehicles you would drive, park and sell." It was further proof of the disconnect between Detroit and its customers.

But there are only so many learning opportunities left. With its market share diminishing, Detroit's old tactics of bombarding the market with dozens of vehicles and hoping some of them stick in consumers' minds is simply not the answer. "It's getting to be overkill. It's really overwhelming for someone who hasn't been in the car market for six or seven years. They end up asking their friends, what kind of car should I get?" said Pinelli. When the noise is loudest, sometimes what gets the most attention is a quiet voice. Karl Brauer, Edmunds' editor in chief, wrote that buyers would even be forgiving of some minor quality issues if their vehicles "speak" to them in ways that please them. Despite Mercedes's quality issues, Brauer said, some buyers would not own anything else.

Wrote Brauer, "I'm heartened by the apparent improvements in reliability for domestic cars and trucks. But reliability ratings are only one aspect of vehicle ownership. Let's hope Chrysler, Ford and GM can 'speak' to the rest of them."

Indeed, the cacophony coming from the Big Three trying to lure buyers ultimately may have the opposite effect—sending customers to the foreign brands, whose lineups speak crisply and clearly about what they have to offer. In this case, in the words attributed to Buckminster Fuller, less is more.

4. QUIT TAP DANCING ON THE ENVIRONMENT. AMERICANS HAVE PROVED THEY CARE.

In approaching the environment in the 1990s, the biggest difference between the management philosophies of GM and Toyota was simple: Toyota executives believed in the market potential of hybrid-electric vehicles and what they mean to the future of the car market. Their counterparts at GM did not, despite the lip service and hoopla they paid to the concept. And that simple element of philosophy is why GM has been badly outplayed by Toyota on a field where GM could have easily dominated the game. It is not GM's capability, and indeed, not a lack of technical prowess on the part of Detroit companies that have led Japanese rivals to eclipse them on alternative fuel vehicles. Detroit's engineers are equally as good as their counterparts anywhere in the world. The difference is leadership.

GM could have easily launched a range of hybrid-electric vehicles as far back as a decade ago, as its former CEO, Robert Stempel, can attest. Bill Ford Jr. has been an enthusiastic proponent of environmental causes during his adult life, and Ford has had a bevy of engineers working to develop fuel-efficient vehicles. Moreover, Zetsche at Chrysler has the engineering background to explain the properties of hybrids and make them appeal to a new generation of consumers. But it is Toyota, joined by Honda, that made hybrids happen, because their executives not only believed in a need for hybrids but ordered them to be made available to consumers in a form and at a price that would be appealing. And they were patient in waiting for them to catch on. The failure to do the same is a misstep that has cost Detroit dearly, not only in sales, but in its relationship with its potential customers. By miscalculating the appeal that hybrids have generated, Detroit proved yet again that it had not understood the psyche of American consumers.

To be sure, when Toyota first introduced its original Prius in 1997, many viewed it as a foolhardy venture. It lost money on every car it sold, even at its original price tag of about $32,000. Honda's Insight, available only with a manual transmission, and with its upside bathtub appearance, was hardly practical for the majority of buyers. But both companies shared a belief that eventually hybrids would catch hold once they had the right configuration of performance, price and styling. And they were right. By the spring of 2004, the Toyota Prius was the most fashionable car in Hollywood. Movie stars drove them to the Academy Awards instead of riding in limousines. By then, Toyota dealers were virtually sold out of the Prius, which would easily eclipse its sales in 2003.

Though it got the most publicity from movie stars, the Prius in fact is just as likely to be driven by thrift-minded grandmothers as by trendsetters. While fuel economy was its main draw, its popularity spoke to something else: American curiosity. What Detroit companies seemed to have missed is that buying a hybrid is as exciting for its owners as the purchase of a sports car is for others. A hybrid Civic might not have the sex appeal of the Corvette, or the sheer power of a Hemi-equipped Chrysler, but a hybrid brings about its own tingle of delight to customers so inclined. And with Toyota poised to introduce two hybrid SUVs and perhaps even a hybrid pickup truck over the next few years, and with Honda planning a hybrid version of the Accord, that feeling will only spread to a greater audience.

Even as Detroit scurries to enter the hybrid market, led by the Ford Escape in late 2004 and a flock of vehicles from GM in the middle of this decade, executives continue to point to hydrogen fuel-powered vehicles as the real wave of the future. In this, they have the government on their side. President Bush has declared hydrogen to be the country's "Freedom Fuel." And in April 2004, the Department of Energy announced $350 million in grants to companies developing hydrogen fuel cell vehicles. Yet *New York Times* reporter Matthew L. Wald, writing that same month in *Scientific American*, questioned whether hydrogen vehicles would ever fulfill their promise. He pointed out that a hydrogen fuel cell cost roughly 100 times per unit of power as an internal combustion engine. Such fuel cells might have an efficient use in cellular phones or laptop computers, Wald wrote, but it was unlikely that many would be found on automobiles. In fact, he said, the timetable for developing hydrogen fuel cell vehicles was much like that for NASA's launch of a manned mission to Mars. But then, deflecting attention to the future has always been a Detroit specialty.

Long term, hydrogen vehicles may indeed be the answer. But short term, it would be much more realistic, no matter how late in the game, for Detroit executives to get behind hybrid development wholeheartedly. They may not have much credibility as environmentalists, given all the battles they have waged in the past against higher fuel-economy standards, said analyst Pinelli. But unlike the hydrogen fuel cell vehicles that Detroit insists are the solution, hybrid-electric cars are already on the road. They have become a part of the automotive scene. And, ultimately, like family cars and luxury vehicles, hybrids will be yet another market where foreign companies have the firmest grip, not the companies from Detroit.

5. DON'T DECLARE VICTORY AFTER ONE TOUCHDOWN

To be around Detroit in the spring of 2004 was to believe that prosperity was back—at least, if you were an auto executive. GM and Ford surprised Wall Street during the first quarter with good results, which for Ford marked the first time since 2000 that its automotive profits had exceeded those of its financing operations. Even Chrysler, whose parent company was again mired in crisis, this time over Mitsubishi, sent signals that a profitable year lay ahead after its losses in 2003. News agencies jumped to conclusions of a "broad recovery" in the automotive sector, never mind that all kinds of businesses had reported earnings surprises that spring.

In Detroit, it seemed time to exhale and in some cases, wag a finger at the naysayers who doubted it could again pull off a comeback. Bill Ford did just that on a conference call with industry analysts. "I hope that after our ninth consecutive quarter of beating our own projections, you will begin to believe when I say that our goal is to underpromise and overdeliver," Ford told his audience. Of course, Ford's own projections had been conservative, and it would have to repeat its performance for numerous quarters before it could make up for the deep losses it had suffered during the early years of the decade, but no matter. Across the city, executives saw another sign of better times return: bonus payments, which the industry considered such a critical element in managers' compensation. The same was true even at GM despite its 2003 market share losses, which wiped out the gains made in the previous two years: The company said they were merited because it had met targets in other areas. But for anyone tempted to celebrate the glimmer of good news, there was a vivid reminder not to rest. That, in a word, was Nissan.

Five years after Carlos Ghosn arrived in Tokyo, Nissan was a bona fide success. Ghosn could boast some of the biggest profits and the highest operating margins in the global auto industry. While Ford was still working its way through the revitalization plan that Bill Ford had articulated in January 2002, Nissan had pushed past the goals it set in two successive programs—the Nissan Recovery Plan and Nissan 180—and was embarking on a third, which it called Nissan Value-Up. While Ford was congratulating itself for beating its internal goals, Nissan had trounced its public ones. Its profit margin in 2004 was 11.1 percent—the highest among the industry's mass-market brands and well above the 8 percent it had promised it would achieve in its Nissan 180 recovery plan. Along with a complete restructuring of the company came an impressive array of new vehicles, whose popularity had boosted sales in the United States by 18 percent in 2003.

And he was not yet finished. Ghosn's goals for the future include making Infiniti a global luxury brand, something that GM and Ford have each tried to do with Cadillac and Lincoln. He is pushing the company to expand in Asia, particularly China, which all of Detroit's car markers see as a battleground. And Ghosn is determined that by 2007, Nissan's worldwide sales will grow by another 800,000 vehicles, to about 4.2 million, with the help of two dozen new models across the lineups of Nissan and Infiniti. Whether Ghosn can make that happen will be a challenge given that he will serve as CEO at both Nissan and Renault, based primarily in Paris, starting in 2005. "Do not expect me to be a part-time CEO but, rather, a full CEO with two hats," he said. Indeed, Nissan faces a number of challenges, including improvements in the quality of its newest models, the big Titan pickup truck among them. It also must deal with the fact that it may be harder to sell a Japanese pickup than it initially expected. But given

Ghosn's track record, Nissan will not ignore the problem for long. And as Ghosn said, no one will be held accountable for failure but himself.

Ghosn's philosophy is the same one that Detroit companies will do well to remember as they do battle with foreign brands. In 1992, when Jack Smith was handed the unenviable task of fixing GM, he operated under the principle, "Deeds, not words." As GM, Ford and Chrysler go forward, that is exactly how American consumers will be judging them. Detroit's automobile companies have broken too many promises and too many hearts to ever have the grip on the American car market that they once enjoyed. But there is still time for Detroit to stabilize itself and play a role in the most exciting competition for customers on earth. And certainly, there is the opportunity to earn a lot of money while doing so. The most important thing for them to remember is that one touchdown does not win the game. Declaring victory too soon, as President Bush discovered in Iraq, can come back to haunt you.

It is far better to acknowledge achievements for ten minutes, as Toyota does, then get on with the next tasks at hand. Prosperity is never assured. A single bad quarter can knock all the steam out of a turnaround drive, as Chrysler has learned twice in the last three years. A mishap with one vehicle can cost a company its chief executive, drain profits and demoralize employees, as Ford learned with the Explorer. No matter how much effort a company makes to incorporate new manufacturing systems and boast of its capabilities, the customer still decides who wins, something GM knows only too well. And miscalculating customer demand can result in huge fire sales that are devastating to a brand's image, as the Detroit companies saw in the summer of 2004.

The UAW's Fraser says he sees hope in the sense of humility that became more apparent among Detroit auto executives during the early years of the decade. "They were humbled. That's a step in the right direction," he quipped. Zetsche, meanwhile, is determined Chrysler will remain on an upward march, boosted by the new 300C and the Dodge Magnum. "It's up to us to prove that what you were saying doesn't come about," he told me. But both the Chrysler chief executive and the retired union leader understand just how hard it ultimately will be for Detroit companies to dominate the industry once more. Says Fraser, "We will not get back until the cars are well-engineered, well-designed and the quality is nothing less than excellent."

There is no better cure for Detroit's ills than that.

ACKNOWLEDGMENTS

IN ALMOST EVERY CORNER of this country, and around the world, people are fascinated with and affected by automobiles and the companies that make them. It is an industry that touches us all in one way or another, from manufacturing and marketing to labor relations, politics and finance, not to mention those heart-stopping vehicles that stir flights of fancy in any language. It has a rich history, a complicated present and a future marked with myriad questions. In short, one can spend years studying it and writing about it, as I have, and still only begin to understand all that goes into it.

I was drawn to write this book by my own experience as a car owner. Except for the Dodge Dart that I drove in college, whose peppy but erratic slant-six engine died with 177,000 miles on it, I have always owned imports. My first new car was a Toyota Tercel, bought in 1982 for $5,200. My current car is a Lexus RX 300, which I leased after becoming disenchanted with a Volkswagen New Beetle whose gorgeous Vapor Blue paint and zippy ride masked substandard quality that tried my patience. Moreover, my own family is a microcosm of what has happened to Detroit. My brother was actually the first member of our family to buy an import, a yellow Toyota Corolla on which I practiced driving a stick shift. My mother was a loyal Oldsmobile buyer for nearly 30 years, but she has become a Lexus owner, too. My friends own everything from Hondas to Volkswagens to BMWs. I didn't have to look far to test my theory that a growing number of consumers have turned to imports. The reality is right there in my address book.

Writing this book was a joy that was made possible by the cooperation and support of many people. I am grateful to my agent, Russell Galen, at Scovil Chichak Galen, for suggestions that helped me frame my book proposal in precisely the right way. My editor at Random House, Roger Scholl, was wonderful to work with, and my assistant, Lisa Robinson, was diligent and creative. I especially want to thank Andrew Sacks for shooting my book jacket photo.

I am indebted to my editors at the *New York Times*, particularly Glenn Kramon, Lawrence Ingrassia, Jim Schachter, Jim Cobb, Mark Stein and Pat Lyons, for their insight and encouragement. Special thanks go to Detroit bureau chief Danny Hakim, for his humor and camaraderie. Thanks also to Howard French, Jim Brooke and Ken Belson in the *Times*'s Tokyo bureau, who made me feel so welcome during my stay there.

My 2002 media fellowship from the Japan Society of New York allowed me the once-in-a-lifetime opportunity to spend three months crisscrossing Japan, visiting factories and car companies. My thanks to William Clark, Jr., John Wheeler, Ruri Kawashima and Brian Byun. I also would like to thank the staff at the International House of Japan for their kindness, along with Kazuko Koizumi-Legendre at the Foreign Press Center for her wonderful assistance in arranging translators and interviews.

I appreciate the cooperation shown me by the car companies that were generous with their time and resources. At Toyota, I wish to thank James R. Olson, who opened doors and supported this project from our first conversation about it at the New York Auto Show in 2001. Daniel Sieger was tireless in arranging my interviews in the United States and abroad, and Jennifer Chung was of tremendous help in California. In Japan, I am grateful to Hisayo Ogawa for her professionalism and friendship, and I also wish to thank Tetsuo Kitagawa. At Honda, Jeffrey Smith was another early supporter who was invaluable in helping me understand the Honda Way. My thanks also go to Yuzuru Matsuno and Edward Miller. In Japan, I was greatly assisted by Masa Nagai and particularly Tatsuya Iida, who patiently answered my endless questions about Japanese language and culture.

Thanks also go to Gina Pasco, Fred Standish and Galen Medlin at Nissan. At Hyundai, I would like to thank Chris Hosford and Steve Morgan, and Martha McKinley at BMW was extraordinarily helpful. Among the Detroit companies, I appreciate the help of Steve Harris, Tony Cervone and Tom Kowaleski at GM, Jon Pepper at Ford, and Ken Levy, David Barnas and Jason Vines at Chrysler. I also wish to thank former United Auto Workers president Douglas Fraser for his insight. In Alabama, my appreciation goes to Linda Paulmeno Sewell at Mercedes-Benz, Steve Sewell and Barbara Thomas, Mayor Lew Watson of Lincoln, and particularly Theodore Von Cannon, for being such a gracious host during my visit to Birmingham.

This project would not have been possible without the many experts on the auto industry who know it as well as anyone inside. I would like to thank for their gracious expertise Jeremy Anwyl, Karl Brauer and Jeannine Fallon at Edmunds.com; James Womack at the Lean Enterprise Institute; Joseph Phillippi at Auto Trends Consulting; Peter DeLorenzo at Autoextremist.com; Greg Kagay of Auto Market Scope; Steve Girsky at Morgan Stanley; John Casesa at Merrill Lynch; Chris Cedergren and Wes Brown at Nextrend; Ron Pinelli at Autodata; Art Spinella at CNW Marketing Research; Scott Sprinzen at Standard & Poor's; and George Petersen at AutoPacific.

At the University of Michigan Business School, thanks go to Professor David Lewis, who knows more about automotive history than anyone on earth; to my department head, Cindy Schipani; and to Paula Caproni for being my patient academic mentor. My students, many of whom work for the auto companies, have given me a terrific inside view of the challenges they face in their daily lives. I have learned as much from them as I hope they've learned in my classroom.

My friends around the world provided invaluable encouragement and feedback. Thanks to Judith Burns, Keith Naughton, Fara Warner, Antoinette Melillo, Christine Tierney, Tom Squitieri, and Amy Resnick. I also would like to thank my family: my mother, Bernice G. Maynard; my godmother, Maxine Clapper; my brother, Frank Maynard; my sister-in-law, Lisa Barry Maynard; and my nephews, Benjamin Maynard and Parker Maynard, who now have a book from Auntie Micki all their own.

In closing, I want to pay tribute to Chris Parks, my bureau chief at United Press International in Lansing, Michigan, who set me on the path to becoming a business journalist. Thank you for everything, Sluggo.

■

THIS BOOK IS BASED primarily on hundreds of hours of original research, along with my reporting on the automobile industry for the *New York Times* from the years 2000 to 2003. In most cases, direct quotes are drawn from the interviews that I conducted in the United States, Canada, Europe and Japan. I visited manufacturing plants in Alabama, Indiana, Kentucky, Michigan, Mississippi, Ohio and Ontario, as well as a number of factories in Japan. Almost all of these interview subjects agreed to speak on the record, but there were some people who felt more comfortable being interviewed without attribution. The articles and books mentioned below supplemented my reporting in specific chapters, and my thanks go to the journalists who shared their work with me.

CHAPTER TWO: A FALLEN COMRADE

Brown, Peter, "Incentive Wars: GM 1, Rest of Industry, 0," *Automotive News,* January 20, 2003

DiPietro, John, *A Ford Taurus/Mercury Sable History*, Edmunds.com, December 2, 2001

DiPietro, John, *A Honda Accord History*, Edmunds.com, December 6, 2001

DiPietro, John, *A Toyota Camry History*, Edmunds.com, December 12, 2001

"Ford Executive Pays Rare Tribute to Toyota Camry," *Reuters News Service,* February 12, 2003

McNamara, Mary, "The Great SUV Divide," *Los Angeles Times*, January 29, 2003

Naughton, Keith, "The Fast and Luxurious," *Newsweek*, January 12, 2003

Stiffer, Harry, "Dr. Range Cuts, Industry May Bleed," *Automotive News*, January 20, 2003

Walton, Mary. *Car.* New York: W.W. Norton & Co., 1997

CHAPTER THREE:
TWO PATHS TO THE SAME CONCLUSION

Meredith, Robyn, "The 'Ooof' Company," *Forbes* magazine, April 14, 2003

CHAPTER FOUR: JOURNEY FROM THE INSIDE OUT

Shirouzu, Norihiko, "Honda's Ambitions Pressure Detroit," *Wall Street Journal*, July 10, 2002

CHAPTER FIVE: HOT DOGS, APPLE PIE AND CAMRY

Gwynne, Sam, "New Kid on the Dock," *Time* magazine, September 17, 1990

Taylor, Alex III, "America's Sweetheart," *Fortune* magazine, November 26, 2001

Taylor, Alex III, "Competition: Here Come Japan's New Luxury Cars," *Fortune* magazine, August 14, 1989

CHAPTER SIX: THE CHALLENGER

Magee, David. *Turnaround.* New York: HarperBusiness, 2003

CHAPTER SEVEN: NIBBLING FROM
THE BOTTOM AND THE TOP

Andrews, Edmund L., "A Loyal Survivor Rises at BMW," *New York Times*, January 6, 2002

Hakim, Danny, "BMW Design Chief Sees Art on Wheels; Some Just See Ugly," *New York Times*, November 29, 2002

CHAPTER EIGHT: DETROIT SOUTH

"Alabama Criticized Over Benz Deal," *Associated Press,* December 29, 1993

Corbett, Brian, Alisa Priddle, and Drew Winter, "Southern Hospitality," *Ward's Auto World,* August 1, 2002

Lyne, Jack, "Hyundai's $1B Plant Alabama Bound," *Site Selection Online,* April 2, 2001

"The 1980s Have Not Been Kind to America's Auto Workers," *Time International,* August 7, 1989

"Nissan Workers in Tennessee Reject UAW," *Reuters News Service,* October 3, 2001

"UAW to Try Organizing at Honda," *Associated Press,* October 4, 2001

CHAPTER NINE: THE END OF DETROIT

Detroit Free Press, various stories about Ford Motor Company, October 31, 2001

Detroit News, various stories about Ford Motor Company, October 31, 2001

Garfield, Bob, "GM Ad Demonstrates Marketing Ineptitude," *Advertising Age,* June 2, 2003

Hakim, Danny, "A Family's 100-Year Car Trip," *New York Times,* June 15, 2003

Hakim, Danny, "In Their Hummers, Right Beside Uncle Sam," *New York Times,* April 5, 2003

The History of Saturn, Saturncarsatlanta.com, January 19, 2003

Mackintosh, James and Jeremy Grant, "Ford Approaches 100 With Optimism," *The Financial Times,* June 12, 2003

Welch, David and Gerry Khermouch, "Can GM Save an Icon?" *Business Week,* April 8, 2002

White, Joseph B. and Norihiko Shirouzu, "Backfire," *Wall Street Journal,* October 31, 2001

CHAPTER TEN: WHAT DO CUSTOMERS REALLY WANT?

Hakim, Danny, "Hybrid Autos Quick to Pass Curiosity Stage," *New York Times,* January 27, 2003

Rechtin, Mark, "Altered State," *Automotive News,* February 24, 2003

EPILOGUE: THE WORLD IN 2010

"The Stars of Asia—Managers," *Business Week,* July 2, 2001

"Toyota's 'Prince' Prepares for His Reign," *Associated Press,* November 12, 2000

SELECTED BIBLIOGRAPHY

Ghosn, Carlos. *Renaissance.* Tokyo, Japan: Diamond Co., 2001.

Honda Motor Co. *A Dynamic Past, An Exciting Future.* Tokyo, Japan: Toppan Printing Co., 1999.

Ingrassia, Paul, and Joseph B. White. *Comeback.* New York: Simon & Schuster, 1995.

Magee, David. *Turnaround.* New York: HarperBusiness, 2003.

Maynard, Micheline. *Collision Course.* New York: Birch Lane Press, 1995.

Maynard, Micheline. *The Global Manufacturing Vanguard.* New York: John Wiley & Sons.

Togo, Yukiyasu, and William Wartman. *Against All Odds.* New York: St. Martin's Press, 1993.

Toyota Motor Corp. *Toyota: A History of the First 50 Years.* Toyota City, Japan: Dai Nippon Printing Co., 1988.

Walton, Mary. *Car.* New York: W.W. Norton & Co., 1997.

ABOUT THE AUTHOR

The New York Times

Micheline Maynard is a business reporter for the *New York Times*. Her work has appeared in *Fortune, USA Today, Newsday* and *U.S. News & World Report*. She has been a lecturer at the University of Michigan School of Business Administration and is the author of two books, including *Collision Course: Inside the Battle for General Motors*. She lives in Ann Arbor, Michigan. For more information, please visit www.endofdetroit.com.